The Globalization Myth

The Globalization Myth

Why Regions Matter

Shannon K. O'Neil

A Council on Foreign Relations Book

Yale UNIVERSITY PRESS
New Haven & London

Published with assistance from the foundation established in memory of Calvin Chapin of the Class of 1788, Yale College.

Yale University Press books may be purchased in quantity for educational, business, or promotional use. For information, please e-mail sales.press@yale.edu (U.S. office) or sales@yaleup.co.uk (U.K. office).

Set in Galliard Old Style and Gotham Medium types by Integrated Publishing Solutions. Printed in the United States of America.

Library of Congress Control Number: 2021952952
ISBN 978-0-300-24897-5 (hardcover : alk. paper)

A catalogue record for this book is available from the British Library.

This paper meets the requirements of ANSI/NISO Z39.48-1992 (Permanence of Paper).

10 9 8 7 6 5 4 3 2 1

The Council on Foreign Relations

The Council on Foreign Relations (CFR) is an independent, nonpartisan membership organization, think tank, and publisher dedicated to being a resource for its members, government officials, business executives, journalists, educators and students, civic and religious leaders, and other interested citizens in order to help them better understand the world and the foreign policy choices facing the United States and other countries. Founded in 1921, CFR carries out its mission by maintaining a diverse membership, with special programs to promote interest and develop expertise in the next generation of foreign policy leaders; convening meetings at its headquarters in New York and in Washington, DC, and other cities where senior government officials, members of Congress, global leaders, and prominent thinkers come together with CFR members to discuss and debate major international issues; supporting a Studies Program that fosters independent research, enabling CFR scholars to produce articles, reports, and books and hold roundtables that analyze foreign policy issues and make concrete policy recommendations; publishing *Foreign Affairs,* the preeminent journal on international affairs and U.S. foreign policy; sponsoring Independent Task Forces that produce reports with both findings and policy prescriptions on the most important foreign policy topics; and providing up-to-date information and analysis about world events and American foreign policy on its website, www.cfr.org.

The Council on Foreign Relations takes no institutional position on policy issues and has no affiliation with the U.S. government. All statements of fact and expressions of opinion contained in its publications are the sole responsibility of the author or authors.

Contents

The Globalization Myth

Introduction: The Untold Story of Regionalization amid Globalization

Akron, Ohio, made its name in tires. The city's rubber industry began by fitting out bicycles in the 1890s and soon followed Henry Ford into cars. During the two world wars, Akron's rubber companies scaled up to meet the military's demands, churning out tires, shoes, tubing, guns, blimps, and planes. They continued to flourish in the peace, as Eisenhower's interstate highway system spurred a shift from rails to roads and baby boomers earned their name, the newly minted parents buying their first family cars. By the middle of the century, five companies in "the Rubber Capital of the World" were churning out nearly 60 percent of the globe's tires.[1]

Money flowed. Goodyear founder F. A. Sieberling held forth from a sixty-five-room Tudor manor on the well-heeled west side of town. Over a dozen golf courses and country clubs sprang up to fill the leisure time and social calendars of the upper crust; Firestone built PGA-tournament level links as an employee perk. The thick society pages of the *Akron Beacon Journal,* the initial paper of the Knight Ridder news empire, chronicled the dresses and seating charts at luncheons, cocktail parties, and the annual debutante cotillion held in Goodyear Hall.

Life for the less tony set was looking up, too. Tire making was dirty but well paid. More than one home in the new east-side neighborhood of Goodyear Heights emulated their benefactor's Tudor style in miniature, company buses shepherding homeowners to and from their factory shifts. Eastern European migrants clustered in Firestone Park on the south side of the city. Weekends were filled with Industrial League games, Good-year's Wingfoots facing off against Firestone's Non-skids in a hometown rivalry, or taking on Peoria's Caterpillars, Milwaukee's Harnischfegers, or Denver's Chevvies on the court and field.[2] Akron's prosperity drew laborers from hundreds of miles away. Sunday nights Route 21 would fill with West Virginia licenses headed for early Monday shifts; Fridays the pickups would head back toward Wheeling.

This wasn't the Akron I knew. In 1982, news photographers and *Time* reporters watched as Richard Mayo, a General Tire worker, pulled the last tire off an Akron factory line, ending nearly a century of local industrial history. As the smokestacks cooled, the bars and diners across South Main Street from the factory gates also went dark. During the 1980s, four of Akron's big-five tire companies would be sold off to foreign competitors. Tens of thousands of jobs, and even more people, disappeared from Akron. A once thriving city became a defining example of late-century Rust Belt decay.

What had happened? It is easy to peg Akron as a victim of globalization: a once-proud American industry and prosperous city brought to its knees by outsourcing and offshoring. Yet this isn't the whole story. Part of it was new radial technology from abroad that let French and Japanese tires outperform and outlast their American counterparts. Volatile labor relations pushed tire factories south, beyond the reach of the combative United Rubber Workers Union.

But a big part of Akron's hard luck was the nature of the international competition it faced. The city's struggles reflect less the vagaries of globalization than the costly consequences of the United States' limited regionalization. By the late 1970s, Japanese tire and car production spanned East Asia. French and German makers had embraced Europe's Economic Community. With NAFTA negotiations still a decade away, Akron's companies had no partners to turn to in the face of burgeoning Asian and European manufacturing supply chains. This gave companies such as Michelin and Bridgestone an upper hand over their U.S. rivals. Left to go it alone, U.S. tire companies, and their hometown, went nowhere.

Globalization. You love it. You hate it. You embrace it. You blame it. But it isn't the only, or even the real, story of the global economy over the past four decades. Yes, the world has internationalized. But it hasn't really globalized. It has regionalized. This distinction helps explain who has gotten ahead and who has been left behind; those who engaged with their neighbors gained a competitive edge. It also provides a path forward for what the United States—and other countries, for that matter—should do to help their citizens and communities thrive economically. Isolation and autarky aren't the answers. Nor is unfettered globalization. The Goldilocks middle of regionalization propelled a number of nations forward over the past forty years. And even in the wake of technological, geopolitical, and demographic shifts, geography still counts for a lot. Embracing and deepening regional ties is a way to succeed in an internationally connected and competitive world.

Regionalization Surpasses Globalization

The overlooked reality of regionalization, as opposed to globalization, plays out in many areas. Tourists may travel from country to country, but they hop continents far less often. Students who venture abroad more often attend classes nearer than farther away. Trade officials, defense ministers, and secretaries of state tend to turn to counterparts in their geographic neighborhood first and foremost when negotiating agreements. So too do cross-border news readers, video watchers, and internet surfers.[3]

The regionalization of international ties is most pronounced in economics and markets. The story of economic globalization has been told and retold in books, speeches, articles, and news clips. Yet this conventional narrative largely misses the geographic limits of the majority of international commerce. When companies, workers, money, patents, goods, and services head abroad, they don't go just anywhere. More often than not, they stick close to home. What's happening to the global economy is better termed "regionalization" than "globalization."

The "global" in "global supply chains" in particular is a bit of a misnomer. Sure, some manufacturing processes do span the globe. The Boeing 787 Dreamliner, for instance: it brings together wings from Japan, engines from the United States or the United Kingdom (UK), flaps from Canada or Australia, horizontal stabilizers from Italy, landing gear from France—over forty suppliers, in all, and triple that number of sites worldwide. Pfizer's COVID-19 vaccine, invented by Turkish immigrants living in Germany, begins with DNA spinning in U.S. steel vats insulated by Mexican liners. The mRNA joins Canadian-crafted lipids chilled in Chinese ultracold freezers monitored by Icelandic thermometers. Indian or Mexican glass vials sealed by Chinese packaging carry the lifesaving serum to tens of millions of arms.[4]

But usually, when manufacturing goes abroad, it doesn't spread so far or so thin. Companies find the parts they need nearby. Suppliers sell to foreign customers close to home. The world has become more international but not nearly as global as the news would have you think.

Since the great manufacturing dispersion began some forty years ago, commerce between neighbors and within regions has far exceeded that across continents. The power of proximity holds particularly true for the intermediate goods that are stamped, welded, sewn, or inserted to make final products. For every airplane part coming from the other side of the world, dozens of literal nuts and bolts come from next door.

The manufacturing of cars, trucks, and SUVs exemplifies this trend. Take the Ford Edge. Its seats start life in Tennessee, where locally made foam cushions are covered with fabric from South Carolina and embellishments from Ciudad Juarez. The seats are attached to rails molded in Matamoros and shipped to Ontario to be fitted to metal frames. The Edge's braking system, battery, engine, and transmission all make their way to the final assembly line along similarly convoluted—but almost entirely North American—paths.

On the other side of the Pacific, the Chinese carmaker Great Wall Motors brings together transmissions, chassis, and bumpers from Japan, South Korea, and Taiwan to create its best-selling Haval H6 SUV. In Europe, at Audi's main plant on the Danube, the German company pulls in Swedish power steering, Italian water pumps, Czech wheels, and French circuits to make its sporty two-door A5.

Vehicles aren't the only industry to regionalize. Lenovo ThinkPads start life in a Japanese research and development (R&D) center, where technicians add features and hone designs. When ready, they are handed off to logistics specialists in Malaysia who cull materials and parts from a network of factories across Asia: ceramic capacitors come from Japan, hard drives from Thailand, glass screens from China. South Korean technology powers the semiconductors and processors. These and dozens of other components are then handed over to Taiwanese managers for assembly in Guangzhou plants before heading out to distribution centers across the world.

The aerospace industry also offers similar tales. At Airbus's Toulouse compound, home to more than twenty thousand workers, executives spend their days orchestrating a pan-European dance of processes and parts to build the company's commercial planes, helicopters, and satellites. French engineers hold conference calls with colleagues in Spain and Germany to iron out flaws in their 3D models. A few offices over, managers keep tabs on Swiss assembly lines making wing skins and carbon-fiber shells, on testing results from Bremen-designed-and-manufactured lift systems, and on the machining of keel beams and engine nose cowls in Nantes. Wings from northern Wales, fuselages from Hamburg, rudder spars, landing-gear doors, and tail boxes from outside Madrid all take to the roads, rails, and skies bound for southern France. They sail down the Garonne River in specially equipped barges and wind their way through the small village streets of Colomiers on midnight deliveries. Even here, at the heart of one of the most complex supply chains in existence, over half the parts come from Airbus's home region.

This is true for more than just manufacturing supply chains. It pertains to economies as a whole. Contradicting Thomas Friedman's take, the world is not flat.[5] Moving things is still expensive. Even with monster ships able to carry over twenty thousand containers on each sea crossing, "oceans away" still means time and money. And it's not just about the cash: the need for teamwork also encourages keeping it local. Zoom, Skype, Slack, and dozens of whiz-bang digital analytics and management tools can't erase the advantages of similar time zones, languages, and cultural cues or of shorter plane rides for face-to-face meetings. Government incentives to stay regional—free-trade agreements, visa waivers, cheap loans, and other enticements—help too. So does peer pressure and industrial clustering. Once a few companies set up shop next door, suppliers follow, as do consultants, eager to pave the way for others. And regionalization has proven a way to keep at least some of the benefits of factories, offices, and jobs at home in the face of stiffening international economic competition.

Three Regional Hubs Emerge

Regionalization is the economic story of our time, but not all regions are created equal. Three big hubs, in Asia, North America, and Europe, dominate manufacturing. Asia's is the largest, churning out nearly half the world's goods. North America and Europe together supply another 40 percent of global products. The rest of the world—Latin America, Africa, the Indian subcontinent, Central Asia, Russia, the Middle East—are left to divvy up the remaining 10 percent.[6]

Not only do the three big hubs make the vast majority of the world's goods, but they do it largely independently of other regions. Over two-thirds of Europe's trade remains within the European Union (EU), as Europeans make things together and buy from each other. Asia's trade ties, too, have deepened in recent decades. Over half of Asia's international commerce remains within the continent. North America is the least intertwined; under half of its trade takes place between Canada, Mexico, and the United States.[7] Still, this trade is far more interdependent than that in the remaining regions of the world.

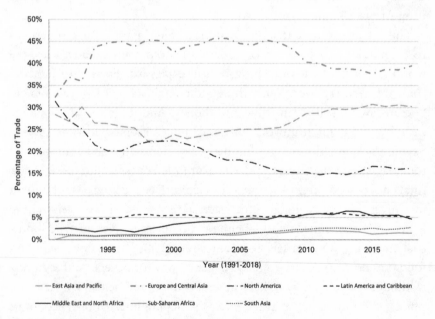

Trade by world region. Source: World Bank

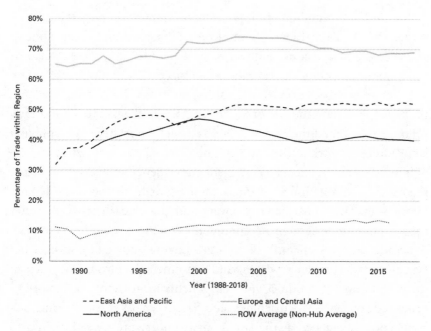

Intraregional trade. The World Integrated Trade Solutions (WITS) database aggregates countries peripheral to the economic hubs analyzed in the book in its denoted regions, meaning intraregional trade in the European and Asian hubs is stronger than depicted.

Europe's integration began in the ruins of the postwar world, as former enemies learned to trust each other through trade. From Rome to Brussels, Maastricht to Amsterdam, Nice to Lisbon, a stream of eponymous treaties bound Europe's members, economies, companies, workers, and populations together. With each ratification, Europe's ties thickened, its integration deepened, and the number of countries in the club grew. The expanding latticework of institutions, agreements, regulations, and court decisions came to govern not just commerce but also the daily lives of citizens in over two dozen countries. Despite frequent squabbles and several full-blown crises, the nations strove to uphold a single European vision, choosing to cede power to regional supranational institutions to propel and promote integration.

Asia's binding together involved fewer diplomats; instead, CEOs backed by state bureaucrats led the charge. East Asia was the first to knit itself together. As Japan rebuilt after the war, its government-supported industries turned to factories in Taiwan, South Korea, Singapore, and Hong Kong to assemble cars, televisions, and footwear. A decade later, these "Asian tigers" were rich enough to repeat Japan's success for themselves, farming out their own production to neighboring Malaysia, Indonesia, Thailand, the Philippines, and the rest of Southeast Asia. In the late 1970s and early 1980s, China joined the assembly line as its neighbors began outsourcing labor-intensive work to the country's new special economic zones.

It was the North American Free Trade Agreement (NAFTA) that spurred the rise of a production platform spanning North America. The United States, Canada, and Mexico had always traded with each other. But after the 1993 free-trade agreement, continental commerce quadrupled in size. A decade on, U.S. manufacturers were buying and selling more from Canadian and Mexican producers and consumers than from any others in the world, moving modules and components from factory to factory to make cars, planes, MRI machines, and flat-screen TVs. North America's connections weakened as the twenty-first century progressed, thanks to China's rise and the hardening of borders after 9/11. But even today, well over a trillion dollars' worth of trade crosses North American borders each year, sustaining thousands of businesses and millions of workers.

These three regional manufacturing hubs compete for companies, brands, and consumers. Asia's vast workforce and its ability to quickly scale production has given it the edge in electronics. Companies like Foxconn, LG, and Lenovo churn out millions of smartphones, LED lights, and nine out of every ten computers. The EU's more formal integration created built-in markets that enabled companies such as Novartis to succeed in pharmaceuticals and Bosch in car parts. In North America, NAFTA's market-based approach honed productivity, advancing world-class companies like Honeywell, United Technologies, and Medtronic in aerospace and medical equipment.

The United States' Reluctant Internationalization and Regionalization

Despite the rise of a North American manufacturing platform, the United States has been slower than others to enter the global trading fray. It remains one of the more closed economies in the world, with trade as a portion of gross domestic product (GDP) less than half the world's average.[8] The United States continues to be less integrated with its neighbors than its European or Asian commercial rivals, as more of its trade still goes to countries outside its region than within it.

A large domestic market and substantial wealth have made it easy enough for most companies and their workers to focus only on consumers at home. A significant portion of the economy is in services, which have been much slower to cross borders. And while overall U.S. tariffs and other barriers are quite low, in some areas—ships, apparel, shoes, chemicals, and many agricultural products—protection has effectively kept most others out.

Still, the United States hasn't avoided international integration entirely. U.S. trade has more than doubled over the past two decades.[9] Much of the growth in U.S. exports has been in intermediary parts sent off to be combined into computers, cars, planes, and thousands of other products. U.S.-made heavy machinery, tools, trucks, and tractors—known as capital goods, because they're used to produce other products—are used by farms and factories all around the world. Add in raw materials—iron ore, cotton, petroleum, copper—and close to two-thirds of all the things the United States sends abroad go into making something else.[10]

This round of regionalization and globalization has brought real, if generalized, economic gains to the United States. Businesses, workers, and families have all benefited from more and cheaper goods; the sheer number of items and the fall in prices together enable today's middle class to own far more gadgets than its predecessors did. Nostalgia blurs the vision: during the supposed middle-class golden age of the 1950s, one in five households didn't own a car, and fewer than one in ten had a television. Today, the average home has two cars, three televisions, and a proliferation of other screens—nine out of ten have a computer, three out of four Americans a smartphone. A middle-class lifestyle includes former luxuries turned basics: air conditioning, washing machines, and dishwashers. Abundance has come in large part from technological breakthroughs. But mass ownership is also the result of supply chains that draw on many different factories and countries to make goods cheaper for all.

According to a study by the Peterson Institute, a think tank for economics, the average U.S. household gains the equivalent of $10,000 in real disposable income from trade every year.[11] Working-class families benefit the most, as cheap manufacturing turns extravagances into staples. Today's TVs are bigger, their screens crisper, and their prices just a quarter what they were a decade ago. Toys, kitchen supplies, and sneakers all cost a fraction of their former price tags, thanks largely to trade.

Trade doesn't just help consumers. Whatever the conventional wisdom says, the reality is that when U.S. companies make goods abroad, they create jobs at home. One study of U.S. multinationals found that for every job companies filled abroad, nearly two new jobs opened up in the United States.[12] Another study, by two Harvard professors and a colleague at the University of Michigan, found that when U.S. companies hire people abroad, U.S. jobs, wages, and investment all increase too.[13] Foreign companies that set up shop in the United States also boost local prosperity. As well as hiring workers, they buy 80 percent of their parts from local suppliers. And they pay their employees nearly a third more than do companies that aren't tied into global markets.[14]

Why does creating jobs abroad also create them at home? The answer is straightforward: cheaper manufacturing means more sales, and more sales means more workers are needed to run operations in the United States. Outsourcing allows companies to find cheaper parts and cheaper manufacturing processes. It can also mean higher quality, as companies exploit specialized materials or manufacturing skills not available at home. Operations abroad open up new markets, giving companies the chance to sell to a whole new group of consumers. When brands can offer the same or higher quality products at lower prices to more people, they sell more. And when they sell more, they need more designers, engineers, managers, marketers, and a whole host of other U.S.-based suppliers. Multinational sales, whether in one or a dozen countries, link U.S. offices and operations to the global economy. And the resulting jobs are the "good jobs" politicians often talk about, well paid and reliable.[15]

Of course, not all Americans enjoy the fruits of globalization. Interconnectedness has left many U.S. companies, workers, and communities vulnerable to shifts in international manufacturing. Disruptions in production elsewhere, whether from natural disasters, political spats, economic downturns, or even pandemics, can delay or cancel the contracts that keep U.S. factory lines running, sales reps on the road, and store shelves stocked.

And the deepening of regionalization elsewhere has cut out U.S. suppliers, as they turn to sources and factories closer by.

Many of the new positions that are created aren't in the same place or the same kind of jobs that have disappeared. Those who are accustomed to working a factory line aren't likely to easily transition to designing, coding, or marketing. And over the past three decades, trade is one of many factors that has helped make jobs in the United States more transient. The average American worker will hold nearly twelve different positions over their lifetime; the median time in each job is less than five years. And while job churn has risen, wages for the middle and working classes have not. This stagnation has many causes that play a bigger role than trade: automation and technological changes, the decline of unions, the erosion of the minimum wage by inflation, fading entrepreneurship, and for many, not enough or the wrong kind of education.[16] The COVID-19 pandemic has further disrupted the situation, especially for lower-skilled workers, as millions lost jobs during lockdowns. While less influential or important, these pressures also reflect the rise of international supply chains, as many manufacturing steps are now done more cheaply elsewhere.

Most Americans understand these complexities. Polls show nearly three-quarters of Americans believe trade benefits the United States as a whole. A majority believe trade, broadly speaking, creates jobs, even as they recognize the costs that some Americans do often pay.[17]

Many local politicians understand the advantages of trade. The governors of forty states and mayors of dozens of cities have opened some two hundred outposts abroad to attract foreign investment in the United States. From Beijing to Mexico City, entrepreneurial politicians showcase their facilities, workers, and locales to far-off companies and help their local businesses woo global consumers.

The United States' national politicians are, sadly, less nuanced. On the left and the right, leaders denounce trade, blaming it for everything from lost jobs and devastated communities to rising inequality and government deficits. In the wake of the coronavirus pandemic, they have added national security concerns, pointing to stretched-out global supply chains to explain the scarcity of medical equipment and medicines that left Americans vulnerable to the virus.

The truth is that while trade benefits the United States as a whole, some kinds are better than others. Regional ties help U.S. workers and businesses more than global ones do. Studies of communities hit by offshoring demonstrate this crucial difference. A well-regarded investigation by the economists David Autor, David Dorn, and Gordon Hanson estimates that during the first decade of the twenty-first century, up to two million U.S. jobs were lost to imports from China (though they did not try to measure jobs gained from increased exports).[18] At the same time, studies of NAFTA have found limited effects on jobs and communities from trade with Mexico and Canada.[19] How could one kind of trade undermine towns and entire industries and another cause barely a ripple? The answer lies in how regionalism works.

When U.S. companies buy and sell within North America, more work stays at home than if they set up shop farther away. And these jobs aren't just researchers, marketers, or headquarter managers; they are also machinists and assembly-line workers in U.S.-based supplier factories. Because of the trade in intermediate goods, the average Mexican import is 40 percent U.S. made; the average Canadian one is 25 percent U.S. made.[20] These ties with Mexico support an estimated five million U.S. jobs; the ties with Canada support another seven million.[21] Combined, that's as many Americans as can be found working in the entire U.S. manufacturing sector. As for a product coming in from China? Just 4 percent of it was made in the USA.[22] Rather than being "the worst trade deal ever made," NAFTA was probably the best for the United States, protecting U.S. industries and jobs through a more united front.

This same dynamic benefits other manufacturing hubs as well. When imports come from nearby, they tend to have more parts or inputs from home, providing more support for local factories and jobs compared to wares made farther away. The French Peugeots sold in Berlin showrooms are filled with German parts made by German workers. The same goes for Mercedes-Benz A-Class sedans sold in Paris, which use French Renault engines. More than two out of every three traded intermediate pieces in Europe come from within the region, meaning more work in European factories and offices. Regionally integrated production chains get the best of both worlds; by drawing on different skills and cheaper labor, they make products more competitive, boosting sales, and by keeping production near at hand, they support more jobs at home. Through lower prices due to economies of scale and higher quality through specialization, regionally made goods become more globally competitive and more likely to edge out similar products made in just one place or country that tries to go it alone.

The lack of regionalization helps explain some of globalization's losers. In Latin America, Africa, India and South Asia, and the Middle East, less than a fifth of trade takes place within each region.[23] Not coincidentally, these countries have grown more slowly than many of their emerging-market peers have.

Development economists have long struggled with why so few nations have been able to join the ranks of the rich over the past six decades, all but a handful getting stuck in what they call the "middle income trap."[24] In a similar vein, the economist Dani Rodrik has found that the most historically successful path to wealth—manufacturing—is closing off to many developing countries in what he calls "premature deindustrialization."[25]

Both of these economic discussions tend to blame globalization. Yet the geographic disparities in the data hint at the saving graces of regionalization. Of the thirteen countries that have made it into the high-income ranks since 1960, ten are part of one of the global regional hubs. Latin America and Africa have seen the biggest losses with regard to manufacturing jobs and output; Asia has bucked this trend and become a manufacturing powerhouse.

Scholars of international supply chains (which they tend to call "global value chains") show how taking part in the international production process helps attract investment and technology, teach workers new skills, and enhance managerial know-how.[26] Over time, local factories can upgrade and make more sophisticated and higher-priced goods.

Without strong commercial ties to nearby nations, workers and consumers are largely left on the ends of global supply chains, relegated to sending out raw materials and bringing in final goods. The lack of neighborhood ties means most imports have little local content. Unlike in the regional hubs, these goods from distant shores compete with, rather than support, local manufacturers. This all leaves these nations in the economic slow lane.

Global Supply Chains to Get More Regional

The forces that pushed the world toward globalization, some forty plus years in the making, are now shifting once again, and regional trade is set to win out even more than in the past.[27] Commercial dispersion has peaked. For the past decade, growth in trade flows has lagged growth in GDP. In part, this reflects the long hangover of the 2008 financial crisis; more recently, COVID-19 temporarily threw the brakes on trade. But this deceleration also stems from longer-term structural shifts in the costs and benefits of globalized supply chains. Many of the economic, technological, and political factors that once gave the edge to far-away factories have begun to fade.

Labor costs, which once drove companies abroad, are often less important. Rising wages have made China's labor force less of a bargain. Robots and 3D printing, alongside semiautomated assembly lines, warehouses, and inventories, enable businesses to do more with fewer workers. And in a world of faster turnaround times and guarantees of overnight or even same-day delivery, being near your customers has become more valuable. Finicky and rapidly changing consumer tastes also undermine mass production and economies of scale. The promise of custom-made goods, from shoes to glasses, threatens the advantages of large, monolithic factories across the oceans.

Politics are changing, too. Economists often claim that globalization is inevitable, that it is the result of market forces too powerful for any government to control. But in reality, globalization was always a choice. And today, politicians are choosing different things. Around the world, policies that increase barriers to trade and close borders now outpace those that aim to open them up. The United States is questioning the open trading order it helped build. And China is pulling back, importing less as it strives to become more than a final assembly hub.

Yet as politicians promise to bring factories and jobs back home, and companies look into shifting their production sites and sources, the benefits of regionalization continue. The multicountry advantages of diverse workforces, labor costs, technology, access to capital, free-trade agreements that harmonize rules and regulations, combined market size, and diversifying risks enable companies and their workers to make better products for less, even in a world of smaller batches and faster delivery. As more nations join together for a competitive edge, it leaves the laggards at a further disadvantage. For the United States, the best way to compete with the other regional manufacturing hubs is still to build its own.

Even if the reaction against globalization means making things become less global, sales may become ever more so. To thrive, brands must now court choosy consumers from Kuala Lumpur to Prague—and compete with cutthroat foreign brands on their home turf. Without cheaper and more innovative offerings, U.S. brands will lose the race. Already, South Korea's Samsung smartphones outsell all others in Indonesia, Argentina, and Egypt. Its Galaxy phones are edging in on the iPhone's popularity in American hands. China's Great Wall Motors goes head-to-head with General Motors (GM) in Italy, Australia, and Russia. And India's Tata Consultancy is nabbing information technology (IT) and digital services customers from IBM and Accenture throughout North and South America. Competition has gone global.

Sixty years ago, the United States built half the world's products. U.S. companies faced little competition from devastated European and Japanese factories and farms that were barely able to meet the needs of their own populations, much less those of other countries. Dominating the world is no longer so easy. Today, Asia and Europe make nearly two out of every three products sent abroad. Their success stems, in part, from their regional embrace. By integrating their markets, investments, and chains of production, European and Asian companies have become more globally competitive, creating jobs, wealth, and profits at home. The United States, meanwhile, hasn't yet made the most of the opportunities that can come from commercial ties to its neighbors.

As competition internationalizes and, crucially, regionalizes, so too must the United States. It needs to expand and deepen the North American integration that NAFTA once spurred. Exploiting the three countries' variations in capital, labor, and natural resources, in sources of information and clusters of innovation, allows North American companies to make products faster, cheaper, and better than they could in one nation alone. Integrating North America creates a larger home market and lets U.S. suppliers benefit from Canada's and Mexico's more expansive free-trade agreements with the world. That will create and protect U.S. jobs.

To compete abroad, the United States also needs reform at home. Doing globalization on the cheap—without adequate safety nets and labor rights, without ample levels of publicly funded science and research, without comprehensive health-care coverage and competitive schools—makes it hard to help those who are disenfranchised by trade and to better equip more Americans to reap the benefits. The United States needs a real safety net. It needs to enhance workers' voices in trade discussions. It needs to invest in education, training, and infrastructure, and in basic science and commercial research, to keep its technological edge and prepare more citizens to take jobs tied to the rest of the world and to the future.

A new kind of globalization is on the horizon, one of new technological tools, demographic shifts, climate changes, and a billion new online consumers. Many of these trends play to the United States' strengths: clear legal rules, world-class universities, a growing working-age population, open markets, wealthy consumers, advanced technology, and globally recognized services and brands. The United States can handle competition. But it will be easier and done better with partners. If it continues to leave the benefits of regionalization to the rest of the world, more Americans will get left behind. The country will see less of the innovation and entrepreneurship that make it great, and embracing protectionism will only breed stagnation.

To keep up with and compete against Asia's expansive reach and Europe's industrial prowess, U.S. politicians, entrepreneurs, and workers need to recognize that we do better when we work with those who are closest to us. Regionalization brings variety, fosters innovation, enhances resilience, and creates a much stronger home base. To bring economic vitality back to Akron, and so many communities like it, the United States needs deeper integration with its neighbors.

1

The Rise of Regional Supply Chains

Globalization is one of the most heralded stories of the past forty years, and justifiably so. When Ronald Reagan entered the White House in 1981, annual trade between nations totaled $2.4 trillion. Today, it nears $20 trillion. International capital flows jumped too, from $500 billion a year in the early 1980s to over $3.5 trillion today.[1] People took flight as well—the number of international trips rose from less than 300 million in 1980 to 1.4 billion in 2018.[2] Ideas and inventions, international patent filings, and royalty payments from overseas are all growing rapidly too.

This internationalization of goods, services, people, ideas, and money has vastly improved living standards in dozens of countries and lowered consumer prices in many more. It has sped invention and innovation through specialization and clustered expertise. And it has upended industries and livelihoods, particularly in advanced industrial economies such as the United States.

This isn't the first time that "globalization" has reshaped the world. International trade has ebbed and flowed throughout history, creating towns and cities, building governments and nation-states, starting and ending wars. What is different today is the nature of trade.

A century ago, most of what crossed borders was ready to be consumed— olives from Italy, wine from Spain, furs from Canada; later on, cars from Germany, sewing machines, printing presses, and cash registers from the United States. Sure, resource-rich countries shipped iron, copper, and coal to power far-away factories. But trade generally involved things made or grown in one place and sold in another.

That began to change after World War II. Rather than making the final sale, more companies became suppliers, sending parts to meet up with those made by others for assembly. As companies sliced up manufacturing into discrete parts and processes, they looked abroad. Through offshoring, outsourcing, and subcontracting, international commerce and connections grew. Trade in intermediate goods rose.

Commercial ties between countries increasingly no longer meant just buying and selling goods to and from each other but also creating things together. Supply chains, or what scholars often refer to as "global value chains," began to link up countries, economies, and societies.

Today, 80 percent of trade involves raw materials or intermediate goods.[3] The specialization of factories and firms within production chains has led to new ways of building companies and doing business.[4] C-suite decisions are less about whether the company should bring in parts from abroad— that is usually a given—and more about whether it should own the natural resources, parts makers, and factories in its supply chain or instead buy inputs from others. The sunglass maker Luxottica decided to bring everything, from concept to retail outlet, in house. The design and colors of its Wayfarer Ray-Bans are tweaked in its studios, hundreds of thousands of pairs are put together in wholly owned workshops, the boxes are then shipped out by its internal distribution team, and the sunglasses are sold at the thousands of Luxottica-owned outlets: Sunglass Hut, LensCrafter, Pearle Vision, and Sears Optical. Ikea, a Swedish company headquartered in the Netherlands, also owns most of its supply chain, including tens of thousands of acres of Romanian forest, Polish wind farms and factories, and even a Dutch plastic recycling plant. In contrast, U.S.-based Apple mostly relies on other companies to make its iPads, iPhones, and watches. And Nike doesn't own even one of the 523 factories in forty-one countries that make its signature swoosh.[5] These different corporate choices influence where things are made, who owns innovations, how goods are marketed, and how profits are divided among the many firms that take part.[6]

Still, the narrative and the reality of globalization have diverged fairly dramatically. Trade tripled over the past four decades; nearly a third of what the world makes now leaves its country of origin.[7] But those products don't go just anywhere. If distance were truly no object, the average international sale would involve a 5,300-mile journey (the average distance between two randomly selected countries).[8] Instead, half of what is sold internationally travels less than 3,000 miles, not much farther than a flight from New York to California, certainly not enough to cross oceans. As companies have gone abroad in search of better and cheaper components, as they have built out their own operations or contracted others to do it for them, they have mostly stayed close to home. They haven't typically gone global; they've gone regional. This is particularly true for the more complex production chains in electronics, machinery, and transportation equipment.[9]

The internationalization of the making of things required fundamental changes in transportation, information, and financial flows. It depended on treaties, free-trade agreements (FTAs), and favorable international norms. Usually seen as the drivers of globalization, these factors pushed the more prevalent and intense regionalization that has occurred.

Transportation and Technology Push Production International

Some of the innovations that enabled the expansion of international supply chains were deceptively simple—the unassuming shipping container, for instance. Until the 1960s, goods traveled on ships intricately stacked by longshoremen, whose work was rather like packing an enormous car trunk for a vacation. Barrels of olives, bales of cotton, baskets of oranges, drums of chemicals, pallets of furniture, and any imaginable mix of cargo collected from waterside warehouses would pile up on the docks, tens if not hundreds of thousands of items in all. Skilled longshoremen would load them into irregular ship spaces, from the narrow bottom to the widening top, the bulkhead to the curved sides, building temporary walls out of lumber and the goods themselves, mixing cartons, sacks, boxes, and barrels to keep the wares still on rough seas.[10]

It was time-consuming, dangerous, and costly work. Ships would take days to load and unload; a teetering stack could, and often did, come crashing down, crushing anyone below. Goods arrived broken or disappeared into the hands of unscrupulous workers. Often, organized crime's grip on many waterfronts swelled the costs of getting into and out of port. All told, the loading and unloading process absorbed easily a third of the cost of a transatlantic voyage.

That all changed in 1956, when a crane in the Newark docks lifted the first steel box from a truck bed onto a ship bound for Houston. Over the next two decades, these stackable boxes transformed the way things were sent around the world. Every container ship could be loaded and unloaded in the same way. No more messing about with unwieldy crates of bananas or teetering stacks of cotton bales. Filling the containers took work, of course, but this was now done at warehouses and on factory floors, not at the docks. The result was that shipping costs per ton plummeted from six dollars to sixteen cents, making it dramatically easier for companies to buy raw materials and components from farther away. Today, millions of containers circle the globe, picking up bananas, wheat, tires, electric switches, and furniture and sending back bicycles, televisions, toys, and clothes.

Just as trade on the seas transformed, so did trade in the skies. In the early 1970s, an American entrepreneur by the name of Fred Smith spun out an idea from an undergraduate economics paper he had written a decade earlier to speed up U.S. deliveries by flying his own planes. He called the company Federal Express and started by flying small packages on Dassault Falcon jets from his Memphis headquarters to Kansas City, St. Louis, Atlanta, and a scattering of other cities in middle America. Then came flights to the West Coast and up and down the East. After a rocky start—once, unable to meet that week's payroll, Smith headed with the company's last $5,000 to Las Vegas, where a lucky blackjack table saved FedEx from ruin—the business caught on. FedEx made the one-time luxury of overnight delivery common. Within a decade, dozens of FedEx planes filled with tens of thousands of packages were crisscrossing the United States and Canada every day.

The same decade that Smith started FedEx, Adrian Dalsey, Larry Hillblom, and Robert Lynn, the founders of an upstart transportation enterprise called DHL, set their sights on becoming couriers for the world. Based in San Francisco, DHL first looked across the Pacific, connecting West Coast companies to their outposts in Hong Kong, the Philippines, Japan, Singapore, and Australia. Multinationals came to rely on DHL's neon-yellow packets to send bills of lading for ships en route, invoices, orders, legal contracts, and other time-sensitive documents across the international date line. DHL's delivery services quickly expanded worldwide, adding parcels to papers along the way. By the twenty-first century, DHL had joined forces with Deutsche Post and become the world's largest logistics company. Every year it fills and ships over four million seabound containers and flies cargo weighing as much as one million cars.[11]

As important as creating faster and cheaper ways to move physical goods was, it wasn't enough to transform manufacturing. Just as important was the ability to work efficiently with people a country or a hemisphere away. To achieve that required new revolutions, this time in communications.

When AT&T began offering international calls in the 1920s, they cost so much that only the rich or desperate used them. Prices fell in the following decades. Yet even by the 1970s, overseas calls still weren't cheap; they were plagued by echoes and voice delays and limited to fewer than ten thousand at a time. In 1980, the average person or business was making just a couple of international calls a year.[12]

The two decades that followed transformed international communication. Easy, real-time, and nearly free connections with colleagues and computers next door or half a world away became common. That made international supply chains possible.

As underwater copper cables gave way to fiber-optic ones, exponentially more voices and data could travel along each wire. The number of possible calls jumped from thousands to tens of millions at a time. Mobile networks joined and then later surpassed these land lines in linking people and operations. In the early 1980s, first-generation, or 1G, cell towers enabled uninterrupted connections not just between individuals but also between the office and the shop floor. A decade later, 2G technology let texting and document sharing proliferate. With 3G, mobile could rival broadband and let users see as well as hear people on the other end. 4G now streams big data almost seamlessly. And 5G promises enough power to instantly download movies, guide industrial robots, and drive autonomous cars. With each generation, speed, volume, and efficiency have grown, making the answer to "Can you hear me now?" more often "yes" than "no."

Devices transformed too. Cell phones morphed from glorified walkie-talkies to always-online handheld computers. In 1983, Motorola launched its two-pound DynaTAC brick. After charging for ten hours, the $4,000 clunker boasted a whole half hour of battery life. It didn't take long for smaller, sleeker, cheaper, and longer-lasting models to arrive. Motorola released the first flip phone in 1989. Nokia created slimmer open versions, its biggest hit the colorful and durable 1100 series, which sold a quarter billion models before it too became obsolete.[13]

As cell phones grew more sophisticated, businesses found new uses for them. New models incorporated calculators, calendars, and currency converters. They added cameras and email. BlackBerry's miniature keyboard allowed managers to type out missives from anywhere and staff to respond in kind.

Computers changed rapidly too. In the 1980s, they entered homes and offices en masse. IBM's personal computer, the PC, hit stores in 1981. But Big Blue quickly lost control of the retail market: upstart Compaq's lighter-weight models were soon outselling IBM's by eight to one.[14] Dell jumped in, marketing its customized computers and kits direct to consumers in trade magazines and catalogs. And Toshiba took computers off desks and put them onto laps.

With each iteration and model, computers got faster, smaller, and cheaper. Computing speed and storage expanded exponentially. Room-size mainframes gave way to desktops, then to laptops, and finally to tablets. Prices plummeted: a 1970s Hewlett-Packard (HP) business computer cost over $500,000 in current dollars; a more powerful Dell desktop retails at just $150 today.[15]

In the early 2000s, undersea cables multiplied as Microsoft, Google, and Facebook joined telecoms carriers to lay new lines across the Atlantic and Pacific floors. Prices plummeted, and the psychology of picking up the phone changed. Quality improved, too; dial-up service gave way to DSL lines, and cable companies piped the internet into tens of millions of households alongside HBO, Showtime, and ESPN.

As transmission size and speed multiplied, so did the sheer number of ways to communicate. Voice over internet protocol (VoIP) made it almost free to call people whenever, wherever. Video conferencing, once the domain of the biggest corporations with dedicated video rooms, became commonplace and virtually costless thanks to Skype, Zoom, and Google

Meet. The sharing of hundreds of millions of digital packets—snippets of conversations, emails, data sets, spreadsheets, texts, and songs—was now limited by only the speed of light.

Computers and phones merged in 2007 with the introduction of Apple's iPhone. Users connected with friends, listened to music, took photos, and played games all on their phones. Businesses brought phones and tablets to the office and shop floor, connecting employees anywhere from a few feet to several countries apart.

Software and apps emerged to exploit the powerful new devices. Computer-aided design, or CAD, software let designers and engineers draw, test, and revise their ideas, 2D and 3D sketches hopping from computer to computer and phone to phone, sending files across time zones as easily as handing off pencil-smudged plans across the hall.

Computer modeling let engineers test joints and fittings without having to visit a workshop, smoothing out the kinks before a product hit the assembly line. And through all the iterations and revisions, designers, engineers, and factory workers never needed to be in the same place. CAD programs quickly became so ubiquitous that thousands of companies, including Boeing when designing its 777, simply threw away pencil and paper.[16]

Software also sped up trade by streamlining logistics. Tracking went virtual. Barcodes allowed managers to follow a product from supplier to warehouse to assembly line to delivery truck, store, and front door. Global positioning system (GPS) tracking located each screw, screen, insole, battery, and microphone to within an inch of its position. Parts could be reliably traced and thus come from farther away, and the assembly-line dance could become more and more complex.

Manufacturers had always toiled over how to calculate the supplies they needed, the best way to set up their shop floors, and how to provide the cheapest, fastest, and safest delivery to their customers. Now, supply-chain software eased these tasks. Physical ledgers and files gave way to digital spreadsheets, databases, graphs, and interactive maps. They could calculate more efficient trucking routes and help decide which assembly lines and machines should work when and for how long.

A whole industry of companies arose with specialized applications that tied together procurement, accounting, human resources, financing, and marketing—almost every aspect of day-to-day business. Software from Oracle, SAP, and Microsoft processed customer orders and sent them to distribution warehouses, monitored inventories and automatically reached out to suppliers when stocks were low, kept track of compliance test results, and traced ingredients for faster recalls.

A $40 billion customer relationship management (CRM) industry emerged, its technologies helping other companies store, share, and manage data. Salesforce, HubSpot, Zoho, and dozens of others offer digital platforms on which sales teams can store contacts, log calls, send reminders, and share targets. Marketers use them to create websites, automate mailings, monitor open rates on emails, and run events. By tracking customers, the platforms help companies target their social media campaigns. Some run other companies' ecommerce sites for them.[17] These connections, devices, and software made it possible and even easy to set up international manufacturing supply chains.

The Internationalization of Money

This slicing and dicing of production could never have gotten so far, so fast without an explosion in international finance. In the 1980s, at the same time as production was going more international, banks were eyeing lucrative foreign markets, too. Over the next few decades, new policies, technologies, and participants would unleash a torrent of capital across borders. These international financial flows enabled companies to expand their work around the world.

Money had not been part of the post–World War II trade opening. After the financial collapses of the 1930s, the Keynesian economists at the economic helm of many nations believed capital controls were the best way to head off speculative booms and busts and rein in financial panics. Across the United States, Canada, Japan, and much of Europe, laws kept out foreign banks, limited foreign exchange flows, and taxed international transactions. The 1944 Bretton Woods agreement reinforced this approach, fixing European exchange rates against the U.S. dollar and, ultimately, gold. For developing countries, capital restrictions went hand in hand with government plans to protect local companies and promote homegrown industrialization.

This orthodoxy began to erode in the 1970s. Mainstream economic thinking shifted as Keynesian economists fumbled through recessions and stagflation. More market-driven neoliberal thinkers gained currency in academic departments. Their intellectual godfather, Milton Friedman, won the 1976 Nobel Prize for Economics.

By the 1980s, a new generation of graduate students trained in the importance of free markets were joining the International Monetary Fund (IMF), the World Bank, and finance ministries around the globe, ready to put their ideas into action. Notably, U.S. president Ronald Reagan and British prime minister Margaret Thatcher embraced the shift. So did the growing number of multinational corporations looking to fund their various operations and repatriate profits from abroad.

After Bretton Woods collapsed in the 1970s—the result of rising U.S. inflation and current account deficits—many members let their currencies float freely against one another. By the 1980s, most Organization for Economic Cooperation and Development (OECD) countries had ended foreign exchange controls. Banking rules relaxed at the same time, opening up once tightly controlled financial markets to foreign entrants.

As policy makers loosened the rules, new technologies made it easier to move first billions and then trillions of dollars abroad. In the 1970s, the big banks replaced a clunky World War II–era Telex messaging system with the faster and more secure SWIFT network. Soon, other new software systems could clear dollars, pounds sterling, and other foreign currencies electronically, speeding international transactions.[18] Throughout the 1970s and 1980s, Visa, Mastercard, and American Express moved from regional credit networks to building their own global payment systems, backing the international transactions of tourists and companies alike.[19]

Cross-border loans grew as commercial bankers moved into new markets. International bonds and equities came next as investment bankers and money managers followed commercial bankers abroad. Financial whizzes on Wall Street and in the City of London brought hundreds of companies from around the world to list on their stock exchanges and issued hundreds of billions of dollars in international debt. In an important move for supply chains, they began extending loans to exporters on the strength of orders. Now that exporters had access to money for cement, steel, plastics, electronics, auto parts, and other orders yet to be delivered, many more companies had the necessary capital to participate in international manufacturing chains.

Over the same period, the big money managers helped open up the developing world to international investment. In the 1980s, Vanguard, Fidelity, and Oppenheimer opened dedicated "emerging markets" funds, and Morgan Stanley and JPMorgan launched emerging markets stock and bond indexes. Far more capital than before began flowing from rich countries to poor ones.

An explosion of futures, options, swaps, and other cross-border financial instruments helped companies and bankers hedge against currency risks. And, in 1999, the introduction of the euro ended the need to deal with foreign currencies for transactions between countries making up almost a third of the world's GDP. This all made it easier to lend, list, issue, and conduct international financial transactions.

Foreign direct investment, which involves making deals and setting up operations in foreign countries, accelerated too. Trillions of dollars flowed abroad to buy land, oil fields, mines, buildings, and plants and to set up subsidiaries, labs, research centers, and thousands upon thousands of factories making everything from nanochips to computers, solar panels to wind turbines, cars to high-speed trains. Joining General Electric (GE), Procter & Gamble, IBM, Dupont, BMW, and others with long-held international operations were relative newcomers like Gillette, Nike, Samsung, and Costco. And alongside the public-company heavyweights were thousands of midsized firms—auto-parts and crane makers, refrigeration and steel-bar specialists, candy makers and furniture builders.

In the early 1980s, some $500 billion crossed borders each year. Now, nearly six times that amount flows abroad every month. Together, bankers, businesses, and new technologies made it possible, even easy, to send and receive money across borders, time zones, and currencies. This flood of capital from foreign direct investments, loans, lines of credit, stocks, bonds, and other financial instruments helped manufacturers and their suppliers join international production chains. The heightened capital flows challenged governments, weakening policy tools even as they intensified financial crises. By the twenty-first century, foreign direct investment had grown to forty cents of every one of the trillions of dollars headed abroad.[20]

A Pro-Trade World

The rise of international supply chains hinged on a global pro-trade consensus. The groundwork began between the world wars. Smarting from the swift worldwide retribution to the country's Smoot-Hawley tariffs in the 1930s, a chastened United States began to rethink its protectionist past. Newly empowered congressional Democrats under President Franklin Delano Roosevelt pushed through legislation to slash tariffs and turn over future negotiations to the historically more pro-trade presidency.

This open outlook accelerated after the war. Democrats and Republicans both turned away from protectionism, coming to see trade as a weapon against a return of Hitler's nationalist appeals, an antidote to creeping communism, and a boon for U.S. companies facing little competition from devastated European and Japanese factories and farms.

In 1947, the United States orchestrated the first worldwide trade agreement, the General Agreement on Tariffs and Trade, or GATT, which brought together twenty-two nations, including the United States, Canada, the UK, and much of mainland Europe and its former, or soon to be former, colonies. From the outset, GATT's members promised to charge each other the same tariff rates on particular goods (called "most favored nation" rules) and treat imported goods the same as those made at home.[21] Over the next four decades, the club would deepen its mutual commitments. Through nine separate rounds of negotiations, its members repeatedly cut tariffs, lowering average rates from over 20 percent to just 5 percent by the 1990s. They took on other barriers too. In the 1960s, members limited what is commonly called "dumping," the practice of selling goods abroad for less than they go for at home in order to gain market share and push out competitors. In the 1970s, part of the group agreed to slash export subsidies, cut out onerous import licenses, and relax quotas on products like tropical fruits, beef, and dairy. Some nations promised to let foreign companies compete for government contracts.[22]

As the requirements grew, so did the membership. Japan and many northern European countries signed on in the 1950s. The 1960s brought a host of newly independent African nations eager to sign on. GATT continued to grow throughout the 1970s and 1980s, reaching 128 countries by the early 1990s.

In 1995, GATT evolved into the World Trade Organization (WTO). The new organization's mission expanded beyond regulating goods to include rules for services, investments, and intellectual property. It gained the power to judge and punish member nations accused of flouting the club's regulations.

It was within this trade-friendly environment that long-excluded economies reentered the global fray. In the 1980s, China emerged from its economic isolation, Russia and eastern Europe came out from behind their curtain, and West and East Germany united. India began undoing the protectionist policies that had been set up at the time of its independence. Across the Global South, country after country began lowering tariffs, pushed by international institutions and pulled by locals hoping to entice emerging international supply chains to their shores.

Regionalism: The Overlooked Story

Yet with all the talk of globalization, international trade truly transformed the economies of only about two dozen countries. Bangladesh, Hungary, Mexico, Poland, Romania, and Vietnam are among the handful that have seen trade more than double as a proportion of their economies since 1990. For eighty other countries, including Chile, Egypt, Kenya, and Norway, trade barely budged or actually shrank as a percentage of GDP.[23] The remainder are somewhere in between. Clearly, cheap shipping, virtually free communication, sophisticated software, and flowing capital don't tell the whole story.

That's because the world regionalized more than it globalized. As the international flows of goods, services, money, information, and people grew over the past forty years, more than half moved between neighbors and other nearby nations.[24]

Most of the winners of this latest round of globalization tied themselves to countries next door. China's era of double-digit growth began with regional inputs; similar ties helped neighboring Vietnam leave behind years of economic stagnation. Many eastern European countries surged as they integrated with "old Europe." NAFTA helped Mexico's economy more than double in size.

Companies' forays abroad, especially initially, have been more regional

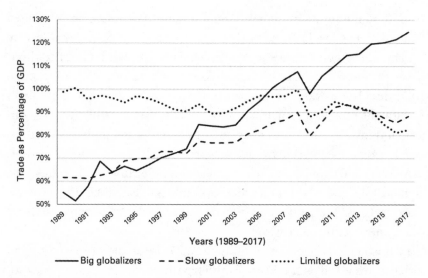

Globalization's limited reach. The graph divides nations into three categories. Big globalizers aggregate the twenty-four nations in which trade as a percentage of GDP more than doubled since 1990; limited globalizers, eighty-four countries in which trade stagnated or declined as a percent of GDP over that time; and slow globalizers, the other seventy-six nations that have seen trade's weight in their economies rise at a slower pace. Source: World Bank

than global. Sweden's Ikea expanded first to Norway and Denmark. Ford Motors' inaugural international plant was just across the Detroit-Windsor Ambassador Bridge in Canada. Foxconn started on its path to becoming the biggest electronics maker in the world with a factory in Shenzhen, less than five hundred miles from its home in Taiwan.

Tens of thousands of smaller corporations followed their higher-profile colleagues in going abroad but also, when doing so, sticking close to home. European companies have invested over a trillion dollars in their brethren nations in the past two decades, far more foreign direct investment (FDI) than came from outside the Union. In Asia, roughly half of all greenfield investments (in which a company creates a new foreign subsidiary and builds and outfits its own factories or offices) comes from other Asian nations, a percentage that has been rising over time. And while foreign direct investment in North America is less regional than elsewhere, Canadian companies outpace all but the British in setting up shop in the United States. Scotia and TD bankers have opened offices from New Orleans to

New York; the auto-parts maker Magna now has more plants in the United States than in Canada. And for Mexico and Canada, U.S. corporations are by far their biggest outside investors; Walmart, GE, Ford, GM, and thousands of others have laid out hundreds of billions of dollars in the two countries. The world over, fifty cents out of every dollar of foreign direct investment stay within their home region. If distance truly were no object, and investors followed GDP growth patterns and global opportunities, less than twenty cents would stay so close.[25]

Mergers and acquisitions tell a similar story. Starting in the 1990s, foreign firms increasingly bought local operations to ease their way into new markets. Cross-border deals grew to one-third of all transactions. But here, again, most ventured nearby.[26]

In Europe, German Siemens bought up British rails and Danish wind turbines, while the once midsize British pharmaceutical player Zeneca leap-frogged in size by merging with the Swedish ulcer medicine maker Astra. Air France acquired the Dutch carrier KLM, while Switzerland's biggest cement company took over French rival Lafarge. Overall, local EU buyers have outpaced outsiders by half.[27]

North American and Asian acquisitions lean regional too. Burger King bought the Canadian burger and donut chain Tim Hortons. Walmart bought the Mexican retail chain Cifra to kick off its southern expansion. Mexico's biggest baker, Bimbo, picked up Mrs. Baird's cookies, Entenmann's pastries, Sara Lee's danishes, and Arnold's bread, coming to dominate the U.S. baking market. In Asia, South Korea's Samsung broke into flat-screen TVs by acquiring Sony's liquid-crystal display (LCD) operations. Thailand's biggest bank beat out Japanese and Singaporean competitors to buy up one of Indonesia's financial mainstays. Chinese conglomerates have snapped up Singaporean warehouses, Burmese ports, and Thai fashion brands.

Research backs up the idea that businesses have gone more international but not necessarily more global. One study of the Fortune Global 500—a set of companies explicitly chosen for their international reach—shows that more than two out of every three dollars of their revenue come from sales within each company's home region. That number hasn't changed much for over two decades.[28] Other studies of multinationals show an even greater concentration, with four out of every five dollars brought in close to home.[29]

In fact, only a handful of companies live up to the "global" hype. For every Coca-Cola, Nokia, Sony, or Canon that has conquered the world, there are many more Carrefours, Siemens, Sumitomos, Whirlpools, Wal-marts, Alibabas, Cisco Systems, General Electrics, and Mitsubishis that have expanded mostly next door.[30] And these regionally focused corporations mostly outpace the globe-trotters.

Making things is, if anything, an even more regional business than selling them. Ikea stores may span the globe, but two out of every three of its products are made in Europe. The fashion house Zara similarly sews a good portion of its trendy clothes in Spain and Portugal, then sells a third of them in Asia and the Americas. Canon's cameras are put together between Japan, Taiwan, China, and Malaysia for consumers in the United States and Europe. As a sector, electronics is the most global in sales. But when it comes to actually making and assembling computers, cell phones, and Fitbits, the process looks distinctly regional.

Finance, too, is more regional than most people recognize. Over half the money moving across borders circulates exclusively within the European Union. Another big chunk moves within Asia, led originally by Japanese financing for the Philippines, Vietnam, South Korea, Taiwan, and China. The 2008 global financial crisis only deepened this regional focus, as chastened U.S. and European banks curtailed their global aspirations, leaving even more to local and regional players.

Of the well-known big banks, none is truly global. Deutsche Bank may have offices in over fifty countries, but two-thirds of its clients and profits come from Europe. Bank of America, Barclays, and JPMorgan are as, if not more, regional in nature.[31] The financial sector as a whole is even more concentrated—three out of every four dollars made by banks come from within their home region.[32]

Even portfolio holdings, the hottest of international money, don't live in a borderless world. When buying stocks and bonds, the average investor goes no farther than the distance between Singapore and Tokyo. And cash, the most versatile asset of all, travels mostly next door when it ventures abroad.[33]

People tend to orient their lives regionally. Most don't leave their own country. But for those who do plan a holiday abroad, nearly three out of four go nearby. The vast majority of tourists taking European vacations are Europeans. The same goes for North Americans vacationing in North America and even more so for Asians in Asia. Students are an unusually global bunch, sometimes crossing continents to attend world-renowned universities. Yet almost half of those who study abroad do so in their international neighborhood. And in the day-to-day of phone calls, news, or internet surfing, those who venture beyond their national borders most often connect with people and websites in surrounding countries.

In total, over half of the flows in international trade, investment, money, information, and people occur within regions.[34] Globalization is, as much as anything, a regional affair.

This shouldn't be all that surprising. The whole point of offshoring and outsourcing is to become more competitive. Sticking close by allows companies to benefit from different costs, skills, and access without losing the trust and understanding that make operations hum.

Manufacturing is particularly susceptible to distance. While research and services can travel almost instantaneously through calls, videos, emails, and file sharing, parts and products have to physically move from here to there. Even when shipping costs plummet, distance adds time. A transatlantic crossing by boat can take well over a week, a transpacific one a month. For companies buying inputs or parts, longer lead times mean they need to keep more inventory and pay more for storage. For fast fashion and other trendy retail products, long shipping times lose customers and revenue.

And just because it is cheap to talk to someone on the other side of the planet doesn't make it easy to coordinate long, complex manufacturing processes. Lower wages or the promise of new consumers often can't offset the intangible costs of doing business outside your comfort zone.

This starts with language. Even talented linguists can get tone and meaning wrong when using their second (or third or fourth) tongue. Profits can literally be lost in translation. As a result, almost a fourth of all trade takes place between countries that speak the same language.

Cultural cues are just as important. That doesn't just mean greeting practices. They include understanding what "tomorrow" means for a supplier, whether you're more likely to convince your boss with an example or a logical argument, and whether you'll get further by addressing conflict discreetly or head-on. Culture can determine whether merit-based pay and promotions will motivate workers, whether third-party contracts or wholly owned subsidiaries make the most organizational sense, and whether marketing campaigns should (or should not) try to be funny.

The ups and downs of offshored call centers reflect these challenges. Once seen as the easiest of businesses to send abroad, since all one needed was a room with computers, headsets, and an internet connection, call centers turned out to have hidden costs that have led many companies to reconsider. Sure, wages may be lower elsewhere, but language barriers, missing cultural references, and poor understanding of company values and ethos leave customers angry. Even when operators adopt local personas— the IT-support technician in Bangalore who tells you her name is Debbie and chats about the weather in St. Louis—the veneer easily wears thin. Many companies, Dell, Capital One, and JPMorgan among them, have moved customer service back home.

Running a business far afield can be tough as well. Any management book will tell you that collegiality and trust are vital things in the workplace. Building teams with enough in common gets harder the farther away you go. Human interactions, and the understanding they bring, lessen with the miles. On top of that, legal rules and accounting standards differ across the globe, requiring companies to double up on accountants and lawyers. Everything from the laws surrounding workplace sexual harassment and how management deals with it (or, too often, does not deal with it) to whether gifts constitute shows of respect or illegal bribes to whether children should be allowed on a shop floor can flummox international executives. Getting things wrong costs time, money, and employee goodwill. Sticking close to home means that basic rules and customs are more likely to be similar, or at least mutually intelligible.

Trade agreements matter too, as they lower tariffs, strip out barriers, and give the participants an edge over countries outside the club. These treaties, more often than not, get signed by neighbors. After Israel, the United States turned to Canada and Mexico when looking for free-trade partners. Brazil joined with Argentina, Australia with New Zealand. Belgium teamed up with Luxembourg and the Netherlands before heading into the (also nearby) European Economic Community. The free-trade area of the Association of Southeast Asian Nations (ASEAN) binds together Indonesia, Thailand, and Malaysia. The Regional Comprehensive Economic Partnership (RCEP) brings together fifteen Asian economies; megaglobal agreements, such as the Comprehensive and Progressive Agreement for Trans-Pacific Partnership (CPTPP), are the exception, as regional arrangements make up a majority of formal trading ties.

Selling to customers in other countries is a perilous business. For every Hollywood blockbuster that goes global, dozens of others get lost in translation. Even sophisticated brands have made bloopers when trying to go international. Ford's Pinto failed in Brazil as its name suggested diminutive male private parts. Pepsi's "bring you back to life" campaign scared away Chinese drinkers worried about their ancestors rising from the grave. KFC tried to tell Chinese customers that their chicken was "finger lickin' good," but an overly literal translation informed viewers that it would make you "eat your fingers off." Sweden's main appliance maker tried to sell its vacuum cleaners in the United States with the tagline "Nothing sucks like an Electrolux."[35]

The differences go beyond slogans to basic tastes, preferences, and ways of managing people. GM's halfhearted attempt to build a smaller car, the Opel, for the European market failed, as management couldn't shed its SUV mentality. Starbucks hasn't caught on in Israel's classy coffee culture. And Home Depot's do-it-yourself vibe foundered with upwardly mobile Chinese who saw manual labor as beneath them.

Walmart's international setbacks exemplify these challenges. In the 1990s, after conquering the U.S. market, the world's largest retailer set its sights abroad, moving into twenty-seven countries, from Argentina to Zambia. Twenty years on, Walmart's Mexican and Central American operations have blossomed. Mexico now boasts almost twenty-five hundred Walmart stores; Central America has more than eight hundred. In Canada, some four hundred stores cover almost every province. These outlets send billions of dollars back to Walmart's headquarters in Bentonville, Arkansas. Operations farther afield have often floundered. Despite the same sophisticated distribution systems and heavy pressure on suppliers' margins, the world's largest retailer ended up pulling out of Germany, the UK, Argentina, and South Korea altogether and scaling back its operations in Brazil and Japan.

Today, Walmart has more stores abroad than in the United States, but nearly 90 percent of its half trillion dollars in annual revenue still comes from North America.[36] The big-box giant remains a regional company.

The British telecoms company Vodafone reveals a similar story of the promise and peril of global expansion. The once relatively unknown company catapulted through acquisitions to become, at one point in the early 2000s, the largest wireless carrier in the world. Yet it too ultimately retrenched to a regional business.

Vodafone's international push began in the 1990s. Over the course of the decade, it set up in fourteen countries across Europe. Then, in 2000, it orchestrated the biggest takeover in the world at the time, acquiring German competitor Mannesmann. These bets mostly made good: Germany grew into Vodafone's biggest moneymaker, and the company became Europe's largest mobile and data services provider. Ventures outside Europe went less smoothly. In 2001, Vodafone took control of Japan's third-largest mobile operator, J-Phone. Things went south quickly. J-Phone was slow to match its competitors' new 3G phones and other sleek offerings, and the company proved tone deaf, marketing its products with European celebrities. Vodafone lost a chunk of market share and billions of dollars before selling the remains to Japan's Softbank in 2006. Vodafone's Indian ventures never paid off either, losing money and ground to cheaper local competitors. After more than a decade of investments, the company pulled out of the United States, selling its wireless stake to Verizon in 2013. And in 2019, it let its New Zealand network go too.

Today Vodafone has operations in two dozen countries and boasts nearly seven hundred million subscribers. Yet it remains European in essence: operations on the continent ring up three-quarters of its sales and profits.[37]

Organizational gurus at McKinsey have found that the experience of Walmart and Vodafone holds more broadly. Looking at over five hundred companies, they concluded that even the best-run multinationals pay a "globalization penalty."[38] The more spread out they become, the harder it is to set standards, connect to customers, innovate, and maintain company esprit de corps.

McKinsey's study complements work by academic scholars. One study of over a hundred U.S. manufacturing multinationals found that those that expanded regionally brought in higher profits than both those that went farther afield and those that stayed home and that their earnings diminished with distance.[39] New York University professor Pankaj Ghemawat illustrated the globalization penalty in a study of washing machines and white goods. In the 1990s, the United States' Whirlpool, Europe's Electrolux, China's Haier, and Japan's Matsushita expanded their global footprints, battling it out in market after market. These four all now bring in more revenue than any of their competitors do. But none of them is anywhere near the most profitable maker of washing machines. That distinction goes to more regional players: Turkey's Arcelik (sold throughout Europe) and Italy's Indesit (bought by Whirlpool in 2014 in a ploy to lift its weaker profit margins).[40]

Operating abroad can bring big profits. Otherwise, corporations wouldn't do it. Talent pools, wage rates, access to natural resources, tax incentives, tariff barriers, and logistic costs differ across countries. Megafactories can achieve economies of scale. New markets and new customers are waiting across the border.

But stray too far, and you may run into trouble. International supply chains haven't dispersed as far as either globalization's cheerleaders or its skeptics assume. Businesses have found that sophisticated supply-chain software and systems can only take you so far—a few countries away but often not much more than that. Familiarity, intuition, collegiality, and proximity matter. Some things can't be packed in a shipping container. For so many companies, it has been better to stick to the Goldilocks regional middle: not too close, not too far.

Three Hubs Emerge

As supply chains came to dominate the manufacturing world, three distinct regional hubs formed: Asia, Europe, and North America. By combining regional understanding and cross-country advantages, companies found that they could more effectively compete in the global economic race. Countries that have become part of a regional bloc now have a distinct advantage over those that remain outside.

Recognizing regions isn't all that new. Throughout the 1960s and 1970s, scholars debated the good and bad of regional economic and geopolitical blocs for global trade, security, the spread of authoritarianism, and, later, a wave of democratization.[41]

With Japan's rise in the 1980s, the former McKinsey Tokyo head turned business writer Kenichi Ohmae popularized the idea of global economic "triads."[42] In his telling, multinationals from the United States, Japan, and Europe were dividing up the world.

In the 1990s, economic regionalism picked up speed on the ground. The United States, Mexico, and Canada signed NAFTA. Europe built on its single market, laying out a decade-long integration roadmap for one passport, one monetary policy, and one currency. The newly founded Asia-Pacific Economic Cooperation (APEC) finally added trade to the diplomatic docket in Asia.

Yet by the start of the twenty-first century, the popular and scholarly focus on regions dissipated. Emerging markets captured the collective imagination. Goldman Sachs's research head Jim O'Neill christened the geographically dispersed BRICs—Brazil, Russia, India, and China—the next global economic power bloc.[43] Fareed Zakaria announced the "rise of the rest."[44] Pundits opined on the "multipolar world." And "globalization" spattered the titles of hundreds of books, thousands of reports, and millions of articles. But even as the idea of globalization caught on, the reality of regionalization kept going. It is time to revisit this trend, its distinct evolution in each part of the world, and what it means for the United States.

2

Europe: Regionalism through Diplomacy

Stuttgart, the German city originally known for breeding horses for the royal cavalry, has a long history of being industrial and industrious. Daimler launched its first automobile there in 1886. Ferdinand Porsche settled there too, leading the team behind the famous Volkswagen Beetle before opening his namesake company's first office next to the railway station in the 1930s. Then came World War II. Years of Allied bombing devastated the city, and after the war, its companies were tarred by their collaboration with the Nazis. Stuttgart didn't stay down for long, however. Today, "the cradle of the automobile" is once again at the beating heart of German industry.

Stuttgart's comeback began as part of Germany's broader postwar revival. Daimler-Benz (the two companies had merged between the wars) anchored the city's renaissance. After returning to private hands, it rode the wave of Germany's economic boom. In the 1950s and 1960s, German car sales jumped from thousands to millions a year; Mercedes captured a good chunk of them.[1] Daimler-Benz's bus business also took off as West German cities upgraded public transportation.

But Stuttgart's economic success is more than a German story. It was in large part thanks to the wider European project that the city became one of Germany's wealthiest. After conquering the German market, Daimler-Benz soon looked abroad, taking advantage of Europe's newly minted customs union. No longer held back by layers of licenses and import quotas, the stately lines and elegant backseats of its sedans caught the eyes of CEOs, celebrities (*La Dolce Vita* star Anita Ekberg drove a roadster convertible, director Federico Fellini favored a black sedan), and heads of state across the continent. By the 1970s, Mercedes had become Europe's leading luxury car. At the same time, Daimler-Benz delivery trucks and buses became mainstays on the streets of Amsterdam, Paris, Rome, and Copenhagen.

Mercedes captured the European imagination, but Stuttgart's more mundane auto-parts makers actually played a bigger role in the city's ascent. Hundreds of medium-sized enterprises—Germany's famed *Mittelstand*—scattered factories on its hills and along the bank of the Neckar River. They expanded throughout Europe's core, courting Fiat, Peugeot, Jaguar, Renault, and others with their transmissions, axles, pistons, brakes, and steering wheels. Bosch and Mahle used this regional base to become two of the world's biggest providers of powertrains, fuel injection, wiper blades, ignition parts, and batteries.

As cars grew more sophisticated, Stuttgart transformed into a technology hub. Glass office blocks went up alongside Gothic buildings. Research institutes and labs proliferated. Stuttgart's flagship university added mechanical and electrical engineering faculty at a blistering pace, minting thousands of aspiring engineers, managers, and, more recently, start-up founders each spring.[2] Stuttgart led its state in joining with Lombardy, Rhône-Alpes, and Catalonia as one of Europe's "four motors" for regional innovation and research collaboration.[3]

At the turn of the twenty-first century, the European Union looked east, and so did Stuttgart's industrial stalwarts. Its companies ramped up investments in eastern European nations prepping to join the EU. Mercedes opened assembly lines in Romania and Hungary. Bosch began making batteries, wipers, and other auto parts in Romania, Slovakia, and the Czech Republic. Lesser-known names invested heavily too, selling to or buying from the factories proliferating in an expanding Europe's newest members.

Today, Stuttgart is still a seat of Germany's auto industry. Inside its multinational headquarters, thousands of engineers design and build the internal computers and write many of the one hundred million lines of code baked into each new car. They manage regional manufacturing chains, tracking components as they traverse Austria's autobahn to and from Hungary or across Germany's famed speedway to operations in the Czech Republic.

Stuttgart's industry has made the city one of the wealthiest and best educated parts of Germany, leading the nation in research and development outlays and in patents filed. It also leads in exports: sixty percent of its manufactured goods head abroad.[4] The cradle of the automobile has grown up to become the center of a now Europe-wide auto supply chain as well as a global industry leader.

The regional agreements that made Stuttgart's comeback possible had their origins in the same war that destroyed the city in the first place. After 1945, western European leaders, scarred by the devastation of two world wars, began grasping for ways to resolve future disputes without guns. Private companies were equally desperate to rebuild. The answer, for diplomats and CEOs alike, was economic and political integration. Over the next six decades of fits and starts, European governments, businesses, and some 450 million citizens would surmount significant challenges and bind themselves together into a common market, much of it with a common currency, united by a host of councils, committees, courts, banks, and legislatures. They would agree to set the same standards for safety, health, and working conditions and for collective bargaining and property rights, recognize each other's professional licenses and university credits, and even jointly award scholarships. After the end of the Cold War, thirteen more nations would join, signing onto the growing number of rules and responsibilities for those within the club.

As diplomats dismantled barriers and expanded the club, regional supply chains multiplied, as companies Europeanized more than they globalized. The design, manufacturing, and marketing of wares spread across countries. Professionals started moving too: Polish workers coming to make Portuguese leather boots, Spanish architects designing Swedish buildings, Hungarian seamstresses working in Milan's fashion houses, and Luxembourgish bankers investing in Rotterdam as if at home.

Much of Europe embraced a single currency, using the same coins and bills for a baguette in Paris and a strudel in Vienna. Whether it's goods, services, capital, information, or people, two-thirds of what goes abroad from European countries stays within Europe—a higher share than in any other

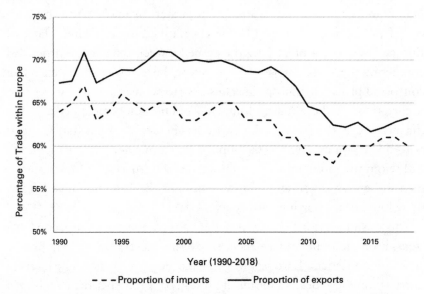

Intraregional trade in the European Union. This graph includes data for Austria, Belgium, Bulgaria, Croatia, Cyprus, Czech Republic, Denmark, Estonia, Finland, France, Germany, Greece, Hungary, Ireland, Italy, Latvia, Lithuania, Luxembourg, Malta, Netherlands, Poland, Portugal, Romania, Slovakia, Slovenia, Spain, and Sweden. Source: Eurostat

regional hub. This has led even the most national of brands—Germany's Mercedes-Benz, France's L'Oreal, Switzerland's Credit Suisse—to become, in their essence, European. This process has, in turn, made Europe the biggest manufacturing exporter in the world.[5]

Making Europe European: Trade Agreements Kick-Start Regionalism

Europe's countries had known only a few consecutive decades of peace in their long history, with battling powers being the defining characteristic of the political landscape of the region. Yet the sheer physical, economic, and human toll of the Second World War provided an opportunity for lasting connections to take root. So did fear of a growing Soviet Union menace to the east, helping to bring once-rival nations together.

To start down the path to integration, Europe needed its archrivals,

France and Germany, to learn to live together. In 1946, Winston Churchill, fresh from the Potsdam Conference, called for a "United States of Europe" as a means of keeping the peace between the two countries and countering the Soviet menace.[6] Even before the armistice, the French had concocted plans for "European states . . . [to] constitute themselves into a federation," and the Italians founded a political movement dedicated to the idea.[7] After the war ended, new leaders in Germany and Italy grabbed onto this vision as a way to pick up the economic and diplomatic pieces and rejoin the international community. And in 1950, the French statesmen Robert Schuman and Jean Monnet put the first substance behind these lofty ideals, starting with coal and steel.[8]

This wasn't a case of leaders pushing cooperation on unsuspecting citizens. From despondent farmers to recovering factory owners, shopkeepers to union leaders, Europe's workers and business owners saw international commercial ties as a means of putting back together their economic lives. To find raw materials, fill their shelves, sell their wares, and create desperately needed jobs, they would have to look to their neighbors. Only cooperation could end the devastation.

The United States too was a big proponent of European integration. With Europe's treasuries empty, its national savings depleted, and its security threatened by the looming Cold War, the United States stepped in with aid. The 1948 Marshall Plan channeled $13 billion—$135 billion in today's money—to the region. Over four years, the money helped Britain, Germany, France, and thirteen other nations buy fertilizer and fuel, build houses, fix bridges and roads, reopen mines, refurbish plants, and import machinery. As a percentage of GDP for the recipient countries, the aid remained mostly below 6 percent (Austria was an outlier at 14 percent), but the Marshall Plan did more than just give out money. It backstopped the exchange of it—Deutsche marks for French francs, Dutch guilders for Italian lira—making it easier to buy and sell wares between nations. It gave guarantees to private companies ready to make investments. And, importantly, it pushed recipients to open their domestic markets to each other and to share their national economic plans, seeding the European cooperation that would follow.[9]

In just a few short years, shortages of food and fuel eased, coal and steel production rebounded, and industrial output nearly doubled. Europeans got a first and quite successful taste of working together for economic gain. The Marshall Plan also got European institutions going. Part of the deal was that the sixteen nations had to figure out how to allocate U.S. funds together. The result was the first pan-European organization in 1948: the Organization for European Economic Cooperation, which later became the Organization for Economic Cooperation and Development (OECD).[10]

With western European infrastructure on the mend and the U.S.-backed North Atlantic Treaty Organization (NATO) security blanket in place, Europe's central countries expanded cooperation further. West Germany, France, Italy, Belgium, the Netherlands, and Luxembourg started with heavy industry. The 1951 European Coal and Steel Community created a common market for these basic inputs. It had defensive roots: the idea was to erase Germany's military advantage by giving every nation access to the raw materials of war (and to stop future battles between France and Germany over the industrialized Alsace-Lorraine). It also played well economically and politically, making manufacturers happy and appeasing powerful unions. As tariffs crumbled and taxes evaporated, the new club's steel and coal trade almost doubled.[11]

The next big diplomatic step was the creation of the European Economic Community, or EEC. Here, the smaller Benelux countries—the Netherlands, Luxembourg, and Belgium—took the lead, orchestrating the economic marriage of historical enemies France and Germany and sealing their vows in a customs union.

The 1957 Treaty of Rome formalized the EEC. It enticed French farmers with promises of generous subsidies and guaranteed prices. It favored German manufacturers with bigger and freer markets and side benefits for companies caught in the East-West divorce. Italy got money, while Luxembourg, Belgium, and the Netherlands brought their collective labor bargaining practices to the rest of the group.[12] Within their protected club, the six member states agreed to market rules of the road: no more tariffs, quotas, dumping, price fixing, or divvying up of customers and markets. They set common agricultural prices and doled out subsidies. And they talked aspirationally about community-wide industrial policies, atomic energy cooperation, transportation grids, even political union.

Businesses took advantage of the insider perks. Over the decade and a half following the treaty's start in 1958, imports from outside the group halved. Trade between the six treaty-bound nations grew ninefold, rising from just over a quarter to over half of all commercial exchanges by the early 1970s.[13] As the economic miracle spread, whole industries blossomed. German aluminum, synthetic rubber, machinery, and ship making recovered and prospered. French paper, radios, airplanes, and basic computers spread across the continent. And once-scarce delicacies—French cheese, Belgian sugar, Dutch chicken, and Italian vegetables—became commonplace as farm yields and trade grew.

As the six nations' economies recovered and commerce intensified between them, so did productivity: German, French, and Italian industrial workers outpaced their American and British counterparts by over two to one between 1950 and 1962. GDP leapt ahead, as did wages, and unemployment fell. In roughly one generation, between 1947 and 1975, incomes grew more than they had in the previous 150 years.[14]

The German transmission maker ZF Friedrichshafen AG was one of the companies making the most of Europe's new ties. ZF's post–World War II life began in receivership to France to atone for the sin of powering German tanks and military vehicles. Around the time of the signing of the Treaty of Rome, it regained its freedom as a private company. Now on its own, it took advantage of not just Germany's rebirth but Europe's too.[15]

ZF's reboot began with a postwar boom in German car and truck sales, as its traditional clients—Daimler-Benz, Hanomag, Klöckner-Humboldt-Deutz, and MAN—quickly upped their orders. With the EEC rules in place, so did others from across Europe. In the 1960s, Peugeot, Alfa Romeo, and Maserati chose ZF's three-gear automatic transmissions for their new car lines. In the 1970s and early 1980s, Citroen, Range Rover, and Jaguar joined a growing client base for steering systems, axles, and transmissions. ZF in turn opened sales offices and servicing centers in the Paris suburb of Rungis, Nottingham, Copenhagen, Milan, and, as Spain negotiated its entrance to the EEC, Madrid.

The company went farther afield during these years too, setting up shop in Brazil, Norway, the United States, South Africa, and Japan. Still, in 1980, as its sales hit over two billion German marks (roughly $1 billion), the commercial benefits of the EEC ensured that the vast majority of that revenue came from Europe.[16]

Europe's centrality to ZF's profits continues today. The company got a jump-start on an expanded Union, leveraging Soviet-era licensing deals to move in early to a reunited East Germany, Hungary, and what was then Yugoslavia. It joined Audi, Mercedes-Benz, and Opel when they opened up in Poland and Slovakia. These operations took off once eastern Europe joined the EU, with ZF's local sales doubling. Although ZF is now one of the three biggest auto suppliers in the world, it still has more plants in Europe than in the rest of the world combined. It sells more—and earns more—at home than anywhere else.[17]

The coal and steel community created a host of governmental structures: an executive, a court, and two legislative bodies, one akin to a parliament. In the Treaty of Rome, the European Economic Community mostly absorbed these and recrafted its own version of three supranational branches of government. These would be continued, expanded, and added to as the EEC was subsumed into the EU in the 1990s.

The European Court of Justice was the first to override national rules. Its initial decisive 1963 case involved formaldehyde. A Dutch importer complained about new tariffs on barrels coming from Germany and asked Europe's highest court for his money back. The seven judges decided in his favor, holding that the Treaty of Rome trumped Dutch law. Just as important, they set the precedent that not only states but also citizens could appeal to Brussels for justice. In 1979, in a dispute over imported Cassis de Dijon liqueur, the court affirmed that a product made in one member country generally had to be allowed for sale in another. Over time, the European Court became the last legal word for members, striking down local laws over health codes, equal pay, and differences on everything from packaging to hiring practices.[18]

Two bodies came to share legislative power. The Council of Ministers brought together nations' cabinet members. The European Parliament was made up of first appointed and later elected officials. Together they hold the purse strings, allocating funds to seed small businesses, set up satellite services, pay for student scholarships, and back thousands of other infrastructure, energy, education, and research projects. They oversee dozens of policy areas from agriculture to fisheries, transportation to intellectual property, drinking water to clean air, bypassing local governments and national parliaments and shaping the lives of nearly 450 million citizens.

The European Commission became the executive branch, governed by commissioners sent from each nation and a president appointed by the European Council (and approved by a majority in the European Parliament).[19] It proposes legislation, leads trade talks, and in general makes regional policies a reality.

As integration deepened, more technical bodies emerged, each helping to bind Europe further together. A regional central bank, auditor, ombudsman, investment bank, even a data privacy protector came into being. Merit-based exams screen technocrats, with the posts divvied up among nations.

For many years, the European Council presided above all; now it often tends to cogovern with the Parliament. Led by heads of state, the Council has pushed integration at crucial moments and through crises, creating the common market, the European Union, and the euro. The Council was the one to abolish internal borders and later broker a solution for millions of Syrian refugees. And it directed the Commission to negotiate an end to the UK's membership.

These institutions represent Europe to the rest of the world. They negotiate free-trade agreements and sit on the WTO, Group of Seven (G7), and United Nations (UN), while EU central bankers help set global financial rules.

Through Economic Challenges
European Integration Prevails

The postwar twenty-year burst of prosperity enticed others to join the treaty-bound EEC. The UK was among them, overcoming earlier ambivalence to being part of a European project. As the continent picked up economic steam, Britain had faltered, dragged down by its collapsing empire and uncompetitive industries. Denmark and Ireland wanted in too, drawn by potential markets and subsidies alike. And by 1973, the three countries had overcome French resistance to join. Greece, Spain, and Portugal followed in the 1980s. These additions brought 120 million new customers and nearly $600 billion in new markets to the Economic Community.

Yet in the 1970s, even as new countries entered the club, Europe's economic prowess began to fade. Dramatic foreign-exchange swings and a global oil crisis took a toll. Inflation and unemployment rose; economic growth and trade declined. And though tariffs had all but disappeared, other barriers had not. Together, these held back regional integration.

Germany banned plastics like those used in the UK-made Paddington Bear's yellow boots. Italy wouldn't let in pasta made with durum wheat. The Dutch kept out French-made brioches on the grounds that they were hazardous to their citizens' health.[20]

Even if not explicitly forbidden, products often faced armies of inspectors and hundreds of permits. These nontariff barriers seemed to come into existence faster than clunky European committees could negotiate them away. In this game, Germans leaned on quality standards, the French on taxes and subsidies. Other nations threw up a whole host of customs forms, sanitary tests, and procurement restrictions to get a leg up on their supposed partners. Even the successes illuminated the hurdles: it took twenty-five years to decide what qualified as jam (as opposed to marmalade).[21]

Big multinationals often dealt with these hurdles by going domestic everywhere, creating federated structures to serve each national market. For instance, Philips opened separate plants in every nation, some 250 in all, manufacturing seven different types of TV sets (each with different components), and over two thousand kinds of lightbulbs to meet all the local requirements.[22]

But these extra operational layers weren't possible for smaller firms. By limiting economies of scale and scope from more regional sales, they held back the global competitiveness of European companies and brands.

By the 1980s, afraid that Europe was falling behind, the continent's diplomats (encouraged by their CEOs) negotiated an end to many of these impediments. A pro-market Britain found common ground with an export-oriented Germany and a France turning away from "socialism in one country." European Commission president Jacques Delors, looking to make a mark, took advantage of the confluence and championed a business-friendly Commission white paper. Its solution was to double down on regional integration. The result was the 1986 Single European Act, a grand bargain that marked the start of a true regional marketplace. National quotas disappeared, as did voluntary export restrictions between members. The main workaround was mutual recognition. Governments no longer had to pass the same laws or enact the same regulations. Nations would just recognize that whatever met another member's standards met its own, too. Products sold in one country could be sold in all.[23]

There were, inevitably, exceptions. Countries could still reject things deemed dangerous to health or the environment. The Dutch couldn't sell hashish to Sweden, and Denmark kept out Ovaltine and its additives. But for the most part, customs officials now had to give goods coming from other members the benefit of the doubt.[24]

The nations also largely agreed to a one-and-done system for tests, permits, and certifications. Audis crash-tested in Munich could head straight to Swedish showrooms. Italian calcium chloride could keep Austria's Autobahn free of winter ice. French perfumes could be sold in El Corte Inglés department stores throughout Spain.

Labeling, too, became more regional in nature. Discrepancies in font size or background color no longer disqualified sales next door. With a "CE" stamp, standing for "Conformité Européenne," or "European Conformity," Finnish-made Lumene eye shadows could fill pharmacy shelves from Lisbon to Larissa. Danish-made LEGOs could entertain children in Oviedo and Naples.

When mutual recognition wasn't enough, countries hashed out common legal standards. To do this, European officials designated technical groups affiliated with industry to lead the charge. These made Europe-wide regulatory calls on standards for telecommunications, food processing, chemicals, and a whole host of sectors. They set rules for everything from engine fuels to safety masks, security alarm systems to smart grids. Europe's highest court cemented these regional guidelines through its rulings.

Electrolux had already gone on a spending spree throughout the 1970s and 1980s, buying up dozens of local brands across fifteen countries. Its vacuum cleaners, washing machines, and refrigerators had a strong hold on Europe's appliance sales. Yet national differences in rules and regulations kept its operations siloed. And the added layers of products and the proliferation of plants in each nation dragged down its profit margins.

With the arrival of the common market, Electrolux rationalized its production process.[25] Managers for refrigerators and coolers, as well as steamers, ovens, and microwaves, congregated in Stockholm. Those making and selling laundry machines and dishwashers headed near Venice. Some factories and warehouses closed as the company consolidated around fewer distinct products and plants. Others opened or expanded, now able to supply stores and dealers across the Union. As real economies of scale became possible, European sales and profits jumped.

Carrefour, too, took full advantage of the common market. The French retailer began in 1960 with a modest supermarket at a crossroads—a *carrefour*—in the lakeside town of Annecy just as the EEC was taking off. Its first large-scale hypermarket came three years later just outside Paris. Within a decade, Carrefour had transformed French shopping, with nearly four dozen big-box stores.

In the 1970s and 1980s, Carrefour made a push into France's European neighbors: Switzerland, Belgium, Germany, Italy, and Spain. Some of its ventures succeeded, but many didn't, as Carrefour's outposts were flummoxed by zoning rules, legal limits on what it could sell where, and tough local competition. These regulatory differences made it hard to leverage its purchasing power over local stores. Defeated in Europe, Carrefour ventured farther abroad, into Brazil, Argentina, the United States, and even the Dominican Republic. Success was decidedly mixed, as it was in Carrefour's later Asia expansion.[26]

The creation of the single market gave Carrefour a renewed European impetus, tearing down many of the barriers that had previously stymied its expansion. Throughout the 1990s and early 2000s, Carrefour rolled up local retailers in Spain, Belgium, Italy, Romania, Greece, and its home turf of France and expanded into Poland and Turkey. The retailer centralized purchasing and pushed its store brands: paint and motor oil, beer and coffee, shoes and socks. With thousands of new stores, it served over a billion customers a year.[27] Carrefour now trails only Walmart in size on the global stage. Yet beachheads in Latin America and Asia aside, its scale— over three-quarters of its twelve thousand stores and €80 billion in yearly sales—comes overwhelmingly from Europe.

At the same time as diplomats were hashing out rules and harmonizing regulations in the common market, they were taking down other barriers as well, making it easier for people to live, work, and travel around the Union. In 1981, burgundy European Community passports replaced the former rainbow of country documents. In 1985, in the picturesque Luxembourg village of Schengen, delegates agreed to do away with internal border checks, visas, and passports. When the rules came into effect a decade later, long lines at Europe's borders disappeared.

Europe made many licenses and degrees transferable between members. Doctors, dentists, realtors, teachers, hairdressers, engineers, and dozens of other professionals could practice from Athens to Bucharest. Students too could move around during and after their studies. Latvians could attend classes at Berlin's Humboldt University and transfer the credits back home, their hybrid diploma recognized throughout the Union.

Free movement made it easier to fill jobs, manage teams, and run operations spread out across countries—no visa necessary, however long the stay. The growing portability of degrees and licenses made it possible to hire the same person to work in multiple offices, as line workers, managers, and back-office employees could move between factories and cubicles as the production process dictated. The new rules spurred trade in services, too. Bankers, construction crews, computer programmers, bellhops, and concierges became importers and exporters in their own right.

Vacations led the way. Italians went to Paris, Belgians to Bellagio, no passports or currency exchange needed. Europe's trains, planes, and roads made jaunts so easy that four out of five trips abroad stayed within the continent. Tourism became the biggest single service export in the Union, and for countries like Spain, Portugal, and France, foreign visits fueled a large chunk of their overall economies.[28]

The new wave of travel wasn't all pleasure. Consultants from one country could now advise corporate restructurings, guide new operations, or overhaul digital footprints across Europe. The French government flew in German Roland Berger consultants to study automation in its factories. Spanish film distributors hired Berger's Bonn-based competitor Simon-Kucher to help them figure out how to get more families to watch from the big screen. Danish retailer Flying Tiger turned to Swedish consultants when rethinking its packaging, as did Portugal's natural gas companies to prepare for decarbonization.[29] Engineers traveled to set up electricity generators and waste-treatment plants or to build tunnels and develop mines. As the trade in services grew, it too looked inward, a strong majority of international sales occurring between EU countries.[30]

With the single-market rules in place, others became eager to join. And once the Berlin Wall fell, a host of new candidates emerged. Diplomats set about expanding the Union, bringing in thirteen nations in as many years: first Cyprus, then the Czech Republic, Estonia, Hungary, Latvia, Lithuania, Malta, Poland, Slovakia, Slovenia, Bulgaria, Romania, and Croatia all changed their laws and opened their markets. In most cases, they jettisoned their currency. From 1995 to 2007, the European Union (which subsumed the Economic Community in 1993) expanded by a third geographically, by one hundred million people demographically, and by nearly $1 trillion economically.

Companies joined in the expansion. The Spanish designer Zara employed Bulgarian seamstresses; Germany's Hugo Boss turned to Czech, Romanian, and Slovakian tailors; and luxury Italian handbag makers favored Bulgarian leather tanners. Heineken and Carlsberg started brewing on the outskirts of Warsaw and Zagreb. And the carmakers VW, Daimler-Benz, and Peugeot set up factories in Gyor, Hungary; Jawor, Poland; and Trnava, Slovakia.[31]

As the EU became the world's single largest trading area, its international commerce grew faster than that of the rest of the world, with imports and exports almost doubling.[32] And the regional back-and-forth just intensified as trade became an even bigger part of these economies.[33]

Funding Regionalism: Financial Integration

Money has underpinned the European project. Stable exchange rates, shared monetary policies, and, ultimately, a single currency bound Europe together, promoting more extensive cross-border investment than anywhere else in the world.

It didn't start off that way. In the wake of World War II, it was hard to do something as basic as swap money: French buyers didn't want Deutsche marks, Dutch merchants wouldn't take Italian lira. The United States helped at the start, backing a currency payment clearinghouse to enable international buyers and sellers to settle up. The 1944 Bretton Woods agreement officially tied Europe's currencies to one another and to the U.S. dollar. As it came into operation over the next decade, individuals or companies could be sure that the value of a French, Belgian, or Luxembourgish franc would be more or less the same when deals closed or cross-border bills came due at the end of the month.

Discussion of European monetary integration had started in the 1960s. With Bretton Woods' demise in 1971, Europe had to find a way to stabilize exchange rates on its own again. During the 1970s and 1980s, the nations stumbled through a series of adjustable currency pegs. While they worked for a while, each attempt eventually succumbed to financial pressures and devaluations.

The first exchange-rate agreement was dubbed the "Snake." The idea was to peg Europe's currencies to each other within a narrow band, and then the seven currencies (the mechanism included Britain) would rise and fall together against the dollar. This, its creators hoped, would protect European trade.

The Snake quickly foundered, as underlying economic, political, and social differences made it too hard to hold the monetary line. Britain and Ireland were the first to crash out, with speculators driving down their currencies after only a month. Italy soon followed, with inflationary pressures too much for the lira to bear. The economic aftershocks of the 1973 oil crisis forced France out a year after, effectively ending the experiment.[34]

In 1978, Europe tried again. Led by France's Valéry Giscard d'Estaing and Germany's Helmut Kohl, they bound their currencies together in the European Monetary System. The EMS had more breathing room, allowing currencies to move within a wider band. It also adjusted bilateral exchange rates more frequently and even let countries drop out temporarily during tough economic times.

Britain initially passed, but eight other European countries signed up. The system was rocky from the get-go. In the first four years, countries had to adjust bilateral currency rates seven times. The UK later joined but then crashed out, rather dramatically, when the financier George Soros famously bet (and won) against the pound.[35] Many people complained that Germany's Bundesbank had too much influence, with the Deutsche mark a de facto anchor. Eroding capital controls looked to make the system even less stable, threatening economic growth and stability. So Europe's leaders again turned to expanding regional institutions.

To get rid of the dislocations and disruptions plaguing Europe's currencies, diplomats decided to do away with them all together. In the southeastern Dutch city of Maastricht in 1992, Europe's leaders and their diplomats left the European Economic Community behind for a more expansive European Union. The new agreement strengthened Brussels's hand in foreign policy and military matters and deepened cross-border cooperation among Europe's police and courts. And, most important, it laid out a decade-long path to supersede volatile exchange rates by adopting an overarching currency.

The plan directed central bankers to coordinate lending, reserve requirements, and other monetary policy tools as countries got rid of capital controls. The delegates created a new European Central Bank to oversee monetary policy and set region-wide interest rates. The euro's creators had learned that a currency union was only as strong as its members, so they set rules for aspiring joiners. To adopt the single currency, countries had to get their public spending, debt, inflation, and interest rates under control.

Eleven nations adopted the virtual euro at the turn of the century, with Greece making it twelve as the countries exchanged tens of billions of local coins and bills for Europe's own in 2002. Over the next decade and a half, they would be joined by seven more, making the euro the currency for nearly 350 million people and over a tenth of the global economy.

The path toward this tighter union was far from easy. Germany's initial plans for a European political union were more than many members could bear, while German central bankers shot down France's opening gambit to quickly devolve monetary policy to a higher authority. The British threatened to walk out of the whole process altogether until social policies were pulled out of the main treaty and put into a separate side agreement.

Achieving a single currency didn't cure Europe's financial headaches. For one thing, several nations never joined. Britain rejected the common currency. Denmark's citizens voted down their government's bid to join. Poland still uses its złoty, Hungary its forint, and the Czech Republic its koruna. Monetary union brought a new and different set of diplomatic tensions, particularly when countries went astray from the set debt and deficit guidelines.[36] Germany and France were the first to do so, juicing their economies to stave off downturns. Portugal, Spain, Greece, and Ireland would follow. The rigidity of one monetary policy for a disparate group of countries and economic conditions led to serious debt problems, as some nations overlent and some overborrowed, seeding later financial crises.[37]

But even with its limits, the presence of a single currency made it easier for companies to fund operations, source materials, build supply chains, and sell throughout the Union. Devaluations no longer upset their margins, and companies didn't have to give a cut to currency traders, saving billions.

The euro also spurred foreign direct investment. The EEC had kicked off a mutual interest in each other's markets and enterprises (as well as strong interest from U.S. multinationals, which brought their brands to and made their products on the continent). Over the course of the 1960s and 1970s, European multinationals opened affiliates and expanded subsidiaries across Europe much faster than with the other parts of the world. The single market reinvigorated this regional focus, and throughout the late 1980s and 1990s, Europe's biggest companies turned their gaze—and checkbooks—to each other.[38]

In the early years of the Eurozone, these investments accelerated further. Of the $5 trillion invested abroad globally over the next decade, Europe captured over $2 trillion, most of it from fellow Europeans.[39] From big cities to small enclaves, regional multinationals moved in, investing as much cash in each other as they did in the rest of the world combined. Auto companies led, with big brands and parts makers pouring billions into new operations in eastern and central Europe. Consumer goods expanded too; Ikea opened new stores across most of Europe's nations, and Nestlé broke ground on new factories to up the options for more of Europe's consumers. Mergers and acquisitions tell a similar story. As thousands of companies threw in together, European suitors outpaced outsiders nearly three to one.[40]

One of the biggest transformations happened in pharmaceuticals. Region-wide drug approvals now meant that compounds developed in one country could be manufactured in another, bound for shelves across all the member nations. As a flurry of mergers and acquisitions took off, European medical powerhouses emerged to rival U.S. giants in this capital-intensive industry.

One of the big winners was Sanofi. Today a leading maker of diabetes, meningitis, and cancer drugs and of vaccines, it started out in the 1970s as a modest offshoot from the French petrochemical maker Elf Aquitaine, selling its medicines mostly in France. During the 1980s, it looked to Japan and the United States to boost sales, making inroads with a few of its drugs and its cosmetics. But it was in the 1990s that Sanofi really took off. Repeated mergers enabled it to build scale and take advantage of the EU's single market. In 1999, it joined forces with Synthélabo, a medical spin-off from the French cosmetics giant L'Oréal. In 2004, Sanofi took over the much-larger drug supplier Aventis (itself a recent creation through the merger of a number of French and German operations). As eastern Europe's nations joined the EU, Sanofi expanded its reach there, buying up the Hungary-based Chinoin, one of the area's biggest generic drug suppliers.

Today, Sanofi sells more prescription drugs than all but a few other global firms. Its research labs span three continents, its sales even more. But the impetus behind its exponential expansion came as Europe's markets opened to each other.

Sanofi wasn't the only pharmaceutical company to find global scale after regional success. Novartis came into being through the merger of two Swiss pharmaceutical companies in 1996. Since then, German and U.S. acquisitions, combined with medical breakthroughs for hypertension and breast cancer, catapulted it to become the second-biggest medicine maker in the world. In 1998, Sweden's Astra and Britain's Zeneca merged, propelling the new company from the midrange to the global top five. And Hoffman-La Roche, currently the biggest pharmaceutical company in the world, accelerated its global climb in the early 2000s with acquisitions in Switzerland and the United States. Today, four of the top ten drug providers are based in Europe, and they owe their heft in the global industry in good part to the unification of EU rules and regulations.[41]

Banks went similarly cosmopolitan. Finance hadn't been part of the initial postwar diplomatic deals, as national capital controls and complex financial regulations made it difficult to lend in more than one place. For decades, sovereign borders mattered more than distance did. Zurich's bankers were shut out of nearby Stuttgart businesses; London's financiers were excluded from Normandy-based deals.

Yet as bank clients went international, bankers were eager to follow.

Technology made it possible to send money and settle transactions across borders in real time. It was the rules that had to change for banks to go abroad.

Europe once again opted for a top-down, regional solution. Brussels decided to treat banks as it did citizens, providing a "passport" for them to operate abroad.[42] By 1993, banks could offer savings and checking accounts, provide loans and mortgages, manage retirement funds, and dole out credit cards around the EU. The euro made this all the easier, lowering the risk and administrative costs of working in many places. National regulators still guided and supervised transactions occurring within their jurisdictions, but from Paris to Frankfurt, Milan to Amsterdam, the rules were increasingly the same.

A burst of mergers and acquisitions followed. Italy's Unicredito merged with Credito Italiano and together went on to buy up German and Austrian banks. Spain's Santander moved into the UK. Belgian Fortis took over a Dutch counterpart.[43] As the Iron Curtain receded, Western financiers moved east. Italy's UniCredit, Austria's Erste Group Bank, France's BNP Paribas, and many others bought up Polish, Slovakian, Romanian, and Czech assets. When the former Soviet satellites began joining the EU, more banks followed, and western Europe's institutions came to dominate eastern Europe's financial sectors.

France's BNP and Paribas were two of the financial institutions to take advantage of the new single passport and euro, creating what would become the biggest financial institution in the Eurozone. The two banks had both been nationalized in the 1980s and then reprivatized around the time Europe's new financial rules were taking off. During the 1990s, they each bought and sold a series of smaller banks and ventured beyond France into other markets.

In 2000, after a flurry of friendly and hostile bids and counterbids between France's biggest financial firms, BNP and Paribas joined forces. The new fortified bank doubled down on a pan-European expansion. It took over all of the Italian Banca Nazionale del Lavoro, outmaneuvering Spain's Banco de Bilbao and adding some two and a half million clients to its roster. In Belgium, it bought up Fortis; in Luxembourg, BGL; and in Germany, DAB. Over the next decade, the French behemoth would buy, expand, or start operations in Poland, Bulgaria, Spain, the Czech Republic, Slovakia, Portugal, Bulgaria, Denmark, and Britain.

Today, BNP Paribas holds over €2.5 trillion in assets, more than all but a handful of global banks. Yet three-quarters of its deals, employees, clients, and profits come from the region. Even its logo—four stars transforming into a swallow in flight—is distinctly European.

National governments, anxious about banking behemoths putting local champions out of business, found ways to slow this regional financial march abroad. They hid behind consumer-protection claims, often forcing international newcomers to reregister, beef up reserves, and deal with tougher supervision. Different tax rates, mortgage rules, and credit requirements also complicated matters.

But overall, European financial institutions became more and more the norm. By 2008, French, German, British, and Dutch banks had become the biggest in the world, surpassing U.S. champions in total assets. They did this by turning to their neighbors: on average, just 7 percent of their assets were outside the EU.[44]

Then came the financial crisis. The United States' bad mortgages triggered a European meltdown. Banks froze. Economies soured. Sovereign debt ballooned and then turned to junk. The international crisis hastened Greece's economic collapse and illuminated the precarious nature of other member states' fiscal balance sheets. The euro looked doomed.

At first, countries tried to deal with the shocks on their own. Many governments tried to regain the market's confidence by slashing spending and raising taxes. But the uncertainties were too great, and investors quickly abandoned bonds from Greece, Ireland, and Portugal and dumped a considerable chunk of their Italian and Spanish holdings.

Years of financial integration made it impossible for these countries to resolve things on their own. So regional institutions stepped in. The European Commission bailed out Greece and agreed to backstop Spain, Portugal, and Ireland. The European Central Bank (ECB) slashed interest rates, handed out cash to shore up faltering banks, and eventually bought up what would become trillions of euros in Greek, Portuguese, Italian, and Spanish bonds to calm the markets.

Once Europe's institutions had brought the continent back from the financial abyss, they didn't let go of power. The ECB pushed national regulators aside, permanently taking over supervising, stress testing, and capitalizing big banks. And through their seats on the European Council, the heads of state created a single set of capital requirements, a single way of resolving bankruptcies, and other baseline financial standards within the Eurozone.[45]

Once the emergency passed, national governments and regulators regained some of their day-to-day roles. But the new financial normal meant direction, and control, from above. Regional institutions now oversee big banks and capital markets throughout Europe. Brussels increasingly sets budgets, and Frankfurt (the home of the ECB) financial regulations. And the euro, which many people had thought doomed, instead drew in new members in Slovenia, Slovakia, Malta, Latvia, and Estonia.

European financial integration certainly isn't total. National regulations often carry the day over regional interests. Small-business loans and consumer credit rarely cross national borders. Securities markets remain separated by high settling costs. Aspirations for a true banking and capital market union remain just that. Still, even with these limits, Europe is now the most financially intertwined region in the world.

Building Regionalism: Infrastructure and Technology

Physical ties knit the region together just as much as commercial and financial ones, many of them paid for by the EU. EU-funded roads link Vienna and Bratislava to the Polish port of Gdansk. They switch back over the Alps and connect roadways across Belgium's flatlands. European highways have more than doubled in length since the 1990s, easing trans-European travel.[46]

The same is true of railways. Once, nations purposefully made it hard for their rails to connect with their neighbors' lines, worried about troop surges and blitzkriegs. The EU laboriously (and expensively) took on these differences in loading and track gauges, electrification and signal systems, and operational practices.[47] Together with its member nations, the Union laid down enough new track to ride from Spain to Finland and back. Travel time between Brussels and London fell to two hours, Cologne to Paris to just over three.

Regional money also went to build and modernize shipping terminals, to dredge rivers, and to deepen canals to speed goods from Lisbon to Dublin, London, and Amsterdam or from the Adriatic Sea into Italy's industrial heartland. It built gas pipelines, nuclear power plants, electricity grids, and broadband networks, better linking cities to hinterlands and nations to nations. And under EU-wide rules, airplane ticket prices have plummeted and regional flights tripled.[48]

Europe's infrastructure investments propelled regional commerce. Freight could move easily from seas to road to rail to water and back, going farther, faster, and cheaper than before. Ships carting millions of containers move between Rotterdam, Antwerp, Hamburg, and the world; others make stops in Valencia, Marseilles, or Genoa before heading out through the Suez Canal. Inland waterways speed goods too, with commercial loads heading along the Rhône and Rhine to Lyon, Geneva, and eastern Germany.

Regional funding worked to unite Europe's companies and economies through more than just trade. In the 1980s, Europe's bureaucrats singled out technology, offering billions for companies trying to catch up to the United States and Japan (with decidedly mixed success). EU largesse brought Germany's Siemens and the Netherlands' Philips together to jump into the semiconductor industry. It salvaged the teetering Groupe Bull, providing new money for the French computer maker to revive its server business. And it founded Eureka, an organization that funds research and development collaborations to propel European technology clusters in software, telecommunications, microelectronics, new metals, and smart manufacturing.[49]

Companies could tap into European funds for cheap loans and tax breaks. They used this public largesse to bankroll new factories, offices, and labs. They kick-started corporate research programs and filed patents. Smaller operations got working capital and bridge loans.

The EU incentives sent new ventures beyond the usual stops of Frankfurt, London, and Paris. They gave loans to hard-hit industrial areas, such as the northern French town of Creil, which got funding to repurpose abandoned steel plants to make plastics and pharmaceuticals.[50] EU cash helped the hardscrabble East German state of Saxony-Anhalt make something of a manufacturing comeback after a rough experience during reunification.[51]

Regional funds boosted human capital too. They created health clinics and programs to teach young people to code. They pooled funds for people without jobs to start a business or learn a trade. They helped people coming out of prison adjust to the outside world and paid for programs to help kids in tough neighborhoods stay in school. Poorer countries got the largest slices, but citizens in struggling regions of the founding members benefited too.

Europe isn't the only place to provide cheap loans and tax breaks as part of its industrial policy. In Asia, country after country has used these and other tools to entice investment and foster economic development. In the United States, states offer tax breaks, loans, and infrastructure programs to win new plants and headquarters. But Europe stands alone among the three hubs in its regional focus and coordination.

Managing Regionalism: Corporate Governance

While the legal minutiae of corporate governance rarely make the headlines, the technicalities matter for day-to-day operations. Unifying and simplifying the rules of the corporate game propelled European regionalization. A single rulebook made it easier and cheaper for companies to open offices, plants, and outlets across the continent.

The initial six nations thought about business from the get-go. Countries were supposed to adjust their local rules to let companies come in from across the community, cutting the red tape for new ventures and letting existing businesses move offices and operations from one country to another without having to start anew.

Yet on the ground, countries did little to change the local laws and regulations that made it costly to expand and work abroad. Capital controls made it hard to move cash or get loans for foreign factories and offices. Different accounting rules meant that businesses had to redo their books in each and every place. And tax authorities often went after revenue earned elsewhere, forcing companies to pay levies more than once. Even the legal definition of what a company entailed differed between Frankfurt and Florence, Bruges and Birmingham.[52]

Companies could, and did, hire teams of lawyers and accountants to work around these obstacles. But creating fully separate operations from start to finish in every country cost money. Most just stayed home.

In the late 1980s, the single market flattened many of these operational speed bumps. One-and-done testing and Economic Community–wide standards, labels, and certifications made it easier to run a multinational company. These rules changed how companies such as BASF operated: now its antirust paint, manufactured in Switzerland, could be slapped on Peugeots assembled in France and later Slovakia. Its antifreeze could be sent seamlessly from Antwerp to Clermont.

Just as important were region-wide legal changes, unifying the rules for auditing, reporting, shareholder rights, and mandatory information disclosures. Harmonization enabled businesses to centralize operations and to expand. Research, development, and marketing could be done in one place without running afoul of local laws.

Brussels also streamlined work safety requirements, air pollution limits, and all manner of labor and environmental standards. With the same rules now applying from Germany to Portugal, cross-border legal and administrative costs plummeted.

Other legal changes meant that cross-border mergers no longer cost more than the domestic version. Double taxation ended. Even depreciation rates became uniform, easing the accounting and financial burdens of corporations working in many countries. As the rules became easier, mergers, acquisitions, and foreign direct investment surged throughout the union.

In 2004, Brussels created the legal reality of a European company. Now, if registered as a Societas Europaea (SE), companies can do away with the bulk of the paperwork when they expand or restructure within Europe. They can move their headquarters without creating new subsidiaries, saving on administrative fees and taxes.

Austria's construction behemoth Strabag became European when it kicked off a multicountry acquisition spree. Eastern Europe's fast-food giant AmRest Holdings used European standing to spread its Pizza Huts, KFCs, Burger Kings, and Starbucks throughout the Union. And France's aeronautical national champion Airbus took advantage too, now legally claiming Germany, Spain, and the UK as its home bases. By 2013, there were more than two thousand registered European corporations.[53]

By and large, companies are now governed by one set of rules whether operating across two or twenty-seven nations. The scaffolding erected through agreement after agreement makes it easier to work and locate across nations, taking advantage of the differences in resources, labor, technology, access to capital, and other factors that vary between countries.

Under single-market rules, companies no longer have to adapt designs, production, marketing, and sales for each and every market or conduct multiple and duplicative tests nation by nation. The hundreds of billions of euros put into rails, roads, ports, and airports improved logistics. And EU-funded training along with passports lessened human-resource restraints as well. As tariffs fell, roads connected, markets grew, and money flowed; production spread, and companies specialized. This too helped Europe's companies become or remain competitive.

Zara shows that even in the labor-intensive, cutthroat clothing industry, European ties can make a company competitive the world over. The global fast-fashion brand opened its first shop in Galicia in 1975, the year of the Spanish dictator Francisco Franco's death. As Spain reengaged with Europe in the 1980s, Zara did too. It opened stores in Porto, Paris, Athens, Bruges, Oslo, London, and Milan. It started expanding outside of Europe in the 1990s.[54]

Zara today produces nearly half a trillion items of clothing a year.[55] It has become not only one of the biggest but also one of the most profitable fashion companies in the world, clearing some $2 billion a year from its trendy wear. And during the COVID-19 pandemic, it easily responded to the surge in online sales and was able to streamline its inventories, knocking its average warehouse time down by nine days, even as many of its competitors were forced to bulk up their holdings.

The surprising secret to Zara's success? Most of its manufacturing stayed close to home. While many brands outsource clothing production to Asia, Zara's goods are mostly European made. Fabrics come from Italy, Portugal, Greece, and Spain. Cutting, stitching, and assembling happens mostly in Spain, Portugal, Bulgaria, Lithuania, and Romania, as well as in nearby Turkey (part of the EU customs union) and Morocco (which has a free-trade agreement with the EU). Less than a quarter of its garments are relegated to Asia, mostly just T-shirts and other basic staples.[56]

Proximity allows speed and flexibility. Designers cluster at headquarters near the northwestern port of La Coruña. After soliciting customer comments via salesclerks around the world, they hone existing cuts and try out new ones. These patterns then head quickly to nearby factories, many connected by internal monorail, others just a day or so drive away.

New looks arrive to stores every two weeks instead of two months. They offer more than twice the options and items of an H&M, Uniqlo, or Topshop. Spanish distribution centers ship out new items every few days, already tagged and on hangers so they can hit store racks in just minutes.[57]

With more than three out of every four of the company's workers in Europe, Zara has to pay higher wages than do rivals outsourcing to Bangladesh, India, or Vietnam. But machines take on much of the work of cutting patterns, trimming edges, and pressing fabrics. And combined with the ruthless efficiency of the company's high-tech distribution networks, Zara routinely beats its competitors on getting trends to its stores and into customers' bags. Its small-batch designs give it street cachet and limit the markdowns that hit others' bottom lines. And while it boasts stores on nearly every continent, it is Zara's concentrated European base that has allowed it to succeed even in the fastest of fashion lanes.[58]

Europe's regionalism has been remarkably resilient. Through electoral upheavals, currency crises, and diplomatic spats, it not only held together but deepened and expanded. The incorporation of eastern and central Europe deepened rather than disrupted integration. As factories grew in the former Soviet sphere, so did trade and connections with western Europe.

Trnava, on the outskirts of Slovakia's capital, Bratislava, was once the kind of place the Soviets sent bureaucrats who made mistakes. Yet in 2003, as Slovakia prepared to join the EU, Peugeot executives traveled to Trnava with $700 million and plans to build three hundred thousand cars a year. They followed Volkswagen, which had already set up shop nearby. And they would be followed by Kia and Jaguar Land Rover. They were attracted by a cheap but skilled workforce, long-standing if suppressed cultural ties, the day's drive from Germany's auto heartland, and, not least, the embrace of the EU.

Today, Trnava is a bustling city of seventy thousand people that has mostly merged into Bratislava and is tightly linked to its neighbors. Wages have risen, as have education levels. Alongside hundreds of plants sit universities, vocational schools, and research labs. And Trnava isn't the only part of Slovakia to make good: the country has become the per capita auto king, its five million citizens churning out one million cars every year.[59]

Limits of the EU

European integration hasn't been a one-way street. In the 1950s, the notion of a common European army met a swift demise, as did early calls for a political community. Efforts to invest together in transportation and atomic energy never got off the ground. In the 1960s, France blocked the UK's entrance and insisted on keeping its veto power. By the 1980s, it was Britain's Margaret Thatcher both pushing the single market and also pushing back against European labor laws and rejecting a common monetary policy.[60] Later, nine nations, including the UK, Denmark, and Poland, would stay out of the euro.

States don't always enforce European court rulings or edicts; others refuse to comply. Germany still shuts out Danish flooring despite court rulings finding that its extra tests aren't necessary. Poland requires non-Polish EMTs to complete many more certificates than Polish ones do. Sweden keeps out Danish drain taps with arcane rules.[61] Appealing these problems to EU courts costs time and money. Businesses are often long gone before a ruling comes.

Governments blow through debt ceilings and flout budget limits. Long before the 2008 financial crisis, many nations routinely spent more than the rules allowed. Portugal violated the budget cap in 2001. In 2003, Germany did the same. France, Italy, Spain, Greece, and others have repeatedly missed targets, as control of government spending remains in local hands that are uninclined to kowtow to EU objectives. Taxes remain the purview of national capitals too, at times competing with and undercutting their neighbors. Countries have carved out national control over public health, national security, and social safety nets. Heads of state, members of Parliament, and even Brussels bureaucrats come from somewhere, and when hashing out EU policies, they can put nation above region.

Regional corporate governance has limits too. EU laws don't always harmonize fiduciary duties and the other fundamentals of running a company. States tend to interpret EU court rulings differently. And some still consider the court's edicts optional. Penalties for noncompliance are rare.

The movement of people and professionals hasn't been seamless either. Poland drags its feet registering architects, the French block foreign programmers, and Italy makes it hard for outside accountants to work. Few pensions are portable, discouraging careers that hop from nation to nation. In the end, less than 3 percent of the EU's people actually work in another member state.[62]

And there have been many moments when the whole project looked ready to fall apart. The 2008 financial crisis drove the euro and European Union to the brink, uncovering and accentuating deep and still-unresolved economic disparities between north and south.

The influx of people from elsewhere has often brought political backlash. The Danish worried about Polish plumbers descending on Copenhagen. Other countries have voiced periodic concerns about eastern Europeans taking factory jobs. A surge of Syrian, Afghani, and Iraqi refugees in 2015 provided the gravest threat to EU unity. A receptive German government clashed with more recalcitrant countries across southern and eastern Europe. Anti-immigrant and Euro-skeptical political parties like Austria's Freedom Party, Germany's AfD, the Northern League in Italy, and Viktor Orban's Fidesz in Hungary gained ground with calls to erect fences and "keep Europe for the Europeans."

At first, it looked like COVID-19 would weaken Europe's ties even further. For the first time since the Schengen agreement, governments shut down their borders en masse. They hoarded masks and other protective equipment for themselves. Brussels initially hesitated to bail out hard-hit Italy, Spain, and France, even as their death tolls rose and economies cratered.

But after a rough start, Europe regrouped. Europe's heads of state approved hundreds of billions of euros in grants and loans for the hardest hit areas. They authorized Brussels to become a big borrower in its own right, creating €750 billion in EU sovereign bonds to spend on a region-wide recovery. To pay for it all, the plan is for members to relinquish more in tax revenues to the Union. While this may precipitate a further fiscal tussle, pan-European solidarity grew among regular folks, with opinion polls across the twenty-seven nations increasingly favorable to Brussels's moves. The vaccine rollout too has been bumpy: Brussels's penny pinching along with manufacturing glitches left them with too few doses at the start. Yet as inoculations picked up, these tensions eased. Citizens' trust in the center grew too, with the vast majority in favor of sending more resources to Brussels to help fight pandemics.[63] And even at the height of continental bickering over vaccines, bureaucrats successfully defined and deepened a broader European industrial strategy. All in all, the EU is set to come out of the coronavirus pandemic intact.

The most acute political backlash against European integration has come from the United Kingdom. Britain had long been a reluctant partner, demanding a rebate on its contributions, pushing back against region-wide regulations, and refusing to adopt the euro.[64] In 2016, Britain voted to leave the bloc, with the frustrations of older, whiter, and more provincial voters overcoming over forty years of treaty-bound ties.

Yet Brexit in many ways has reinvigorated Europe's project. The remaining twenty-seven members united against any special deal for the UK, doubling down on what it means to be part of the club. Other countries, watching Britain's wrenching exit and ensuing economic pain, have been reminded of the real costs of being outside the group. As British trade with Europe takes longer and costs more, many companies are scaling back or pulling out of the UK. Honda, Jaguar Land Rover, the tire maker Michelin, and the auto-parts supplier Schaeffler were among those closing down plants. Barclays and Bank of America headed to Dublin; UBS and JPMorgan, to Frankfurt. Lloyds of London, despite its name, is increasingly based in Brussels. Sony and Panasonic are just two of dozens of firms that shifted their headquarters to Amsterdam.[65]

Britain's government forecasts that the country's GDP will shrink by over 5 percent over fifteen years as trade and investment fall, productivity declines, and jobs disappear—a loss of some $2,000 per person each year.[66] The pound sterling has already taken a hit, falling in value and even more so in global importance. Some question whether the United Kingdom itself will survive, as popular support for Scottish independence grows (Scotland voted to remain in the EU) and nationalists gain electoral ground in Northern Ireland.

The UK's difficulty extricating itself shows how deep EU ties run. Hundreds of rules and regulations have had to be rethought, renegotiated, or reaffirmed to undergird roughly half of Britain's trade, from data sharing to plane safety certifications, from medicine approval processes to criminal surveillance. Customs booths and inspection facilities have had to be built, millions of new shipping pallets swapped in (as non-EU members use different sizes and colors), and tens of thousands of customs inspectors hired to handle what will be over four hundred million new forms a year.[67] The first year has shown just how costly it can be: one out of every four small- and medium-sized exporters halted their sales across the Channel temporarily as they struggled to come to terms with the new rules and regulations. For more than a few, the inward turn will be permanent.[68]

In Brexit's wake, the EU's popularity among its citizens has surged to its highest level in decades.[69] Many of Europe's most prominent skeptics, including France's far-right Marine Le Pen and the leaders of Italy's Northern League, have toned down their anti-EU rhetoric, focusing instead on reforming the EU from within.

Predictions of the EU's demise are older than the Union itself. Every crisis brings out the doomsayers. Yet through financial catastrophes, mass migrations, democratic backsliding, expansions, contractions, and threats of withdrawal, the Union has endured. More often than not, the response to existential threats has been to rally around Europe, not to pull back.

Europe has come to guide the daily life of citizens on matters big and small. The twenty-eight nations (before the UK's departure) created, if not the federation of European states that some people had once envisioned, a tightly woven community, led by regional institutions of a kind not present anywhere else in the world. As the cost of moving people, goods, and money fell, mutual understanding and dependence rose. Companies, products, and services become more and more European.

The result? European companies and consumers buy more goods and services from their neighbors than businesses and people do anywhere else. Over $3 trillion worth flow around the EU each year.[70] Fashioned for geostrategic and economic reasons, grand international agreements from the Treaty of Rome to the Treaty of Lisbon and everyday diplomatic and commercial steps in between bound the nations together and created a competitive economic hub that now leads world trade in cars, pharmaceuticals, luxury goods, and a host of services. With trade came wealth: Europe is now home to twelve of the world's thirty richest countries.

This has given Europe a hedge when competing globally, especially with

Asia's burgeoning supply chains. Even as China became a global export juggernaut, internal European trade dipped only slightly. And since 2013, internal EU trade is again on the rise, with automation somewhat offsetting the enticement of low wages far away.[71]

Today, Europe is by far the most integrated of the three global hubs. Three out of every four euros traded in foods, clothes, plastics, and rubber and two out of every three in furniture, electronics, metals, and vehicles come from other EU members. So do most of the equipment, medicines, chemicals, leather goods, and a whole host of other products that Europeans use. Services—banking, insurance, consulting, tourism—are likewise a European affair.[72]

Deep integration has allowed countries to develop their economies, companies to exploit economies of scale, and universities and commercial R&D shops to share information and collaborate in research. The expansive internal market has nurtured world-class businesses: Siemens, Ikea, Renault, Telefonica, LMVH.

And unlike the other blocs, Europe has moved beyond trade and investment. Its institutions unite people, currencies, social policies, even labor laws. Harmonized rules and regulations span the continent, and regional institutions help run it. Goods, capital, labor, and services flow more and more freely among member states. Trade is an ever-larger part of their economies. Europe has won the integration game, and its member countries have in many ways thrived.

3

Asia: Regionalism through Business

In April 2011, five weeks after Japan's worst-ever-recorded earthquake, automatic transmissions stopped arriving at Toyota's Guangzhou plant, some two thousand miles away. Immediately after the quake hit, the carmaker scrambled to shift manufacturing away from its massive Japanese Tohoku compound, which had lost power and was cut off by washed-out roads. But even among Toyota's numerous Asian factories, it was proving hard to find one that could produce replacement transmissions and other specialized parts. So the managers in Guangzhou called early summer holidays, and workers went home to their families in the provinces, unsure when they would return to the assembly line.

It's perhaps not surprising that disruption in manufacturing somewhere often means disruption in manufacturing everywhere. We live in an interconnected world. But it wasn't always this way, certainly not in Asia, where long distances, vast oceans, and poor transport networks once kept business local and trade more limited. It was not until the post–World War II recovery that the countries of the world's largest continent began to integrate their economies. Toyota Guangzhou employees' unexpected summer holiday was decades in the making. This is how it happened.

Economists tend to describe Asia's development model visually. A common image is of flying geese. Early on, a technologically sophisticated Japan led the V, with South Korea, Taiwan, Hong Kong, Thailand, and the others fanning out behind, picking up labor-intensive jobs and gaining intellectual and industrial know-how along the way. Over time, South

Korea and Taiwan caught up to the leader, their more advanced companies and sectors creating their own trickle-down production networks as they too set up factories and plants, sold high-tech parts, and licensed innovations to their less prosperous Asian neighbors.

This hand-me-down industrialization was led by companies, helped along by support from their governments' bureaucrats. Foreign money, technology, and know-how combined with cheap local labor, land, and government support to meet customer demand an ocean or continent away. The state played a supporting-actor role, alternately wooing foreign companies and protecting local sectors and champions. These tight links between the public and private sectors helped countries upgrade from imitators to innovators, from assemblers to inventors, and from exporters to foreign direct investors in their own right. They turned Asia into a manufacturing powerhouse. From the 1990s to the 2010s, the continent went from making one-quarter to nearly half of all global goods, coming to dominate the production of clothes, shoes, and electronics.[1]

The details and timing varied by country. But it more or less worked across much of Asia, lifting tens of millions of people out of poverty. Starting in the 1960s, nation after nation climbed the economic ladder and rapidly closed the gap in living standards with Western countries. In the space of half a century, incomes quadrupled, education levels more than doubled, and the average person lived over a decade longer.[2]

Another reason for Asia's success? A core group of nations turned to each other. East Asia's miracle is, in big part, a story of regionalization.

The Rise of Factory Asia

Asia's economic rebirth started in Japan. And as in Europe, the United States helped jump-start it. As head of the occupying force, General Douglas MacArthur was tasked with resetting the Japanese economy alongside Japanese politics. The interim government took on entrenched land owners, banned many industrial families linked to the old regime, and allowed labor unions to organize. Rather than keeping the spoils of war, it handed Japan's surviving steel mills, cloth factories, and machine shops back to the locals.

In the 1950s, the Korean War fueled the nascent Japanese industrial recovery, as the U.S. Army chose Japan as its rear base and supplier. Ports, now cleared of mines from the last war, filled up with U.S. destroyers, soldiers, and ammunition dumps. Rebuilt factories churned out iron, steel, ships, and machinery. Japan's harbors added new piers to handle the war's industrial loads.[3]

The United States also opened its domestic markets to a recovering Japanese private sector.[4] Even as Japan's entrepreneurs ramped up military production, they looked beyond the battlefield to American consumers. They repurposed the factories that had recently made weapons to kill American soldiers to churn out goods to court American shoppers. Machine-gun factories started making sewing machines; producers of rifle scopes moved onto cameras and binoculars. In the 1950s, Japanese-made Barbies and toy cars, armchairs and coffee tables, women's underwear and men's ties, transistor radios and record players filled ships headed east. Within a decade of the country's surrender, Japan's economy recovered to its prewar highs.

The blistering pace of Japan's rebuilding meant that businesses quickly ran short of workers. Starting in the 1960s, companies looked to Japan's neighbors and, in some cases, former colonies to expand. The Japanese once had come in military uniforms; they now began returning in business suits.

They found mostly willing hosts in still-poor Taiwan, South Korea, Hong Kong, and Singapore. Desperate for growth, governments in those countries offered tax breaks, cheap land, and subsidies to lure in foreign investment, technology, and manufacturing know-how (even as Japan protected its home turf).

It worked. Toyota, Honda, Hitachi, and dozens of other Japanese companies poured in to build factories and warehouses. They imported machines to fill the new plants, sophisticated parts for workers to assemble, and organizational techniques and managerial expertise to run things. Locals got to see how Japanese executives stood up operations, navigated production schedules, controlled lean inventories, and monitored production systems. Through licenses, joint ventures, and technology sharing, they leased and learned.

As governments catered to foreign money, they also tried to help national businesses get ahead. They carved out certain sectors just for locals and orchestrated international joint ventures in others. They paid royalties to bring in foreign technology and funded national research to create their own, some even giving cash bonuses to successful domestic inventors.[5] These governments often provided financing to help local companies bridge the "valley of death" between idea and commercial product. These policies helped pull the four emerging Asian Tigers up the economic and technological development ladder.

As Japan's CEOs ventured abroad, bureaucrats traveled with them. In the postwar reshuffle, the Finance Ministry and the new Ministry of International Trade and Industry (MITI) gained the upper hand overseeing the selectively protectionist, pro-manufacturing, and export-oriented industrial policy behind Japan's economic takeoff. International expansion became a vital pillar and outsourcing a main method of economic growth. So bureaucrats marshaled Japan's economic and financial resources to help companies build regional production chains.

Japan's overseas development aid promoted the corporate cause, financing the infrastructure that its companies needed to get their goods to international markets. In the late 1960s and 1970s, Japanese taxpayer money paid for railways, motorways, and dams in Korea and power stations, highways, and water systems in Indonesia. In the 1990s, Japanese aid paid to connect Hanoi to Vietnam's main port, Haiphong, cutting the trucking time from the capital to the sea in half. Japan would lend tens of millions of dollars to Dalian, China, to build a mammoth office park to house dozens of Japanese companies.[6]

Bureaucrats in Japan's embassies throughout Asia guided the commercial expansion on the ground. They helped smaller Japanese companies make the international jump, connecting them to potential suppliers and buyers. They ran classes to train locals in machining and metal, chemical, and textile work. They even helped manage local labor markets, stepping in to keep Japanese companies from poaching workers from each other.[7]

Public money funded viability studies for industries and companies looking to expand, then often provided cheap financing and insurance for those that chose to venture abroad. And bureaucrats ensured that favored companies had access to foreign currency despite exchange controls.

Japan's postwar economic setup made public-private coordination all the easier. Its famed *keiretsu* conglomerates combined banks and brand names, researchers and suppliers, construction crews, and even power plants in a dense network of operations linked by board members, loans, and ownership stakes.[8] Money, technology, and employees jumped from one to another. Bureaucrats shuttled between company boards and management teams, tying them to the government. Japan had created a one-stop shop for managing international expansion.

Asahi Glass is just one of the companies leveraging commercial and governmental ties to its international advantage. Part of the Mitsubishi *keiretsu*, it began its post–World War II foreign expansion in the 1950s. Asahi, which made windows, windshields, TV screens, and glass electronic parts, ventured first to India. It then set its sights on East and Southeast Asia. In the 1960s, Asahi brought flat-glass manufacturing to Thailand, cornering the market for windows in new buildings and the cars being churned out by Thailand's burgeoning auto hub. Next came joint ventures in Indonesia, the Philippines, and Malaysia. Asahi provided much of the industrial glass and chemicals used by the hundreds of electronics and parts factories breaking ground (often with Japanese money).[9] Over the 1980s and 1990s, Asahi would expand into Singapore, Taiwan, and China. Its flat glass covered the mirrored skyscrapers multiplying across Asia's cities; its high resolution screens sharpened the images of feature-film heroes in living rooms; its shatterproof windshields protected drivers; and its chlorine, preminol, and sodium bicarbonate purified water systems, filled mattresses, and was melted into PVC pipes, respectively.

Asahi's *keiretsu* supported these international forays with money, know-how, and guaranteed clients. Mitsubishi's financing arm, the Bank of Tokyo-Mitsubishi, offered cheap and generous loans. For years, Mitsubishi Electric bought up hundreds of thousands of glass tubes for its rear-projection TVs and later joined manufacturing forces to make flat screens. Mitsubishi Motors installed Asahi windshields in its Galants, Lancers, and Eclipses. And Asahi had an in with the dozens of companies and ventures owned or controlled by the conglomerate: Mitsubishi construction and real estate, its defense contractor and regional jet maker, Nikon cameras, Fuso buses and trucks, chemical makers, and more.

Japan's bureaucrats backed Asahi and Mitsubishi throughout. The Export-Import Bank lent Asahi $50 million to get its Philippine venture off the ground and another $20 million to help Asahi Indonesia restructure. MITI helped finance Asahi testing labs and brought in academic researchers to fill them.[10] In an attempt to protect Asahi's dominant market share, Japanese officials even pressured their counterparts in Thailand to block the rival U.S. glassmaker Guardian from opening a plant there.

Over half a century of international expansion, backed by the Japanese government and its Mitsubishi ties, has made Asahi one of the biggest global glassmakers, as well as a leader in a whole host of industrial chemicals. And while the company now has significant European and U.S. operations, Asahi's Asia hub dominates sales and (even more so) profits. The company's over $9 billion–plus market capitalization depends predominantly on its regional strength.[11]

Business Expansion Fuels Regionalism

Taiwan became Japan's first international stop. The Japanese corporate set first crossed the East China Sea to set up factories making cheap shoes, shirts, and plastics (most destined for the United States). Other manufacturers quickly followed. Many looked for local partners. Toshiba singled out the electric-fan maker Tatung, teaching the low-tech family company to mass produce its TVs. Sanyo joined forces with Taiwan's Dali Electric to make air conditioners and refrigerators. Others set up their own factories. Matsushita, Sony, and Hitachi built plants to make all kinds of electronics from radios to tape recorders. At least for a time, car-making blossomed: Nissan partnered to make parts; Mitsubishi, Honda, and Toyota built their own plants.

Taiwan's government courted Japanese money. It offered tax breaks, export loans, tariff waivers, even cash back on levies paid.[12] It created special export-processing zones that did away with many local rules and regulations. And it provided near-captive consumers by hiking tariffs on outside products and weakening Taiwan's exchange rate.

At the same time, Taiwan worked to build an industrial base of its own. To help local firms get started, it licensed foreign technology, most notably for the integrated circuits that go into almost all modern electronics. It underwrote domestic research to spur homegrown scientific advances. And it encouraged local firms to make the most of the influx of Japanese money, patents, and managerial know-how.

Over time, the public support translated into technological success. Local firms began making their own integrated circuits, LCD screens, PC monitors, and, later, cell phones. They created plastic compounds, chemicals, and reams of steel, glass, cement, and cotton to feed thousands of smaller assemblers and exporters. Taiwanese companies became master makers of others' goods, powering the factories behind Casio pocket calculators, Dell notebook computers, Adidas running shoes, and other brand names big and small. They took a stab at building their own trademarks. Giant bicycles, Acer computers, and HTC smartphones hit markets from Australia to Spain.

Through aid, trade, foreign direct investment, and an undervalued currency, Taiwan transitioned from an island of hardscrabble agriculture to a maker of sophisticated electronics, plastics, and machines. In just a couple of decades, per capita incomes more than doubled as Taiwan joined the ranks of the advanced economies.

A similar story unfolded in South Korea. As the new nation got on its feet after the end of the Korean War, Japan's big players arrived, hungry for workers and customers. Starting in the late 1960s and despite simmering tensions between the two countries—Japan had been an occupying force only a couple of decades before—Japanese companies formed joint ventures with South Korean partners, licensed their technology to South Korean manufacturers, and built factories to be filled with South Korean workers. Local companies jumped at the opportunity. Samsung teamed up with Toshiba to make videocassette recorders (VCRs) and Sanyo to make photocopiers. LG hooked up with Hitachi to build black-and-white televisions, Fuji to make elevators, Tanaka to forge metal products, and Mitsubishi to make a whole host of electronic parts. NEC, Mitsui, Matsushita, and dozens of other Japanese companies set up their own operations in and around Seoul. They imported some components for locals to put together and cultivated local suppliers to make other parts to feed into burgeoning regional manufacturing supply chains.

Japanese bureaucrats encouraged the corporate migration. They convinced South Korea to create its first free-trade zone facing Japan: the Masan port, in the country's south, which quickly filled up with Japanese manufacturers and exporters. Official development aid paid for Seoul's harbors to be dredged and for new highways, railways, and industrial parks filled with Japanese firms. And Japanese government loans underwrote Korean companies' purchases of Japanese-made machines and equipment.

South Korea, like Taiwan, had bigger dreams than serving as Japan's workshop forever, and so the government pushed back on too much money and influence from its former colonizer. To do so, the authoritarian President Park Chung-Hee turned to the nation's traditional *chaebol* conglomerates, personally choosing winners to lavish with tax breaks, cheap money, loan guarantees, tariff rebates, and even lower electricity and water prices, as long as they doubled down on electronics, machinery, petrochemicals, and other "strategic sectors" of his choosing.[13] The government paid for roads, rails, and ports to connect their plants to the world (often granting the contracts to the very same conglomerates).[14] Park protected the *chaebols* from foreign competition, giving them time to learn and grow. But if they didn't grow as he wanted, Park was ruthless with them. For those that failed to export, licenses and access dried up, leading many once-famed businesses and family dynasties to disappear.

The South started out the poorer of the two Koreas. Yet beginning in the 1960s, the country was transformed beyond recognition by an outpouring of Japanese and other foreign investment, combined with a strong state cultivating and driving its own export-driven national champions. Over the next two decades, near double-digit growth turned South Korea into one of the world's twenty largest economies and one of the biggest global producers of ships, steel, semiconductors, and cars.

Hong Kong began its postwar economic climb making Japanese-funded yellow rubber duckies, plastic flowers, T-shirts, and flip-flops, products that put hundreds of thousands of Chinese refugees to work in the new industrial parks rising on the edges of Kowloon and Hong Kong Island. Like its neighbors, Hong Kong quickly graduated from bath toys to appliances, cameras, and watches, guided by Japanese and other international manufacturers. As Hong Kong industrialized, it never lost its roots as a merchant city. Its trading houses flourished, often now joined or owned by foreign shipping and logistics companies, making the most of Hong Kong's vast harbor and British legal institutions to buy, sell, and broker deals for parts and finished goods alike.[15]

Japanese money helped fuel Hong Kong's rise as a financial center, its banks leading the foreign invasion. Dai-Ichi Bank, Fuji, Tokai, and over forty others set up branches, clustering in the office buildings and rising towers along the waterfront at the base of Victoria Peak. Later, when China reengaged with the world, Hong Kong became its gateway to the outside. Money from Causeway Bay offices flowed into Guangdong and Shenzhen factories, and goods flowed out to Hong Kong and the world, both sides getting richer in the process.

Outside money helped upgrade Singapore's industry too. As the city-state struck off on its own from Malaysia in 1965, Prime Minister Lee Kuan Yew courted multinationals with a gamut of benefits—cheap land, tax breaks, and wage controls. He even took care of worker housing for companies that were willing to invest in manufacturing.[16] The United States and Europe played a big investing role from the start in the city-state. So too did Japan, pouring in tens of billions of dollars.[17] Seiko, Sumitomo, and other industrial giants helped Singapore's factories quickly move from matches, mosquito coils, and fishhooks to watches, precision instruments, and petrochemicals.

Like other Asian leaders, Lee Kuan Yew carved out space for home-grown industries led by the state itself. Nearly five hundred government owned or influenced businesses—financed by state-run banks—built ships, forged steel, produced chemicals, processed food, and provided electricity and water. Private companies played a decidedly secondary role in the industrial scale-up, but they too went from sewing clothes and milling rubber to building ships and manufacturing semiconductors.[18]

Singapore's government took advantage of its harbor and long-standing trading ties. It was early to convert to containers, rejigging its berths and docks to welcome freighters laden with hundreds, and later thousands, of colorful steel boxes. By the 1980s, stories-high cranes were loading and unloading mountainous ships all along the waterfront. Just blocks away, residential towers and glass office buildings housed a growing cadre of bankers, accountants, insurers, and logistics specialists who moved not just Singapore's own manufactured goods but also a good portion of Asia's expanding trade.

As the yen strengthened in the 1970s and 1980s, Japan's regional investments accelerated. Tens of billions in today's dollars poured into what were at the time backwater cities: Seoul, Taipei, Bangkok, and Kuala Lumpur. The onetime colonizer underwrote nearly two-thirds of the foreign direct investment into South Korea and over one in three dollars flowing into Taiwan.[19] In the 1970s, fully half the money flowing into Thailand's growing electronics, chemicals, and auto industries was Japanese. And it outpaced U.S. investment in Hong Kong and came close in Singapore.[20]

Japanese investment in Asia tended to focus first on manufacturing and then on deepening commercial integration. Japanese plant managers, once they set up their factories, imported precision machinery, electrical equipment, base metals, and chemicals from home. By the early 2000s, Japan's trade with East Asia alone was larger than that with the United States and EU combined.[21]

As Japanese firms regionalized, their operations also specialized. Taipei became Sony's home for radios, telephones, and VCRs; Seoul made its television tuners; Kuala Lumpur made its TVs and DVD players; Penang made its iconic yellow Walkmans; and Bangkok made its microwave integrated circuits. Plants in Beijing, Wuxi, Shanghai, Huizhou, and Guangzhou would later make camcorders, projectors, batteries, and phones. Toyota took to stamping in Taipei, building engines near Bangkok, building transmissions in Santa Rosa City in the Philippines, and later forging joints in China—all to be collected and assembled into Camrys on the outskirts of Hanoi.[22]

Recipients Become Investors

Years of foreign investment, technology transfers, professionalization, and learning combined with industrial policies and government prodding transformed these economies. Production flourished, and technological sophistication grew. Wealth increased, and domestic wages rose.

By the late 1980s, Japan's former beneficiaries had become innovators themselves. They too began to build factories abroad. And like Japan before them, they looked mostly to their home region. As they expanded, they pulled Thailand, Malaysia, Indonesia, and the Philippines (often dubbed the ASEAN-4), Vietnam, and China into the production process. Regional integration picked up steam.

Taiwan was one of the first apprentices to adopt the role of master. Toshiba's onetime student Tatung became an international contractor in its own right, manufacturing TVs in Singapore, washing machines in the

Philippines, and refrigerators in Thailand. Taiwan's main computer maker, Acer, branched out to make monitors on the mainland, motherboards in the Philippines, keyboards and laser printers in Malaysia, and everything in between in Thailand and Indonesia. Taiwanese makers of calculators, computers, power cables, telecommunication systems, auto parts, and tires went regional, too, building plants, licensing technology, and selling components to be assembled across the nearby seas.

South Korea's *chaebols* morphed from the clients of Japanese companies to their rivals, catching up in many sectors and taking the technological lead in some, such as flat screens and memory chips. They started putting their own brands on the goods they made and exported to the world: LG televisions, Samsung Galaxy phones, Hyundai and Kia cars.

As Korean brands went international, so did production. LG charged into China with nearly a dozen plants making everything from air conditioners and microwaves to flat-screen TVs and LCD monitors. Samsung did the same, choosing up-and-coming industrial cities on the outskirts of Beijing, Shanghai, and Shenzhen. Pusan-based shoemakers headed to export zones in Tangerang, Indonesia. Hyundai took to making containers in Thailand. From makers of polyester fibers to woolen cloth, car parts to all sorts of electronics, Korea's companies joined an exodus across borders and seas to invest throughout Asia.

Not all of this international investment stayed within Asia, of course. LG bought up rival U.S. TV maker Zenith in search of a technological edge in 1999. Samsung set up design centers in London and Milan. Acer moved a good part of its research and development to Silicon Valley, while Honda built one of its largest plants just northwest of the small Ohio city of Marysville to sell its Accords across the United States. Still, Asia got the biggest slice, as investments abroad mostly hovered close by.

Following the Japanese model, governments again supported these private-sector bets. Taiwanese development aid funded industrial parks in the Philippines and Vietnam. South Korean public money built Indonesian and Vietnamese roads, power plants, and rail lines. Export-import banks joined in, funding national companies headed abroad. Seoul bureaucrats fast-tracked approval for dozens of daily flights to mainland China to encourage business.

State-owned enterprises led Singapore's charge abroad, building power plants and industrial parks and even outfitting a whole township west of Shanghai. The government backed private efforts too, underwriting scouting trips for local businesses, giving tax breaks when they made investments abroad, and handing out visas to bring up-and-coming managers back to the city-state for training.[23]

Stalwart Japan joined the newcomers in pushing into Southeast Asia. Mitsubishi helped Malaysia in its quest for a national car. Toyota and Mitsubishi headed to Thailand, seeding what would become Southeast Asia's auto hub. Komatsu tractors went to Indonesia. And Nihon Denkei, Takahata Precision, and Tohoku Pioneer set up all sorts of electronic assembly lines in Vietnam.

These lower-income countries did their best to copy their predecessors' paths. They wooed foreign money with tax breaks and tariffs. They fast-tracked licenses and permits to get foreign-funded plants up and running. They tricked out office buildings and industrial parks. And local governments tried to leverage international interest and money to build up their own economies, carving out strategic sectors and promoting national champions. The strategy did not work quite as well this time around, and advanced manufacturing and technological sophistication proved frustratingly elusive; but nevertheless their economies grew, and standards of living rose.

China's Rise

The biggest success of the Asian development path in its size and speed was China. China would use hundreds of billions of dollars in foreign investment and even more local savings to drive decades of double-digit economic growth and pull 850 million people out of poverty.[24] Along the way, it built up its own industrial and knowledge base. Yet the rise of this economic juggernaut, equal parts exalted and feared, was no sui generis achievement. It too depended on regional integration.

China came late to the development game. For decades after World War II, China's political turmoil and closed communal economy left it out of the integration happening just across the Yellow and East China Seas. Things began to change in the late 1970s. With Mao Zedong buried, Deng Xiaoping shifted his country's economic path, rallying the Party around the slogan of "Reform and Opening Up." The new outlook transformed China. For the first time, Deng allowed farmers to sell their extra harvest, and city dwellers to open restaurants and stores. He also courted international money. The fishing village of Shenzhen and a few other coastal cities became the first havens for foreign investment, with these special economic zones being free of many of the tariffs, taxes, price controls, and rigid labor rules that stifled growth elsewhere. Local officials courted international companies, handing out land, rounding up workers, and matching foreigners with connected locals.[25] They built roads, ports, airports, and railways to carry imports and exports. And the government held down the value of the yuan, making everything leaving its shores a little cheaper for foreigners to buy.

Like other Asian nations, China focused on building up its own industrial base. State banks handed out cheap money, and local governments gave out land as they competed to create manufacturing hubs. The nation's five-year plans laid out the rules for international and local companies alike, carving out strategic sectors, directing government contracts, and squashing competitors to favor national champions. China forced foreign companies into joint ventures or to bring in and share technology in order to gain access to its cheap labor and burgeoning market.

Chinese factories were soon sucking in every part and component imaginable for assembly into final products. Clothes, shoes, and toys arrived first, attracted by the possibility of hundreds of millions of agile, if untrained, fingers willing to work for pennies. Manufacturing quickly moved up the value chain to appliances, high-tech gadgets, autos, and planes.

China's neighbors were its earliest and biggest outside investors. In the 1990s, South Koreans came in scale. China quickly became their largest foreign direct investment bet.[26] Samsung inked an agreement with the local government of Huizhou, just north of the Pearl River Delta manufacturing heartland, even before Seoul's diplomats recognized their Beijing counterparts. Together, they built a manufacturing complex the size of twenty football fields to churn out first stereos and monitors and later MP3 players and smartphones, employing thousands of people and developing the whole southwestern side of the city.

South Korea's Kia got into China in 2002, partnering with the Mao-era carmaker Dongfeng to sidestep high tariffs on car imports. From a perch in Yancheng, an overlooked city not far from Shanghai, it rolled out the TianLiMa, a no-frills four-door compact with a $10,000 sticker price. The car was a surprise hit, particularly among young people: Kia sold ten thousand in the first few months. The joint venture added a minivan, hatchback, and SUV to its lineup and another two plants, churning out just shy of one million cars a year. As Yancheng transformed from a struggling producer of sea salt to a bustling auto hub, its population nearly doubled, with workers filling the industrial parks. Today, broad highways and high-speed rails connect the former backwater to nearby Shanghai and the world.

Taiwan saw the same possibilities just across the straits. Apparel manufacturers and shoemakers were the first to flood in; warehouses quickly filled with rows of cutting tables, sewing machines, and thousands of young women feeding seams, attaching buttons, and stitching shoe soles every hour of the day. Next came electronics. Taiwan's Acer, Asus, and Mitac set up factories in which row after row of plastic chairs were filled with hunched and uniformed workers taping, inserting, soldering, and inspecting pieces. From those assembly lines emerged hundreds of thousands of monitors and motherboards, scanners, and soundcards. By the turn of the century, Taiwan-based companies were making more laptops on the mainland than anyone else, anywhere else in the world.[27]

Japan joined too. Matsushita Electric set up washing-machine plants, Hitachi made color TVs, and Canon outsourced its latest digital cameras. Many Japanese companies piggybacked on their Taiwanese connections to get a head start on the mainland. Others detoured through Hong Kong, channeling money through intermediaries to make instant noodles, car parts, and chemicals.

China competed with its neighbors for new factories, plants, and jobs along the production chain. But its rise didn't snuff out the others. Instead, the powerful centripetal pull of its assembly lines drew in much of what its more industrialized neighbors could produce. They found that together they could make most anything cheaper and faster for consumers everywhere.

Much is often made of the high-profile investments by U.S. and European companies in China, particularly after the country joined the WTO, in 2001. And it is true: Ford, GM, General Electric, Siemens, Bayer, Motorola, Ikea, and many others set up or expanded Chinese operations.[28]

But those investments were in large part secondary. The real story is the regional one. Much more of the international money pouring into factories, warehouses, labs, and R&D centers, powering cities and raising skylines, came from Asia than from anywhere else. By the early twenty-first century, China was importing more goods from its neighbors than from the United States and Europe combined.[29] In the decade that followed, that regional integration only deepened.

Asia's integration differed from that of the other hubs. The making and moving of pieces and parts to become toys, clothes, computers, and thousands of other items linked factory to factory and nation to nation. Yet unlike in Europe and North America, the ultimate buyer remained an ocean or a continent away.

What Asia made, the United States bought. Starting in the 1950s, Eisenhower's highways, new government-backed mortgages and loans, and, for more than a few, prejudice, lured families away from dense city centers. Armed with a mortgage-interest tax deduction that tilted the economic calculus toward owning over renting, millions of Americans settled into fifteen-hundred-square-foot ranch houses or the cozy split-levels proliferating in developments and on cul-de-sacs a comfortable drive away from downtown.

Alongside suburbs came shopping malls. Big department stores and specialty shops, restaurants and food stands, barber shops and salons, travel agencies and movie theaters formed islands on seas of asphalt parking lots. They became a place to mingle, eat, and most importantly, shop. Full-service anchor tenants and discount big-box stores alike turned to Asia to fill the thousands of square feet of show space and miles of displays with products destined for millions of suburban cabinets, closets, rec rooms, and garages. Sears, Kmart, JCPenney, Woolworth, and others began sourcing suits and shoes, blenders and beach towels, luggage and clocks, tables and couches from across the Pacific. Madison Avenue's ad men helped companies spend billions to turn Asian-made tennis shoes into Nikes, basic trousers into Gap khakis, and mass-produced shirts and skirts into The Limited's trendy teen wear.

As international stores and brands pushed Asia for better deals, the continent's factories specialized, divvying up the manufacturing process to gain minutes and save pennies in production costs. Yarn from Korea might be sent to Taiwanese mills for weaving and dyeing. The fabric would then be shipped, along with Japanese brand YKK zippers made in China, to Thailand to be cut, sewn, and finished into pleated pants ready for store shelves across the Midwest.[30] To make running shoes, Indonesian rubber would be stitched together with Chinese foam and Taiwanese faux leather by quick Vietnamese hands, bound for Footlockers and shoe departments across the world.[31]

Electronics developed the most streamlined process of all. The silicon in Samsung's Galaxy phones is extracted, melted, and refined in China before heading to western Japan. There, in the town of Imari, diamond saw blades slice salami-shaped ingots into tiny flat discs. After being polished and cleaned, these wafers head, along with Japanese-made diborane gas and sulfuric acid, across the East Sea to semiconductor chip factories a few hours south of Seoul, where Samsung layers billions of transistors onto them to make finished chips. A few hours farther south, another Samsung operation builds specialized OLED touch screens, combining carbon and hydrogen into thin light-emitting films between conductors (themselves made up of parts from around Asia) to create the crisp images and responsive surfaces swiped by tens of millions of fingers every day.[32]

Chips and screens join with Chinese-made microphones able to decipher different languages and identify individual users, skills powered by research breakthroughs in Hong Kong, Singapore, and Japan. Sony's Japanese operations send the image sensors for phone cameras. Cables, sockets, and plugs are made by Chinese suppliers. These and many other parts take to the skies, seas, and roads to assembly lines an hour north of Hanoi, Vietnam.

There, alongside Thai Nguyen's famous tea plantations, sits Samsung's largest manufacturing complex. Covering an area the size of three Disneylands, dozens of low white warehouse buildings clad with flat blue roofs house vast factory floors, an auditorium, dormitories, an infirmary, and three cafeterias. Inside, tens of thousands of employees assemble motherboards, drill precision holes, insert cameras, tighten screws, and wipe down screens. They test each phone's functions, audio, and battery life before sending 120 million of them out into the world each year.[33]

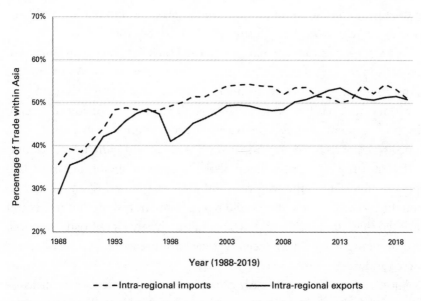

Intraregional trade in Asia. This graph includes data for countries within the East Asia and Pacific regions, as specified by the World Integrated Trade Solution. Source: World Integrated Trade Solution

From 1990 to today, the back-and-forth of goods around Asia grew from a third to over 50 percent of all the region's trade, far surpassing North America's internal ties and closing in on Europe's level of regional intensity.[34] Asia has come to dominate the production of all things electronic, making more than two out of every three phones, computers, pieces of audio equipment, and appliances bought worldwide.

Finished goods are a growing part of regional trade, too. Xiaomi and Samsung phones connect Indian, Vietnamese, and Taiwanese families and friends. The Japanese beauty-product behemoth Shiseido and upstart Korean brand 3 Concept Eyes grace Chinese cheekbones and lips. Haier air conditioners keep Bangkok apartments cool. And TikTok occupies hours every day for tens of millions of teens across Vietnam, Malaysia, Thailand, and Singapore. Nearly a third of the goods made in Asia now stay there, a number that has been edging up since the 1990s.[35]

Asians are selling each other more services, too. Thai hotels fill up with Chinese vacationers during the October holidays. Indonesian patients check into Malaysian hospitals. Filipino maids make beds in Hong Kong and Taipei. Chinese students enroll in Singapore's universities, and Chinese construction workers fill sites throughout Southeast Asia.

Asia's consumers already have more total buying power than European ones, and they are edging in on the North Americans.[36] As Asia's citizens transition from makers to consumers, integration is set to deepen.

Money, too, has helped fuse Asia together. The proportion of foreign direct investment coming from within the region grew from a third in the 1990s to 59 percent today, outpacing European and North American investment.[37] It paid for new chemical plants, semiconductor foundries, laptop assemblers, clothing factories, and food processors. Asian companies bought up each other's office buildings, apartment towers, and hotels and invested in each other's banks. They built each other's railroads, airports, and shopping malls. More recently, they have backed each other's ecommerce and ridesharing apps.

Another good chunk of cash came from overseas development assistance. Japan began the practice, using aid to build roads, ports, water systems, and electricity grids to help its factories abroad start up, run, and connect to the world. The Asian Development Bank has since invested tens of billions of dollars in cross-border rails, roads, riverways, and ports. The newer Asian Infrastructure Investment Bank promises more of the same; it has started off by laying fiber-optic cables across Cambodia and widening highways between Laos and Pakistan. China's Belt and Road Initiative has pledged hundreds of billions of dollars to connect China to its neighbors through ports in Malaysia, Myanmar, and Cambodia and roads, rails, and bridges in Laos, Thailand, and Singapore.[38]

Credit has played a lesser role in tying together the region, as Asia's capital markets aren't as deep as those in Europe and North America.[39] Still, cross-border lending picked up in the early 2000s as Japanese banks followed their conglomerates and clients overseas. Later, other national financiers accompanied their big companies and customers, leading to regional loans today of over $1 trillion.[40] Asia's venture capitalists are just beginning to gain ground. Softbank and other Asia-based funds are building out supply chains and taking the area's "unicorns"—start-ups valued at over $1 billion—into new markets.

Over four hundred million Asians reach for their passports each year.[41] And when they do, they are more likely to go next door, for both work and fun, than anywhere else. Three-quarters venture nearby—exploring China's cities, Thailand's beaches, Indonesia's temples, Macau's casinos, and Hong Kong's malls. Asia's residents now take more trips in their home continent than North Americans do in theirs and nearly as many as Europeans do.

When Asians leave home for good, most do go farther away. Visas for neighboring countries can be hard to come by, especially for less skilled workers. Worries over the abuse of domestic help and day laborers have also led some governments to discourage their citizens from heading to Malaysia and Singapore, in particular.[42] Nevertheless, some thirty million Asians live and work in nearby nations.[43] Filipino nurses care for Japanese patients, Vietnamese laborers clean up Thai construction sites, and millions of Chinese workers tend shops, hotels, and restaurants across the region.

Asia's Regional Specialization

Asia created an economic ecosystem that moves millions of parts back and forth and spreads know-how for as many processes. Countries are now as often buyers as sellers, origins as destinations. As countries have developed, they have specialized. China thrives in heavy industry and consumer electronics. Japan builds premier car, camera, TV, and gaming brands. Taiwan has excelled in mature and cutting-edge technologies: TVs and monitors, desktops and notebooks, commercial lathes and drills, and chip manufacturing. South Korea has developed a similar mix of integrated circuits and LCD screens and has had more branding success in cars and electronics. Thailand has an edge in autos and their parts. And Vietnam is now staking a claim to lower-end electronics, mass producing monitors, radios, and cellphones.

Like any ecosystem, Asia's integrated economy never sits still. For years, China drove integration by serving as the region's finishing school; although it sent trillions of dollars' worth of goods out into the world every year, it produced far less of their final value. This is changing. China's ubiquitous five-year plans and Made in China 2025 all aim to have the country capture more of the value in each circuit, monitor, printer, and phone put together on the mainland. With the iPhone's early 3G, released in 2009, Chinese workers added less than $7 to the $299 sticker price. A

decade later, China's take had grown to over $100 of the more sophisti-
cated X model (which retailed at $1,000), including making the circuit
board, camera module, and battery pack.[44]

In 2000, many of China's factories were essentially assembly shops for
foreign parts: nearly 40 percent of what China exported was made elsewhere. Today, imported parts make up just 17 percent of the value of what
China sends out into the world.[45]

China's growing self-reliance has hurt some of its neighbors economically and at times inflamed tensions diplomatically. South Korea has found
its adhesive products and Japan its machines and flat-rolled steel in much
less demand. Down, too, are sales of Thai rubber, Malay chemicals, and
Filipino medical equipment, once major exports to the mainland.

Other Chinese neighbors are proving luckier. Rising labor costs, the
U.S.-Chinese trade war, and the aftermath of the COVID-19 pandemic
are driving many manufacturers to find new places to make things. And
they aren't going far. Vietnam is absorbing a good portion of the manufacturing of phones, shoes, and TVs. Thailand has seen a jump in auto
parts. Southeast Asia is one of the biggest winners, as Samsung, Nintendo,
Dynabook, Nidec, Panasonic, Sony, and Pegatron shift at least a part of
their Chinese production across the South China Sea.[46]

Chinese companies are becoming big investors themselves, bankrolling
machinery and electronics factories in Vietnam and Malaysia, car-parts and
tire makers in Thailand, and software in Singapore.[47] Flows of foreign investment out of China have accelerated so fast that in both 2015 and 2016
the money leaving outpaced the money coming in, reflecting China's
transition from beneficiary to benefactor on an unprecedented scale. As
China farms out low-cost production, it is exporting more of its components to its Asian neighbors—Chinese-made synthetic fabrics, cell-phone
parts, plastics, and other intermediate goods.[48]

Asia's Marginal Diplomats

Europe's regionalization grew from multiple multilateral agreements creating and defining a formal framework for integration. In Asia,
diplomats played little role in the story of economic integration. After
World War II, a defeated Japan shied away from the international stage,

and its neighbors hesitated to reempower their former colonizer. The United States discouraged any diplomatic clustering that could limit its own influence; its Cold War strategy in the Pacific was to divide rather than unite. Few of Asia's autocratic governments relished the prospect of constraining their power at home with binding international rules.[49] And later on, neither China nor Japan wanted to join an organization controlled by the other.

Sure, there were always summits. Leaders met. The cameras flashed. But little resulted. For decades, Asia had few solid trade agreements. And the continent has never had anything anywhere close to a customs union, a single market, or a single currency.

The first lasting regional association was spurred by politics, not economics. In the late 1960s, Thailand, Singapore, the Philippines, Malaysia, and Indonesia banded together against their communist neighbors, forming the Association of Southeast Asian Nations (ASEAN). Security dominated the new group's agenda; trade was an afterthought.[50] And in any case, without Japan, the region's biggest investor, the association had little economic sway.

It wasn't until two decades later, after the collapse of the Soviet bloc, that trade and commerce took the diplomatic center stage, with the creation of Asia-Pacific Economic Cooperation (APEC). Even then, the "Asian way"—endless "dialogues" on everything from climate change to product standards—meant that little really happened.

Starting in the 1990s, free-trade agreements did finally come to Asia. Yet of the over sixty agreements signed, most remain weak. Few have moved beyond lowering tariffs. Most are riddled with carve-outs and leave in place a host of tests, taxes, and licenses that limit trade. As a result, Japanese-made steel and cars are still rare in Thailand, and Thai condensed milk is missing from Tokyo's grocery shelves. Malaysian beef is unlikely to be used in bibimbap in Seoul, and good luck finding a Korean Hite beer in a Filipino bar. Only a quarter of Asia's exporters actually use the various agreements.[51]

The latest trade effort, the Regional Comprehensive Economic Partnership (RCEP), steps up this ambition, at least partially. The fifteen-nation deal, including China, Japan, and all of ASEAN, takes on tariffs and makes local content rules easier to navigate. This will advantage supply chains between the members, binding the region together more tightly. Otherwise, it mostly combines several existing deals, changing less on the ground. And India's recalcitrance limits RCEP's potential reach and ability to play a lead role in integrating markets that are not already deeply tied.

Formal monetary cooperation hasn't fared much better. The region's central banks share some information, and currency swaps and bond funds have been used sporadically.[52] But no formal exchange-rate cooperation exists, and an Asian Monetary Fund, let alone a single currency, remains a distant aspiration.

The Comprehensive and Progressive Agreement for Trans-Pacific Partnership (CPTPP) may break Asia's poor diplomatic track record. Pulling together Japan, Malaysia, Vietnam, Singapore, and seven other countries, it goes beyond niceties to open up public contracts, protect intellectual property, enforce labor and environmental standards, resolve disputes, and set digital rules and technical regulations. It may reshape Pacific trade. But until it does, the striking fact about Asia's integration will remain how little formal treaties had to do with it.

Overcoming Asia's Remaining Regional Barriers

Getting goods across Asia can be a tricky business. A journey that would last ten days in the Western Hemisphere can drag out for over three weeks in Asia.[53] Customs, repeated inspections, and a hefty dose of paperwork all slow goods at the continent's numerous borders. Many countries have announced electronic single customs windows, which let shippers fill out manifests just once when moving cargo across the East and South China Seas. But just ten have gotten their systems up and running.[54] Even then, data can get lost or corrupted between national systems, untranslated forms confuse customs officers, and some ministries still demand hard copies, forcing shippers to courier documents, slowing handoffs and adding days in storage.

Still, connections are easier than they used to be. Modern container shipping has turned Asia's seas, once barriers between countries, into easy connections. Asia's ports are now the busiest in the world, moving three times the cargo of those in North America and Europe combined. The majority of Asia's sea trade starts and ends within the continent—and this regional trade is growing fast.[55] From Singapore to Hong Kong, China's Shanghai to South Korea's Busan, Japan's Nagoya to Malaysia's Kenang, ships big and small move millions of containers of motors, machinery, ramen, televisions, makeup, and clothes. Specialized carriers transport cars, grains, ores, and oil. Some ports have even specialized in particular goods. In Japan, Tokyo's Kashima port deals in petrochemicals; southern Fukuyama handles iron and steel; and northern Kushiro, timber. Malaysia's Bintulu port welcomes tankers carrying oil and liquefied natural gas, while in China's northern Qinhuangdao Bay, blackened vessels laden with coal fill the berths.

Rails connect places too far for trucks to travel and take deliveries too urgent to go by sea. They run the four thousand miles from Singapore to Kuala Lumpur, Bangkok to Phnom Penh, Hanoi to Kunming. More tracks are in the works to link China to more of Myanmar, Thailand to Malaysia, Malaysia to Singapore. The connections are far from seamless. Track gauges can differ from line to line and country to country, forcing boxcars to unload and reload. Customs paperwork, inspections, and congestion can delay things for hours or even days. But even so, for many routes, trains are quicker than ships and cheaper than planes.

The half-century-long dream of a "Great Asian Highway" is closer than ever to becoming a reality. Cross-border expressways now link capitals and manufacturing strongholds, urban centers and agricultural expanses. The smooth new asphalt lanes, the high bridges above rivers and forests, and tunnels through terraced hills cut a full day off the travel time from China's lush Kunming to Thailand's industrial Bangkok and shortened truck drivers' journeys to Hanoi by more than two days. Meanwhile, Cambodia's Phnom Penh is now an easy day's ride from Vietnam's Ho Chi Minh City.

Regional aviation has taken off too, driven by Open Skies agreements and big financial outlays. Asia now boasts the busiest airports in the world, shepherding millions of passengers and twenty million tons of cargo each year. Daily connections between Kuala Lumpur and Singapore, Hong Kong and Taipei, Seoul and Osaka far outpace those between New York and London or Chicago and Toronto, the other busiest global routes.[56]

Digital connections are multiplying alongside the physical ones. China has more mobile phones than people. South Korea, Japan, and Hong Kong boast some of the world's fastest internet speeds. And while just half of Southeast Asia's citizens are digitally connected, a push to open telecom markets is bringing millions more online.[57]

Asia's infrastructure still lags behind that of Europe and North America. Many ports remain too shallow and roads unpaved. Highways often still stop at the border, abandoning people and cargo on the other side.[58] Gleaming airports and train terminals mostly hug the coasts, leaving large inland swaths cut off. These missing connections can be as costly as high tariffs for trade. But each new rail, each deepened port, and each approved landing pattern ties the region closer together.

Lagging infrastructure is not the only impediment to greater integration. History, geopolitics, and a scramble for natural resources and technology have bred deep animosities. Territorial disputes persist. China and Japan disagree over the East China Sea; Japan and South Korea dispute islands in the Sea of Japan. China's makeshift reefs in the South China Sea impinge on Filipino, Vietnamese, Malaysian, Bruneian, and Indonesian claims.

Other conflicts are existential, and some old wounds have failed to heal. Taiwan bristles at mainland China's increasing presence in and around the island. China and South Korea routinely rehash Japan's colonial cruelty and World War II war crimes. Vietnam still seethes at China's incursions decades ago. And North Korea's nuclear ballistic missile tests periodically threaten to upend the regional balance.

Resentment can threaten or cut economic ties. In 2019, South Koreans stopped drinking Kirin beer and buying Uniqlo's down coats, and they boycotted Sony Pictures' blockbuster *Spiderman* after a flare-up over Japanese wartime reparations. Japan replied by halting the flow of specialized chemicals to South Korea's semiconductor factories, putting high-tech supply chains in jeopardy. China has banned its citizens from booking Taiwanese vacations and shut down Korean Lotte supermarkets over U.S. military ties. It has sabotaged Japanese plants after maritime disputes. In 2019, Vietnam banned DreamWorks' animated *Abominable* film because it featured a Chinese-friendly map of the South China Sea.[59]

Asian companies also worry about losing their intellectual property and proprietary manufacturing methods to Chinese competitors. South Korea and Japan have had to step up prosecutions and ban some foreign investment in response to China's underhanded efforts to acquire semiconductor and screen technologies.[60] And like Western companies, Asian players have been shut out of profitable parts of China's market. China has banned Japanese and Korean WeChat app competitors on supposed national-security grounds. It has effectively kicked out Samsung- and LG-made electric-car batteries and Japanese and Korean industry suppliers by only giving green subsidies to cars with Chinese-company parts. China has even barred Korean K-pop stars from touring on the mainland in order to give its own celebrity-creating machines a leg up.[61]

As diplomatic tensions flare and commercial competition moves from a positive sum to a more cutthroat game, many companies are pulling back. Samsung has abandoned China for Vietnam in making its smartphones. Taiwan is encouraging its chip and computer makers to come back or otherwise stay away from the mainland. Japan has set aside $2 billion in stimulus money to defray costs for its companies wanting to pull out of China. Japan, South Korea, and Taiwan have all announced tens of billions of dollars to help their companies expand research, development, and manufacturing in semiconductors at home. China is doing the same, with the aim of becoming self-sufficient in a number of cutting-edge technologies. U.S. tariffs and sanctions make these moves all the more urgent.

Yet even as the atmosphere has grown frostier, integration has continued to deepen. Over the past fifteen years, trade between China and Southeast Asia has more than doubled. China now sends more to these regional neighbors than it does to the United States.[62] For Japan, South Korea, Singapore, and Thailand, other Asian countries have edged out the United States as the top trading partner, and for the Philippines, they have cut the U.S. share by half. These links probably will only intensify given the regional concentration of investment, production, and—more and more—consumption.

Over the past three decades, as Asia's companies invested, manufactured, and traded, they have turned to each other. This trend toward regionalization has helped country after country climb the economic-development ladder. Japan's success helped seed Taiwan's, South Korea's, Hong Kong's, and Singapore's. Those countries in turn helped raise up Thailand, Malaysia, the Philippines, Vietnam, and China. And now China is returning the favor, investing billions in Singapore, Indonesia, Laos, and Vietnam. As beneficiaries became benefactors, the region has grown rich and prospered.

Asia's economies remain much more heterogeneous than North America's or Europe's, a complex mix of rich and poor, large and small, closed and open. Political and military divides persist, as do a host of commercial tensions. Diplomats have just started to play a more commercial role with formal agreements.

Nevertheless, Asia has knitted itself together. Regional trade is far more tightly bound than in North America and is catching up with Europe. Regional foreign direct investment outpaces that across the Pacific, also edging in on Europe's financial closeness.

Integration has spurred fast growth, dazzling technological upgrades, and unparalleled rises in mass prosperity. It has also given Asia one potential leg up in the next round of globalization, as its consumers come into their own.

4

North America: The Reluctant Regionalist

On July 7, 2020, as Americans shook off an Independence Day without barbeques or fireworks because of COVID-19 lockdowns, Mexican president Andres Manuel Lopez Obrador, commonly known as AMLO, settled into an exit-row seat on a Delta flight bound for Washington, DC, via Atlanta. His reason? To join President Donald J. Trump the next day to commemorate the start of the United States–Mexico–Canada Agreement, or USMCA.

It was an odd celebration in many ways. AMLO is a notorious homebody, and his midpandemic jaunt was his first abroad since taking office over a year and a half before. With Trump in full reelection campaign mode, most foreign leaders were making themselves scarce—the Canadian prime minister and USMCA counterpart Justin Trudeau was nowhere to be seen. And while the bilateral agenda included a dinner with corporate executives, the main business was little more than a photo op in the White House Rose Garden.

Odder still was that these two leaders in particular stood in matching blue suits and ties at socially distanced podiums on a sunny July day to hawk the revised trade agreement. An old-school nationalist, AMLO had long disavowed NAFTA, vocally campaigning against it during his three runs at Mexico's presidency. Trump had bashed the free-trade agreement since his days as a real-estate tycoon and reality star, his diatribes against the "worst trade agreement ever" later honed on the presidential campaign trail. Yet here they were, staking their popularity, and in Trump's case his electoral salvation, on a deal destined to protect and deepen North American regionalization.

The idea of NAFTA began on a snowy January day in the Alps over thirty years before. During the 1990 gathering of the global elite in Davos, Mexican President Carlos Salinas repeatedly pitched his country as an investment destination to his European counterparts. They were too enamored with an emerging eastern Europe to pay him much attention. Disheartened but not defeated, Salinas shifted his appeals closer to home.

This time, he found a more receptive audience. In Washington, he had support from the Texas triumvirate of President George H. W. Bush, Secretary of State James Baker, and Secretary of Commerce Robert Mosbacher. Negotiations for a trade deal kicked off. Brian Mulroney, the free-trade-oriented Canadian prime minister, soon joined, mostly to defend Canada's recent trade gains with the United States.

The process wasn't easy. Twenty months, two dozen negotiating rounds, and seventeen hundred pages of legalese later, the three leaders stood proudly behind their exhausted representatives in warm San Antonio as they signed the North America Free Trade Agreement, or NAFTA.

Then the public battles began, kicking off acrimonious debates that continue to this day. Testifying in Mexico's rubber-stamp Congress, opponents bemoaned the coming fate of local farmers against the Goliath of U.S. commercial agriculture. Canadians decried the loss of sovereignty. In the United States, critics evoked the "giant sucking sound" of jobs disappearing south. It would take another year and a couple of side agreements to get the treaty through the U.S. Congress. The accord finally came into effect on January 1, 1994.

Despite the complaints, obstacles, and limitations, NAFTA anchored North America's economic integration. In its wake, trade between the three nations quadrupled, and investment jumped fourfold.[1] The regional production networks and supply chains proliferating in Europe and Asia began picking up steam in North America too. The making of cars, household goods, medical equipment, shoes, and clothing soon spanned the continent.

Yet while tariffs came down, other barriers remained. Regulatory differences still outweighed convergences. Border infrastructure never got a real upgrade. No money went to address income inequality, curb pollution, or help small farmers. North America chose not to face post-9/11 security concerns or rising Chinese economic competition together.

Compared to Europe and Asia, North America's regionalism has remained shallow. In the end, the three nations couldn't overcome isolationist forces in their respective political cultures: for the United States, suspicions of foreign entanglements and ties; in both Canada and Mexico, deep fears of being dominated by and subsumed into the United States. After the push for NAFTA, the three governments left companies largely on their own to make the most of the improved trading rules among them.

That has hurt the United States. The regional integration that creates and protects jobs, raises profits, and improves companies' global competitiveness didn't take root more broadly, especially relative to other global competitors. North America's tepid integration has left the United States at a disadvantage.

North American Integration

Before NAFTA, North Americans, in the words of one catchy book title, had long been distant neighbors. Sure, goods, people, and money moved back and forth between the three countries. But there were few formal efforts to bind the nations together. For decades, Mexico closed off its economy with high tariffs, quotas, and licenses. The Canadian government wielded a heavy protectionist hand as well: state-run boards set the prices of milk, eggs, and chicken; tariffs and subsidies protected shoes, wheat, furniture, and more. And the United States was more inclined to look globally when it came to trade deals and other official ties.

Starting in the 1960s, the three countries made a few halting efforts to improve cross-border economic ties. Mexico created a special economic zone along the border, where foreign-owned assembly plants could import parts, tariff-free, to be stitched, welded, forged, or fastened together into products sent to stores back north. U.S. and Canadian diplomats set the ground rules for a joint auto industry, ending tit-for-tat tariffs that were threatening to derail the sector in both nations. But for two decades, little else happened.

The three economies were, of course, still linked to one another. The

United States was the main market for Mexican oil, steel, and clothing exports. Canada sent crude oil, natural gas, electricity, and auto parts. And Washington leaned on its neighbors to buy U.S. wheat, soybeans, tractors, and plastics. U.S. brands proliferated to the north and south too: General Motors sold locally made Chevrolets, Kimberly Clark diapers, and Colgate toothpaste, and Coca Cola even became part of Mexico's inflation-defining official basket of goods. But overall, only a small proportion of the goods and services sold in each country crossed borders; the three economies all looked more inward than outward.

In the mid-1980s, things began to change. Canada and the United States signed a fully fledged trade agreement. Mexico began opening up all on its own—slashing tariffs and quotas, privatizing hundreds of state-owned enterprises, and joining the General Agreement on Tariffs and Trade. It then kicked off negotiations for what would become NAFTA.

NAFTA picked up on, accelerated, and transformed the continental integration that had begun. From day one, oranges, spark plugs, oil filters, machine tools, computers, and thousands of other products began moving north and south free of charge. A decade later, almonds, wheat, pork, cotton, and dozens of other mostly perishables joined the free-trade list. Fifteen years after NAFTA's start, most everything was crossing North America's borders tariff-free. Under NAFTA, governments also stripped away import and export licenses, domestic content requirements, and forced technology transfers.

NAFTA was the first trade agreement to define and defend intellectual property. It protected authors' words and compositions for half a century. It safeguarded patents, trademarks, and trade secrets. And the three nations promised to go after counterfeiters together.

Although labor and environmental standards weren't part of the initial draft, they were included in two side agreements. These expanded the legal right to organize, strike, and bargain collectively across the continent. Employers had to make shop floors safer and wages and workplaces fairer. The side agreements set baseline environmental rules for companies, whether operating in Kansas City or Ciudad Juarez. For instance, hazardous waste had to be treated, emissions lowered, and pollutants reduced.[2]

NAFTA was an investment agreement as much as anything. It protected businesses expanding abroad against nationalization and expropriation by foreign governments. It opened up to foreigners many sectors once re-served for locals. And it made sure governments didn't discriminate be-tween homegrown companies and their international competitors. If they did, there were ways to appeal. NAFTA set up arbitration panels for com-panies to turn to if they felt wronged. Judges from all three countries re-viewed complaints, taking on thorny issues from the prices of U.S.-raised chicken thighs to Canadian wire rods to Mexican pipes, tubes, and ce-ment.[3] With the new process, complaints and cases quickly fell. New tax treaties complemented these protections, reducing the costs of operating across the continent.[4]

NAFTA always had its limitations. Complex rules of origin forced many companies to prove where each and every piece came from in order to cross North American borders tariff-free. In textiles, the accord set "yarn forward" rules, meaning that companies had to do all the thread spin-ning, fabric weaving, pattern cutting, and seam sewing within the conti-nent if they were to avoid duties of 20 percent or more on everything from T-shirts to luggage.[5] Companies supplying automakers had to doc-ument where each slab of steel, screw, dashboard, and transmission came from to prove that over 60 percent of the vehicle was North American made.

Many companies didn't bother meeting the complicated requirements, especially if the starting tariffs were low. Tracking, documenting, and fil-ing the paperwork to prove where each thread, button, and fender came from cost time and money: according to one study, about $35 billion a year.[6] Even today, nearly half of the trade coming from Mexico to the United States doesn't go through the agreement.

NAFTA explicitly left many services off the table. Canada defended its filmmakers, publishers, and producers with mandatory airtime for home-grown artists and productions and ensured that print, radio, and film com-panies remained in local hands. It banned foreign banks from providing savings and checking accounts to Canadians. Mexico controlled oil drillers, rig operators, and geoscientists by keeping the energy industry in state hands. Truckers, shippers, and logistics providers faced hurdles, too. And for nurses, engineers, plumbers, and dozens of other professionals, cross-border licenses and certifications didn't exist.

NAFTA hardly touched government subsidies. Washington continued to give billions of dollars a year to corn farmers, Mexico City to bean growers. Canadian airplane makers and U.S. car manufacturers raked in cheap loans and tax credits. Hundreds of local companies still got special grants, slanting the playing field against outsiders.

NAFTA barely recognized, much less addressed, the economic differences among the three nations. At the agreement's start, Mexican workers earned on average just a fifth of what Americans did and just over a third of what Canadians did (not all that different from the wage gaps between western and eastern Europe at the time).[7] Yet while the EU provided substantial support to help close a similar-size gap, no funds were set aside to help Mexico catch up economically. The deal created a North American Development Bank, but it had little funding and less power. Its few billion dollars of capital went to environmental projects along the U.S.-Mexico border.

The three countries adamantly opposed creating continental institutions. NAFTA had no headquarters and no staff. Its arbitration panels had no home, and the judges serve on a temporary basis. Labor and environmental watchdogs languished unfunded. And many of the working groups set up to address issues, from energy to health safety, customs to small business development, rarely, if ever, meet.

NAFTA was, in the end, just a commercial agreement. The far more challenging issues under discussion at the time in Europe—regional courts, legislatures, economic development, shared infrastructure, a common currency, and the free movement of people—were verboten among the North American partners. But even within this limited framework, regional economic trade and production networks blossomed.

North America Integrates

Trade exploded in NAFTA's wake. In the first decade, exchanges among the three neighbors outpaced those with countries outside the club almost two to one.[8] From just under $300 billion in 1993, annual North American trade has risen to some $1.3 trillion today.

The three neighbors are now one another's most important trading partners: the United States exports nearly five times as much to Mexico nd Canada as it does to China, and double what it sends to the European

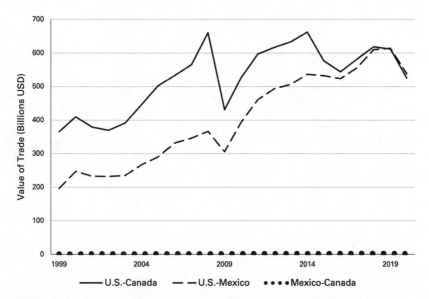

North American trade. Source: World Bank

Union. Michigan sends auto parts, North Carolina pharmaceuticals, Colorado computers, Texas baseball gloves, Nebraska corn, and Massachusetts cranberries. Mexico sells tomatoes, avocados, melons, beer, air conditioners, and computer monitors. Canada delivers airplanes, car seats, wood boards, and oil. By 2000, international sales within North America reached a high of forty-seven cents of every dollar that the three nations traded.

More trade meant new products for North American consumers. Supermarkets in Mexico City stocked Wisconsin cheese; groceries in California sold queso Oaxaca. Hershey's Kisses traveled south, and Abuelita hot chocolate went north. Soon, dozens of brands were crisscrossing the continent's borders for the first time.

NAFTA helped companies stretch supply chains across borders. Parts for cars, phones, appliances, sofas, and shoes were often made in one country and assembled in another. One analysis by an adviser to the U.S. Department of Commerce reckons that before NAFTA, U.S.-made parts constituted just 5 percent of what the United States imported from Mexico; today, that figure is around 40 percent.[9]

The auto industry made the biggest bet on regionalism. Canada and the United States had already been building cars, trucks, and minivans to-

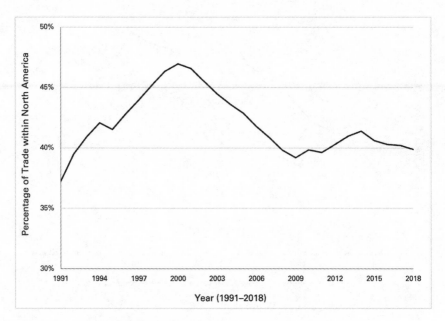

Intraregional trade in North America. Source: World Integrated Trade Solution

gether for decades. NAFTA brought Mexico into the equation as a market and a maker.

Take the U.S. engine maker Cummins. Founded in 1919 in Columbus, Indiana, by a perpetual tinkerer who developed successive improvements on the diesel engine, Cummins expanded from its midwestern base over the decades to make engines, fuel and filtration systems, and power generators for makers of cars, trucks, tractors, boats, trains, and heavy machinery throughout the United States and, increasingly, the world.

Cummins stumbled in the 1970s. The oil crisis killed demand for its signature high-horsepower engines. Rival engine maker Caterpillar cut in on its sales to Ford with a new truck-engine line. In the 1980s, Japanese imports from Mitsubishi, Isuzu, and Komatsu started luring away Cummins's customer base with cheaper, more-fuel-efficient designs.

Then, in the 1990s, thanks in large part to NAFTA, Cummins fought back. It slashed production costs by copying its Japanese competitors' lean management techniques and outsourcing many of its parts—the trade agreement's preferential access let it regain its competitive edge by making, assembling, and selling its products across the three nations.[10]

The 1990s brought a North American vehicle boom: truck and car production jumped by four million during the decade, lifting demand for Cummins's engines with it.[11] With tariffs and quotas gone, the company found new customers in Mexico's diesel-truck makers. Its Jamestown, New York–made engines now power more semis on Mexico's highways than any other brand. Canada's miners turned to Cummins's engines for their excavators and other heavy machinery.

Today, Cummins sells over $20 billion a year in turbochargers, fuel systems, filters, and all kinds of engines. Its hometown of Columbus has become the most trade-dependent community in the United States.[12] And while it brings in clients from across the globe, NAFTA helped keep North America its strongest base, home to well over half its sales.

As well as boosting homegrown companies, NAFTA's rules also encouraged foreign businesses to set up shop in North America. Longtime Japanese, Korean, and German sellers to U.S. consumers became U.S. manufacturers. The brands on Honda Accords, Toyota Forerunners, Hyundai Sonatas, and BMW SUVs may sound foreign, but these days, the cars are North American products.

Toyota opened its first U.S. dealerships in California in 1958. Sales picked up in the 1960s with the Corolla and even more so in the 1970s with the Camry, which became the most popular imported car, edging out the Volkswagen Beetle with its higher-powered engine and, for the time, luxurious heaters and automatic transmissions.[13]

By 1980, Toyota had sold more than three million cars across the United States, all of them made abroad. It wasn't until 1988 that the first U.S.-made Toyota came off a Kentucky assembly line. Even five years later, as NAFTA was about to kick in, the Camrys, RAV4s, and Forerunners on dealers' lots were still mostly shipped in from overseas.[14]

That soon changed, as the growing U.S. market, combined with NAFTA's rules, shifted economic calculations back in Japan. Over the next twenty-five years, more and more of the Toyotas bought and sold in North America would be made there. Like other carmakers, Toyota would create manufacturing chains to build nearly two-thirds of each vehicle on the continent (meeting NAFTA's rules of origin requirements)—and not just anywhere in North America: the vast majority of its new plants would be built in the United States. In the 1990s, workers began putting together Toyota trucks and SUVs and welding and painting sedans in Princeton, Indiana. Toyota built new plants in Buffalo, West Virginia, and Huntsville, Alabama, to make engines.

In the early 2000s, Toyota doubled down on the United States. It opened plants in San Antonio, Texas, a few hundred miles from its new North American headquarters in Plano, to make Tacomas and Tundras, employing some twenty-five hundred workers to churn out around two hundred thousand pickups each year.[15] Dozens of local metal stampers, brake-pedal providers, glove-compartment molders, and other parts manufacturers fill the surrounding blocks. As Toyota expanded throughout the United States, it also broke ground on two factories in Mexico and two more in Canada, helping it specialize and hold down costs. But all told, eleven of Toyota's fifteen North American plants are in the United States.[16]

Toyota's big bet on the United States means that many of the more than two million Sienna minivans, Camry sedans, Lexus SUVs, Prius hybrids, Forerunners, RAV4s, and pickups that Americans buy each year (Toyota is second only to GM in U.S. sales) have a better claim to being made in the USA than their U.S.-brand competitors do. Three-quarters of each Camry comes from U.S. (with a bit of that from Canadian) factories, a higher proportion than Ford's Fusion or Chevy's Malibu.[17] More of Toyota's Sequoia SUV is made in the United States than GM's Yukon or Ford's Explorer.

A map of Toyota's plants shows the new geography of auto production that arose after NAFTA. An international "auto alley" stretches from Windsor, Ontario, and Detroit, Michigan, through Toledo, Ohio; Bowling Green, Kentucky; Fort Wayne, Indiana; and Spring Hill, Tennessee, and onto Matamoros, Piedras Negras, and Saltillo, Mexico.[18]

Car components speed up and down this route daily as thousands of pieces come together into every sedan or SUV. Wisconsin steel is forged into suspensions in Piedras Negras and brakes in Puebla before ending up in Silverados, Yukons, and Suburbans. San Luis Potosi–made front-end carriers head to Chattanooga to meet up with the interior and back end for VW Passats. Cadillac hub bearings from Puebla join the rest of the wheel in Detroit. For most of the autos rolling off Guanajuato or Aguascalientes assembly lines, roughly three out of every four parts come from the north, mostly the United States.

By taking advantage of different locations, skill sets, and wages across the continent, costs have stayed low: the sticker price of the best-selling Ford F-150 pickup truck has barely budged since NAFTA was signed. And that has brought jobs across the three nations, as North American customers can afford to trade in and trade up more often, and exports farther afield have grown.

The auto industry hasn't been the only one to regionalize thanks to NAFTA. Textile makers, players in one of the most cutthroat global industries, also got an initial boost from the agreement. And even after the 2005 changes in global rules, which eliminated the quotas that had held back Asian competition, U.S. workshops still export over $10 billion worth of fine and rugged wool, cotton, and linen each year to be cut up in Mexico's *maquilas* or sewn by Canada's tailors.[19]

Planes, too, lean North American. When Bombardier introduced the Learjet 85, in 2007, it set out to make a true NAFTA jet. The vision started in Montreal, where Bombardier's engineers designed the body, calibrated the navigation system, and calculated the engine propulsion and lift needed for the eight-passenger plane. The plans headed to Querétaro, Mexico, where local engineers and technicians built out the fuselages, cockpits, and tails. By truck and rail (sometimes on railcars also made by Bombardier across the three NAFTA nations), these parts crossed the border at Nuevo Laredo bound for Wichita. Once there, workers attached Canadian-made engines and fitted out the interiors.[20] U.S. pilots put the finished jets through their paces before flying them to businesses and private clients around the world.

Even Boeing, which has among the most globalized supply chains of any aircraft maker, still leans heavily on North America. Aerospace plants across Chihuahua, Sonora, Wisconsin, Ohio, Manitoba, and Ontario build engines and interiors, doors and fuselages, wings and wires, airframes and landing gear. This mosaic of parts heads to Everett and Renton, Washington, to become 747s and 737s, or else it goes to North Charleston, in South Carolina, to become a 787.[21]

NAFTA didn't just transform high-tech industries. Food production and distribution now stretch across the continent. Millions of Canadian-born piglets feed on U.S. corn before being shipped south to grow fat on Iowa farms. They later head to dining tables across the three nations. Over a million Mexican-born calves grow up on Texas and Oklahoma ranges. Much of their meat then returns south for tacos, stews, and *milanesas*. A similar story plays out in the North, where Canadian calves fatten up on South Dakota grassland and others leave Alberta for Illinois slaughter-houses.

Cross-border food sales, long held back by tariffs and protectionist regulations, spiked after NAFTA. For one thing, the agreement all but eliminated tariffs on processed foods. U.S.-made cereals, sausages, pickles, canned fruits, and ketchup soon filled Mexican supermarket shelves. Barrels of high-fructose corn syrup headed south to sweeten Mexico's sodas, chips, and treats. Other rule changes have meant that overall agricultural sales have accelerated throughout the continent as Mexican ranchers buy up feed corn, U.S. consumers eat avocados and tomatoes, and Canadians buy U.S.-grown fresh fruit and vegetables.

Individual companies have seized the opportunity to expand. Herdez, for decades a staple of Mexican grocery stores, began exporting its chipotles and salsas to Mexican clientele in the United States and Canada after NAFTA came into force.[22] The company teamed up with Spam maker Hormel a few years later to market its products beyond immigrant communities, showing up in Walmarts, Wegmans, and Targets across the United States. A new Dallas-based plant started making tacos, flautas, and chimichangas for stores and restaurants. All told, NAFTA helped Herdez build up a U.S. business that brings in tens of millions of dollars every year.

As cross-border sales and manufacturing of everything from beans to planes has expanded, the United States has tended to capture the more profitable start and finish of most goods. Its companies feed raw materials, machinery, and components to Mexican factories for assembly. U.S. headquarters manage the lucrative designing, marketing, and financing. That makes doing business within North America more profitable for U.S. companies, and more conducive to U.S.-based workers, than looking farther afield, since factories in Asia and Europe tend to rely on suppliers, designers, marketers, and banks closer by.

Investing in North America

As NAFTA clarified the investment rules of the road across North America, investment among the three countries soared. CEOs began snapping up neighboring companies, and bankers eyed attractive investment opportunities abroad. During NAFTA's first decade, hundreds of billions of dollars flowed among the three nations.[23]

U.S. and Canadian companies came to play a big role in Mexico's mines, steel foundries, medical laboratories, banks, and insurance companies. Walmart kicked off a three-thousand-store buying and building spree in Mexico, and automakers poured in billions of dollars to build new plants. Of the nearly $500 billion of foreign investment Mexico has received since NAFTA, roughly half came from the United States and Canada.[24]

U.S. companies went north as well as south. Walmart and Home Depot opened up in Oshawa, Oakville, Mississauga, and Toronto. Burger King bought the coffee and donut staple Tim Hortons. Molson merged with Coors. And ExxonMobil bought the fueling giant Imperial Oil.

Mexican and Canadian companies broke into the world's largest consumer market with their own factories, facilities, and stores. América Móvil came to dominate the U.S. prepaid cell-phone market. The Mexican appliance retailer Elektra bought up Advance America, the United States' biggest payday lender. From Lululemon leggings to Mission Foods tortillas, from BlackBerry to Corona beer, brands have swept throughout the region, appealing to recent immigrants and lifelong residents alike.

The Mexican building-materials giant CEMEX offers a good example of how the process worked. In 1906, the Zambrano family began mixing sand, gravel, and crushed stone to make cement in Mexico's northern industrial town of Monterrey, supplying local construction companies and families rebuilding after the Mexican Revolution. Throughout the 1960s and 1970s, the company aggressively bought up other regional outfits in Torreon, Merida, Coahuila, Guadalajara, the State of Mexico, and Mexico City, systematically expanding its hold on the national market.[25]

In the 1970s and 1980s, an oil-flush Mexico shelled out for public works, expanding the capital's subway, constructing oil platforms and refineries, connecting Mexico City and the beach town of Acapulco, and transforming an isolated fishing town along the Pacific coast into the beach of Huatulco. Politically connected CEMEX won the lion's share of these contracts, as well as those for hundreds of roads, bridges, dams, and airports being constructed across the nation. CEMEX dominated retail sales too, selling millions of bags of cement one at a time to Mexicans building and expanding their own homes.

By NAFTA's start, CEMEX had consolidated a near monopoly in Mexico.[26] It then began aggressively expanding abroad. It ventured first to other Spanish-speaking places: Spain, Colombia, Venezuela, Panama, the Dominican Republic, and Puerto Rico.

NAFTA's new rules, along with countervailing duties stymieing exports from Mexico still in place, made opening U.S. operations an attractive play. CEMEX started out by opening its own cement and ready-mix plants, mostly in the South and West of the United States. Soon, its cement was being poured for new Arizona and Texas highways and into the foundations of Enron's Houston headquarters and the Camp Pendleton military base in Southern California. In 2000, CEMEX's acquisition of Houston-based Southdown put it second only to Holderbank in U.S. cement markets overnight. Seven years later, a $14 billion takeover of Australia-based Rinker so concentrated CEMEX's hold on U.S. building materials that the U.S. Justice Department forced it to sell off several of its Arizona and Florida plants to bless the deal.[27]

Over the past couple of decades, CEMEX has gone more global. In 2005, it bought heavily into the European market by acquiring the UK's RMC group, along with a series of other purchases throughout Europe, North Africa, and Asia. CEMEX is now the second-biggest cement maker in the world, but its biggest and best markets still remain close to home: over half of its sales and profits are North American–made.[28]

Cross-border investment didn't just mean companies buying one another. International finance picked up the pace as well. Citibank, Bank of America, and Scotiabank moved south as Mexico's banking sector opened up to foreigners. Royal Bank of Canada and TD Bank set their sights on the United States, hiring bankers and buying up thousands of branches in U.S. cities and towns. And as trade picked up, money followed: stocks, bonds, and cross-border loans proliferated.

Yet regional financial flows never reached the intensity seen in Europe or Asia. Foreign direct investment goes outside North America as often as nearby. So too do bank loans.[29] North America's weaker financial ties reflect the outsized influence of Wall Street and the singular role of the U.S. dollar and Treasury bonds. With the world's elite and governments preferring to park their money in the United States, regional financial flows matter less. Tighter U.S. anti-money-laundering rules have also held up cross-border flows, at least between the United States and Mexico, as some U.S. banks shy away from Mexican accounts to avoid paperwork and scrutiny.[30]

Although cross-border finance and trade haven't taken off to the same extent as in Europe and Asia, deepening regional trade has still created a lot of jobs. During NAFTA's first five years, as trade among the partners grew, manufacturing jobs rose in all three nations. The United States created six hundred thousand positions, Canada four hundred thousand, and Mexico roughly seven hundred thousand.[31] The broader U.S. economy added almost seventeen million jobs in the years after NAFTA's start.[32] Total U.S. GDP grew by two-thirds in the decade following NAFTA. Canada and Mexico saw their economies grow in nominal terms by around half. And North America's share of world production jumped too, rising from twenty-eight to thirty-four cents of every dollar traded.[33]

 In the end, NAFTA mattered more for Mexico and Canada than for the United States. It locked in the economic opening already under way in both nations and cemented access to their biggest export market. For the United States, exports to Mexico and Canada grew more quickly in the trade agreement's wake than with other nations, turning the two countries into U.S. companies' best clients. They now buy more than China, Japan, South Korea, and Singapore combined.[34] Still, sales next door accounted for only a third of the United States' total exports. And trade in general has remained a relatively small part of the much bigger U.S. economy. NAFTA's promise for the United States remains in large part just that, ready to be fulfilled if and when the United States decides to look outward economically.

Why Deeper Integration Didn't Happen

Although NAFTA slashed tariffs and harmonized investment rules, it did much less to take on other issues that slowed down regional

duction and trade. A tyranny of small regulatory differences held back cross-border sales. Crumbling infrastructure slowed down trucks and trains. And the three neighbors dealt with migration, education, customs, and often security on their own. Joint efforts, when they did happen, tended to be bilateral, not recognizing, much less reinforcing, any potential continental strategy.

Petty regulations still hamper trade. Despite NAFTA, Canadian and U.S. beef have to pass through a gauntlet of import controls to get to the other country. Different names for the same cuts add to the general confusion. California peaches routinely get caught up in Mexican quarantine. Layers of rules and tests mean that only a few Mexican states grow avocados for the U.S. market. U.S. potato growers, meanwhile, can sell their spuds only along the Mexican border, shut off from customers farther in.[35]

Trivial but mandatory label differences force companies to repackage their products if they want to sell them next door. The United States requires saturated and trans fats to be broken out in nutritional tables, while in Canada they must be calculated together. Canadian regulators also tend to get overly specific about font sizes and colors. The U.S. Food and Drug Administration (FDA) is much more relaxed than its Canadian and Mexican counterparts are about health claims, allowing cereals to say that they lower cholesterol, vitamins to declare that they reduce the risk of osteoporosis, and cartons to assert that the milk inside supports "brain health" (whatever that means).[36] And each country demands that everything be readable in its own language (or two, in the case of Canada).

The three nations have tried to tackle these barriers. Bilateral regulatory councils and working groups have proliferated, discussing everything from motor-vehicle safety to train emissions, drug approval to poultry tests. There have been some small wins. Negotiators have cleared the way for headphones with microphones, photocopiers, satellite transmitters, and some processed foods to traverse borders relatively pain-free.[37] They have dealt with outbreaks of wheat fungus, hog cholera, and chicken respiratory diseases, finding ways to keep cross-border sales going.

But broader recognition of trading partners' rules and standards along the lines of Europe's single market has never caught on in North America. Even with powerful business lobbies and economic sense on the side of advocates of unrestricted trade, they have failed to end limits on the flow of natural gas, the distribution of over-the-counter medicines, or the freedom to eat Cheerios made on the other side of the border.[38] After hundreds of meetings and thousands of hours of talks, the breakthroughs touch only a small portion of the three-quarters of a trillion dollars in North American trade affected by national barriers each year.[39]

In some areas, the United States has gone out of its way to make trade harder instead of easier for its neighbors. For years, the U.S. government required hamburger patties and pork chops to list where the animal was born, raised, and slaughtered. The labeling forced ranchers to bear, raise, feed, transport, and process foreign-born calves and piglets separately, adding time and costs in an integrated North American market. Though the United States eventually repealed these rules for beef and pork, it has kept them for fish and chicken parts and added them to venison.

Medicines, too, face duplicative hurdles. Getting approval for new compounds to take on depression, high cholesterol, pain, and other ailments means going through three similar, but separate, time-consuming and costly processes. In Canada, the provinces get into the act for many over-the-counter medicines. Regulators from each country must visit manufacturing facilities if medicines are destined for their pharmacy shelves. The finished packages are checked once again when they cross the border. This makes it hard to take advantage of economies of scale in making Advil, Claritin, Zoloft, or any other medicine, prescription or not, for North American markets. Patients, consumers, and companies all lose: the repetition and duplication doesn't make products safer, but it does make them more expensive, shaving profit margins and costing jobs.

The limits on North America's integration are physical as well as legal. As the volume of people, cars, trucks, and goods crossing borders has escalated, roads, bridges, and rail connections haven't kept up. There was an initial burst of money and coordination at NAFTA's start, as the U.S. Congress envisioned new high-priority corridors to link up with the United States' neighbors. But in the end, the vast sums allocated went mostly to local projects in the districts of well-placed members of Congress, many of them not related to the border at all.[40]

Far from building shiny new roads, bridges, and railways at the border, the U.S. government struggles to maintain its existing ones. Most of the current border crossings are old, some dating back to the Eisenhower administration. As repair schedules slip, pavements crack, ventilation systems fail, locks break, and inspection-booth glass clouds over. Antiquated roads, bridges, and terminals force trucks and trains to pile up at the border, costing their owners—and North American consumers—time and money.

For years, successive U.S. administrations have asked Congress for just a few hundred million dollars for the border, even though their own studies show that they need at least $5 billion just to fix the infrastructure to meet existing demand. When they do get funding, a slow bureaucratic pace can mean that it often takes a decade more to build new lanes, booths, and buildings—some of them outdated before they even open.[41]

Of course, the border isn't the only place where U.S. infrastructure is near failure. The American Society of Civil Engineers awards a C- to U.S. roads, bridges, rails, and ports overall.[42] The situation is even worse in Mexico, where less than half the roads are paved, railroad tracks are few, and the ports are disconnected. Canada, while better off, also grapples with well-worn highways, rails, ports, and crossings.

North American infrastructure also suffers from a lack of cooperation. The three countries have no equivalent of Europe's continental fund that provides money for cross-border infrastructure projects or Asia's public development spending. The North American countries rarely ever plan together, which means that even when one country does invest in infrastructure upgrades, the effort can be wasted. In Tornillo-Guadalupe, Texas, for example, the United States spent tens of millions of dollars on a state-of-the-art cargo facility. Yet since Mexico did little to upgrade its side of the border, few truckers used it. After a year and a half, U.S. Customs and Border Enforcement shut it down. At big border crossings like the one between Blaine, Washington, and Surrey, British Columbia, Canadian border upgrades haven't been matched by ones in the United States.[43] And the highways leading up to the crossing still don't go all the way to the border, creating long lines among the thousands of cars and trucks that cross each day.

The money that does get spent at the border is more likely to go to security than to trade. The United States' green-uniformed Border Patrol that watches the no-man's-land between crossings has grown five times in size since the signing of NAFTA. The number of blue-clad officers who check cargo, process forms, and ultimately let in over a million pedestrians, three hundred thousand cars, and tens of thousands of trucks and trains every day has expanded far more slowly.[44] This means that there often are not enough workers in the right places at the right times to speed traffic. Low pay, high turnover rates, and corruption compound the problem, often leaving inspection booths empty.[45] And if open U.S. lanes don't match up with the Mexican and Canadian sides, everything slows down.

Bureaucracy makes things worse. Regulations on vehicle weights and sizes differ, as do safety checks, prohibiting many trucks from driving on the other side. Add in immigration rules, and many drivers have to drop their loads just before the border, handing them over to short-haul trucks. After crossing, these local rigs transfer cargo to still other drivers who drive the final leg to a warehouse or directly to a store. The repeated switching, unhooking, unloading, and reloading all add up in time, money, and extra traffic, complicating the already arduous back-and-forth across the Mexico-U.S. border. NAFTA included a pledge to let truckers drive their full routes between countries, but more than twenty-five years later, the United States still hasn't enacted the necessary rules. For Monterrey-made refrigerators headed to Houston's Nor-West Appliance showroom floor, the need to change drivers can turn what should be an eight-hour trip into a days-long ordeal. The reverse is also true; semis loaded with specialty steel bars made in Whitehall, Michigan, must switch drivers multiple times to deliver their cargo to the company's sunroof factory outside San Miguel de Allende.

On top of driver changes, other crossing woes routinely add a couple of hours of time, sometimes an entire day. While drivers wait for customs officials, vegetables wilt in the sun and delivery dates slip, forcing companies to hold expensive extra inventory.

The news isn't all bad. Some forty-three U.S. agencies, including the FDA, the U.S. Trade Representative, the Animal and Plant Health Inspection Service, and the Census Bureau, have substituted a single electronic customs page for dozens of paper forms and certificates. "Trusted traveler" programs speed trips for those that qualify. These and other bilateral efforts help two million individuals, drivers, and companies move back and forth in relative ease, accounting for just under a third of the four hundred million crossings that take place each year.[46]

Energy integration is another bright spot. Thirty-seven transm lines tie together northern electricity grids, keeping Canadian houses warm in the winter and U.S. apartments cool in the summer, all at lower prices and with fewer blackouts. On the U.S.-Mexico border, gas pipelines flow from Louisiana into Central Mexico, Texas into Chihuahua, Arizona into Sonora.

Some of the most innovative integration efforts have come from states and provinces. Texan and New Mexican personalities, officials, and business leaders came together with their Chihuahuan counterparts to open a whole new border crossing in the 1990s. In Santa Teresa, less than a half-hour drive from downtown El Paso and Ciudad Juarez, the barren desert has been transformed over the past twenty-five years into a border hub of industrial parks and factories.[47]

Foxconn has the largest cluster of sprawling factories, nearly twenty million square feet of workstations and warehouses pushed up against the border on the Mexican side. From its loading docks, a dedicated lane leads directly to the border, speeding dozens of trucks that haul over fifty thousand Dell computers, HP tablets, and other electronics north every day. Nearby are makers of tiles, wind-turbine blades, and candies, each taking advantage of the space and border-crossing speed that Santa Teresa affords over nearby Ciudad Juarez.

On the northern side, offices and industrial parks fill the once-empty expanse, home to metal recyclers, wire makers, and power-cable manufacturers as well as all sorts of computer-chip, screen, and keyboard providers (many products destined for Foxconn's hulking compound just to the south). Cattle corrals, holding pens, and feeding stations grace both sides of the border too, making Santa Teresa the biggest livestock crossing point in North America. Amazon has moved in nearby, joining FedEx and dozens of logistics companies and distribution centers operating along this part of the border.

Preinspection programs allow trailer trucks to sail through special border lanes, having already cleared customs back at the factory. And special dispensation for Mexico's heavier trucks lets them head straight to U.S. warehouses and railyards, cutting transit time by even more.

Nearby El Paso's trade has thrived alongside the bustling border. Here, too, local officials have stepped in to expedite trade. El Paso's customs offices coordinate opening hours with their Mexican counterparts. Local businesses chip in to keep U.S. customs booths open longer. These efforts speed the twenty thousand pedestrians and thirty thousand cars that make their way from Ciudad Juarez to El Paso every day, as well as the two thousand trucks that pass through Texas's sixth-biggest city daily, hauling a good part of the more than $100 billion of trade that moves back and forth every year in this corner where Texas and New Mexico meet.[48]

In the Pacific Northwest, cooperation spans U.S. states and Canadian provinces. Ten of them have banded together to connect power stations, put out forest fires, plan for natural disasters, bring broadband to farms, and knit together their economies and societies. Cooperation has made business at the border more straightforward. Yet these advances remain local, without national and continental direction.

The most visible sign of integration, and its limits, in North America is immigration. One in four U.S.-bound immigrants hail from Mexico, as do eight hundred thousand from Canada.[49] Mexico, in turn, hosts nearly one million Americans and tens of thousands of Canadians—some only in the winter, many year-round. Yet North America hasn't made this movement easy, to put it mildly. Migration was mostly kept off the NAFTA negotiating table; the agreement's only nod was a small program for temporary U.S. visas for Mexican and Canadian professionals, which has just ten thousand takers a year.[50]

Even for those who move next door legally, the three countries make it difficult for people to work in the same field that they did back home. Established Canadian doctors can't take on patients in the United States without repeating hospital residencies, training, and tests. Mexican lawyers can't advise U.S. clients without passing state bar exams. Engineers, therapists, social workers, teachers, and dozens of other professionals have to start over if they want to move from one nation to another.

To be sure, these hurdles are a problem within the United States too. California-trained stylists can't cut your hair in New York without repeating the equivalents of classes they've already passed. Travel guides, interior designers, personal trainers, and manicurists trained in one state often can't ply their skills in another without taking local courses (and paying expensive fees). Licensing regimes hold back Americans hoping to follow l ved ones or make a fresh start. They also limit North American integra′

Education, too, rarely carries across the continent. American s′

are much more likely to study in Paris or London than in Toronto or Puebla. And there are far more Chinese and Indian students than Mexican ones studying for exams at U.S. and Canadian universities.[51] North America's governments do little to support educational exchanges, and what scholarships there are have rarely lasted for long.

And while midwesterners love to get away to Mexico's beaches in the winter, and Mexicans have a soft spot for Houston's malls and Colorado's ski resorts, there is still far less tourism between the countries than there is within Europe and Asia. Roughly half of North American vacationers choose their neighbors, compared to nearly three-quarters of Europeans and Asians.[52]

North America Founders after 9/11

As the twenty-first century started, the shock of 9/11, the threat of Mexican drug cartels, and worries over future terrorist attacks bumped trade from the top of the North American regional agenda. Since then, the focus on security has primarily served to divide rather than unite the continent.

It wasn't meant to be this way. On a brilliant sunny September day in 2001, George W. Bush and Vicente Fox stood on the White House South Lawn as the Army's Old Guard Fife and Drum Corps played the nations' anthems and the U.S. and Mexican flags fluttered behind the two presidents and their wives, kicking off a three-day official visit. That night, dozens of finely dressed ministers, members of Congress, business leaders, celebrities, and other guests sat down to Maryland crab and chorizo pozole, bison, and red chile mango ice cream in Bush's first official state dinner. Bush tried to soften the formality of the occasion by comparing the visit to a family gathering at the "Casa Blanca." The next day, Fox spoke to both houses of Congress before he hit the road with his presidential "amigo" for a joint speech at the University of Toledo in Ohio and a visit to the local Aurora Gonzalez Community Center.

Meanwhile, cabinet members and staffers, having changed out of their tuxedos and evening dresses, met to hash out ways to make it easier for goods, services, money, and people to move around. There were hopes for a deal that would cover what Mexico's foreign minister optimistically called "the whole enchilada."[53] Four days later, two planes struck the World Trade Center in New York, and the border shut down.

At first, it looked as if North American ties would grow after 9/11. The United States created a new military command the next year and invited the Mexicans and Canadians in. In 2005, the three leaders announced their biggest push for integration yet, the Security and Prosperity Partnership of North America, or SPP. The name and setup conjured visions of a holistic approach to the region, as the three nations created committees to work on everything from ecommerce to health care. The gambit was to move beyond trade and take on the red tape, regulations, and border delays that were holding North America back.

It didn't work. At the first meeting, migration and many aspects of trade were taken off the table. That left a set of working groups on important, but ultimately peripheral, issues, such as energy integration and maritime and aviation security.

Conspiracy theorists on the right, including then CNN anchor Lou Dobbs, painted these new technical meetings between bureaucrats as something secretive, even sinister. The left accused the administration of surrendering to business interests. The leaders themselves clashed over what could and couldn't change. No treaties or binding commitments emerged.

When President Barack Obama came into the White House, he quickly shelved the whole initiative. He still met with his North American counterparts in Guadalajara in the months after his inauguration, but there was no mention of the SPP. It had died after just five meetings.

What survived was the focus on security, the issue that most divides North America's nations. Some new cooperation to get the bad guys did span the continent: governments began to share airplane rosters, ship manifestos, and most-wanted lists. They traded intelligence and sped up extraditions. But much more often than not, the new security plans and programs followed separate bilateral tracks with separate budgets and personnel.

Part of that was probably inevitable. The three countries worried about different threats. Mexico faced horrific and accelerating rates of violence from drug cartels and organized crime, while Canada was focused on counterterrorism. The two countries squabbled over their relationship with the United States. Canadians rarely wanted to be lumped together v ico, fiercely clinging to their perceived privileged partnership with their southern neighbor. Mexico didn't always need or want its demographically and economically smaller northern counterpart at the table either.

Without leadership or infrastructure, with stubborn and expensive regulations, and with layers of border security multiplying, NAFTA's benefits were largely exhausted by the turn of the twenty-first century. And as the three nations would quickly find out, a commercial agreement alone would not be enough to meet the challenge that Asia's rise posed for North America's economic competitiveness.

The China Shock

On September 17, 2001, China joined the World Trade Organization, officially ending the isolated status of one of the world's largest economies. Its inclusion tested North America. NAFTA's tariff advantages had narrowed as global tariff rates fell and WTO membership expanded. Deteriorating roads, rails, and ports reduced the benefits of proximity. North American governments provided fewer of the cheap loans, land grants, and other perks that China lavished on its manufacturers. And when China didn't fulfill its WTO promises, it gained an advantage over North Americans who played by the rules. Combined with an expensive dollar, NAFTA's dwindling edge wasn't enough to hold out against Chinese competition.

U.S. economists and politicians usually look only at the United States' losses, counting the companies and jobs headed east. Overlooked is how the global manufacturing shift reverberated throughout the continent. As China's share of world trade rose from just a blip to double digits in the 2010s, North American regionalism began to unravel. The China Shock isn't just a U.S. story.

Within North America, it was actually Mexico that was hit the hardest, as it competed head-on with China to be the region's assembler. Its border plants shuttered by the hundreds as Chinese-made toys, shoes, TVs, cell phones, and other electronics poured into North America. Makers of tables, chairs, and cameras who once fêted Mexico now set their sights across the Pacific.

U.S. exporters lost out as China quickly made deep inroads into Mexico's stores, malls, and street markets. China edged out U.S. makers of printers, faxes, telecom equipment, furniture, and glasses.[54] It effectively ended sales of U.S.-made women's coats and underwear.[55]

It wasn't just consumer products that suddenly had "Made in China" labels on them. Industries that were once deeply embedded in regional supply chains began to exit wholesale. Here again, U.S. exporters suffered as the Mexican industries they once supplied dwindled and vanished.

Mexico had long been a preeminent shoemaker, its cobblers expert in the dozens of steps that go into the making of leather boots, heels, and oxfords, from curing to hole punching, leather piecing to delicate stitching. The United States was a big supplier, sending hundreds of millions of dollars' worth of soles, heels, and buckles south each year.[56]

With China's WTO admission, this integrated supply chain crumbled. WTO rules meant that Mexican duties on Chinese shoes fell from a high of 300 percent to between 15 and 20 percent. Without tariff protection, North American manufacturers could no longer compete with cheap Asian wages and generous subsidies.

Although Mexico still makes 250 million pairs of shoes a year, enough to shod its population almost twice over, it pales relative to the scale of Asia's production. Nearly all of the 900 million pairs of Nikes on the market come from Vietnam, China, or Indonesia, as do the vast majority of the billions of other pairs of shoes shipped to North America today.[57]

Office tech equipment, another once-vibrant North American industry, faltered in the face of Chinese competition. In 2000, three out of every five computers, printers, photocopiers, and faxes brought into Mexico came from the United States. A decade later, that figure was just one in ten; the rest had been replaced by China.[58]

Chinese manufacturers even began to threaten the tight-knit auto industry. As the twenty-first century took off, Chinese-made tail lights, rearview mirrors, exhaust manifolds, aluminum wheels, and dozens of other pieces poured into North America, rising in just a decade from next to nothing to a fifth of imported auto parts.[59]

In the late 1990s, three out of every four dollars' worth of goods that Mexicans bought from abroad came from the United States. With China's rise, this fell to less than one of every two. Just two years after China join the WTO, China had surpassed Mexico in U.S. sales. Before the end of decade, it had ousted Canada to become the United States' largest goods supplier. Overall trade among the United States, Canada, and Mexico fell back to closer to four of every ten dollars exchanged.[60] North America's global position faded, down from a third to a quarter of global commerce.

Jobs suffered too. While the United States gained six hundred thousand manufacturing jobs between 1994, when NAFTA launched, and 2001, it lost nearly a million after China's arrival at the WTO, as old plants closed and new ones opened in China. A million more jobs vanished when regional supply chains unraveled and local economies cratered. And the United States wasn't alone: hundreds of thousands of jobs evaporated in just a few years in Mexico and Canada too.[61]

Scores of furniture factories shut down as the big brands started making bedroom sets and dining-room tables in Dalian and Sichuan. As the factories abandoned the brick buildings lining Virginia's Smith River, for example, local lumberyards, carpentry-tool makers, and accounting offices disappeared with them, as did department stores, restaurants, and theaters. Nearby, Martinsville, Virginia, lost its claim to be the "sweatshirt capital of the world," with just a few fleeces now made on its mostly idle mills and looms. As factory after factory shuttered, so did local thread makers, fabric weavers, and sewing-machine repairers.

Now, almost two decades later, a renaissance of sorts is in the making. The China Shock is largely over. The hemorrhaging of apparel workshops, leather tanners, and appliance assemblers has slowed, and exports of U.S.-made trucks, buses, planes, computers, specialty chemicals, and medical devices are on the rise.[62] North American supply chains are playing a big part.

San Diego and Tijuana are two of the places making the most of this resurgence. San Diego was struggling at NAFTA's start. Defense Department budget cuts had hit the Navy's local air station and labs, as well as the big defense contractors that had set up nearby. Wages had stagnated; unemployment and poverty were on the rise. After 2001, Tijuana took a big economic hit from Chinese competition.

In search of a way back to prosperity, the two cities turned to biotech and medical equipment to power their linked revivals. The life sciences had long been prominent in San Diego. Research heavyweights like the Salk

Institute, the Scripps Institute, and the University of California, San Diego (UCSD), clustered on La Jolla's panoramic mesa. Private companies and investors joined these labs along North Torrey Pines Road, eager to license their discoveries. Biotech start-ups began gaining ground in the 1980s after two UCSD professors created the first blood test for prostate cancer and were bought out by Eli Lilly to the tune of nearly half a billion dollars. The founders and their acolytes would go on to set up dozens of other medical companies in San Diego, fueling a soon thriving biotech ecosystem.[63]

The activity began to attract big pharma and medical-device makers. Novartis, Bayer, Pfizer, Johnson & Johnson, Biogen, and Takeda opened up offices and set up research facilities. Stent maker Medtronic, genetic tester Thermo Fisher Scientific, intravenous-therapy (IV) provider BD, and dozens of other equipment manufacturers opened outposts. World-class research labs, renowned institutes, a high concentration of scientists and technicians, investor money, and 266 days of sunshine a year were a big part of the draw for these companies. So increasingly was Tijuana, just twenty miles south across the border.

Tijuana's growing number of engineers, its base of approved facilities, its free-trade benefits under NAFTA, and its nearness all helped make it attractive to San Diego's medical researchers and commercially vital for San Diego's companies. By locating manufacturing in Tijuana, inventors and engineers could test, tinker with, and modify medical equipment, diagnostic devices, and all sorts of drug-delivery tools without having to wait days or weeks for results and prototypes from farther afield. And once perfected and approved by regulators, manufacturing next door made commercialization faster and cheaper. City and state governments stepped in to ease the path for new entrants, speeding permits and licenses and doling out tax breaks. The city's base of technicians and engineers quickly expanded as local vocational schools and universities beefed up their STEM offerings and designed classes around specific company needs.[64]

Officials on both sides of the border focused on streamlining trade. They expanded the number of lanes, added more "trusted traveler" options, introduced pilot programs to let inspections happen before trucks got in line to cross, and increased the number of simultaneous inspections by Mexican and U.S. customs officials. They even internationalized Tijuana's airport, a cross-border terminal now serving the whole metropolitan area. As a result, the Otay-Mesa crossing has become one of the busiest on the continent, with over one hundred thousand vehicles and people moving back and forth every day.[65]

Today companies in Tijuana make some $600 million worth of pacemakers, defibrillators, feeding tubes, blood-pressure cuffs, artificial respirators, catheters, and all sorts of other medical tools—and employ forty thousand skilled workers in labs and factories to do it. The lion's share of exports heads to U.S. clinics and hospitals. But the devices also go to Japan, Uruguay, Switzerland, and France, letting U.S. companies use Mexico's broader global free-trade platform to their advantage.[66]

Across the border, San Diego's concentration of biotech companies and research institutes outshines all but San Francisco and Boston. Arena Pharmaceuticals, Dexcom, and others have set up their headquarters here, expanding San Diego's professional class. Life sciences has grown into a $40 billion local industry, sending some sixty-five thousand biochemists, biophysicists, geneticists, mechanical engineers, lab technicians, programmers, patent lawyers, and others to work each day.[67] This vibrancy brings dynamism to local restaurants, arts, and services, supporting hundreds of thousands more people in the local economy.

When COVID-19 arrived in North America, the two cities' symbiotic relationship proved lifesaving. Mexico, led by Tijuana, was already supplying more medical equipment to the United States than China was. As Chinese imports shut off, the Mexican medical-manufacturing lines expanded, even during the worst of the coronavirus pandemic. Mexican factories filled U.S. hospitals' desperate orders for ventilators, medical-grade masks, and protective gear. They churned out cloth masks for people across the United States and Canada. And in a sign of the deep ties between the communities, scores of Tijuana-based Americans and green-card holders filled San Diego's COVID-19 wards.[68]

In the past decade, North America has gotten a bit of its regional economic groove back. Trade among the three countries has picked up slightly. Yet commercial ties haven't returned to anything near their levels during NAFTA's 1990s honeymoon days. Nor have North America's nations regained their global market share.

USMCA: NAFTA for Populists

The renegotiated rules that came into effect in 2020 aren't going to significantly move North America's economic ties forward. The United States–Mexico–Canada Agreement (USMCA), the new NAFTA, brings some advances, to be sure. NAFTA was designed before Google, Amazon, or smartphones existed. The new deal sets up rules of the road for data, downloads, and personal information. It updates intellectual property rights, extends copyright and trade secrets protections, and doubles down on ways to combat counterfeit goods, bringing the quarter-century-old agreement in line with newer ones around the world. It takes small steps to streamline the ways medicines, makeup, and chemicals are tested and approved and lowers the number of sanitary checks for foodstuffs. Customs too should get easier as they go more digital. New provisions to ensure better labor standards should help workers, especially in Mexico. And with strong support from both Republicans and Democrats in the United States, it cements preferential trading ties with Mexico and Canada.

But the new agreement threatens to put out NAFTA's regional spark. It ups the protective ante for autos and their parts, making it more, rather than less, complicated and costly to comply. More parts suppliers will have to trace and certify the origin of each and every input if they want tariff-free access to North American markets, adding paperwork and costs that are particularly onerous for smaller companies. Many may just decide not to bother (especially for cars, for which the tariffs are low anyway), opening the option of importing more rather than fewer parts from farther away.

The USMCA undercuts legal assurances for U.S. and Canadian manufacturers that set up shop in Mexico. Companies will now have to resolve disputes through local courts that have not always been known for their fairness. It stipulates its own end after sixteen years (pending renegotiation). And the whole benefit of certainty that the agreement was supposed to bring was quickly upended: within weeks of USMCA's start, Trump imposed tariffs on Canadian aluminum. The acrimonious negotiations and then blatant disregard for the spirit of the new agreement have revived an old wariness between the nations, an unfortunate return given the boost that North American production brings to economic competitiveness.

Crises united Europe. They have driven North America apart. As the China Shock hit, and the blame game for the lost plants, jobs, and hollowed-out communities grew, the United States turned on its neighbors. And while Canadians and Mexicans have generally supported regionalism, suspicions still arise: Mexicans worry that NAFTA helped only the rich, Canadians that it favored the Americans.[69]

NAFTA came to be blamed for everything from stealing U.S. jobs to polluting the United States' air and spurring immigration. Few people came to NAFTA's defense. After its passage, its boosters and beneficiaries faded back into their day-to-day business. Those who paid attention were much less convinced of its benefits.

Economic studies show that the narrative of NAFTA-driven decline is dead wrong. While some factories have closed, others have opened (although rarely in the same place). Some jobs have been lost; others have been created. Nearly all studies done in the years following NAFTA saw little to no effect on overall employment. Some estimate slight gains in the thousands or tens of thousands of jobs each year; others calculate similar losses. Iron, steel, and machine makers won; clothes makers lost. Each job lost represents real suffering, but the overall number of jobs gained or lost is dwarfed by the four million workers who lose jobs every year as part of routine business turnover. The $21 trillion U.S. economy is just too big, and trade just too small a portion of it, for NAFTA to make much of a difference.

Those who tout big losses (one study claims 200,000 jobs a year were destroyed by imports from Mexico) conveniently disregard the equally large estimated gains (the same study showed 188,000 jobs created every year by export sales to Mexico alone, jobs that tend to pay more than domestically focused ones). Taking into account both sides of the employment ledger, NAFTA was a wash. This stands in stark contrast to Chinese trade, which has hit many jobs and communities hard.[70]

Would U.S. workers have been better off without NAFTA? It is always hard to measure a counterfactual. But by divvying up production across countries with different skill sets, wage rates, and access to money within h America, companies became or remained competitive with companies that could exploit cheaper labor in eastern Europe or Asia. Without NAFTA, many of the jobs that stayed would have left too, and new ones that have been created never would have appeared in the first place. North American–made, as opposed to U.S.-made, products can be both higher quality and more affordable. It is this combination that helps them win customers at home and abroad. And when orders rise, so do jobs along the supply chain.

Businesses' ability to diversify where they made components (often sending the more labor-intensive ones south) gave many of them the option to keep a big chunk of their production in the United States rather than ship it all abroad. When factories open in China, Vietnam, Poland, or Romania, U.S. suppliers don't get any extra orders. When plants open in Mexico and Canada, they buy more parts and inputs from the United States to feed into their assembly lines than from anywhere else in the world. Yes, just some of the steps in the manufacturing supply chain stayed in the United States. But alone, the United States probably wouldn't have kept many or any at all, with the final wholesale or retail product eclipsed by those that are made better, cheaper, and faster elsewhere.

The biggest beneficiary of NAFTA has been one of the most integrated industries: autos. During the 1970s and 1980s, the U.S. auto sector shrunk faster than manufacturing overall, as Detroit's big three lost out to higher-quality, more efficient Asian and European competitors. In NAFTA's wake, the industry recovered. Over the next decade, more than one million additional cars and trucks were made in the United States, and the industry added some one hundred thousand jobs, this time outpacing, rather than lagging, general manufacturing.[71] The biggest boost came from new plants. Sure, many opened in Mexico, but even more broke ground in the United States: BMW built its biggest plant in the world in Spartanburg, North Carolina; Nissan chose Smyrna, Tennessee; Daimler, Hyundai, Mazda, and Toyota all set up shop in Alabama.[72] Market size is part of the story: U.S. consumers buy more cars than Mexican or Canadian ones, and there is a cost benefit to having final assembly plants nearer to dealer lots. Also part of the story are solid U.S. legal rules and the general ease of getting the permits and licenses to break ground on new manufacturing facilities. But these automakers built out their U.S. facturing bases in large part because of the ground rules set by N

Able to bring in parts tariff-free from across the three nations, the automakers could now serve the lucrative U.S. market and competitively export their cars and in particular SUVs.

Although U.S. auto plants open and close with some regularity, most of the moves are domestic. When GM's Janesville, Wisconsin, plant shuttered in 2008, Chevy Tahoe production ramped up in Arlington, Texas.[73] In 2007, Ford's best-selling F-150 pickup lines left Norfolk, Virginia, not for Mexico but for Dearborn, Michigan, and Kansas City, Missouri.[74] The Ford Ranger, once made in Minneapolis, was revived in Wayne, Michigan. The internal geography of car making has changed, as Detroit lost out to cities across the South and Southeast. Yet Ohio and Michigan politicians seem reluctant to blame Tennessee, Arkansas, and Alabama for their communities' losses.

Auto jobs did decline in the twenty-first century. The car industry took a big hit after the 2008 financial crisis despite the federal bailout. Over the next few years, automation took hold industry-wide. Today, half of all the robots in the United States are in auto plants. So even when output began growing again, jobs did not.[75]

Despite the China Shock, the financial crisis, and rising production in Mexico and Canada, the United States now makes about twelve million cars a year, roughly a million more than it did before NAFTA's signing, a period when U.S. sales rose from roughly fifteen million to just over seventeen million vehicles a year.[76] The United States remains the biggest automaker in the region, assembling two out of every three North American cars.[77]

Even the examples most used by NAFTA's detractors show, if you look more closely, how North American production helps U.S. auto companies and their workers. In 2019, Lordstown, Ohio, stopped making Chevy Cruzes, as GM moved all its remaining lines to Guanajuato, Mexico. Yet the reason was the car's declining popularity with U.S. consumers (combined with the low margins on sedans as compared to SUVs). Without NAFTA, GM would have just stopped making Cruzes altogether. By shifting assembly to Mexico, GM will save enough on production to allow the sedan to live on in North America, as will contracts with its U.S.-based suppliers and parts makers.

The United States shows few signs of abandoning its regional skepticism. When the Obama administration set out to negotiate the Trans-Pacific Partnership, or TPP, it only belatedly let in its neighbors. During trade talks with the EU, the United States again went ahead on its own. Its neighbors followed suit. Canada closed a new trade deal with the EU, and Mexico updated its previous agreement, while the U.S. negotiations stalled. By failing to work together, the three countries have made life harder for their companies. Canadian recognition of France's exclusive right to make Brie de Meaux and Italy's to Parmesan means that Wisconsin dairy farms can use those labels in the United States but must change them when they export to Canada. Clashing auto rules of origin could move Mexican assemblers away from U.S. suppliers for their Europe-bound models.

Migration remains the most serious sticking point, despite the benefits it brings to North America and the United States in particular. Mexican and Canadian immigrants have enriched U.S. society and fueled its economy, bringing everything from Kind granola bars to Revlon cosmetics, Kraft cheese to Superman comics, and running tens of thousands of local stores, restaurants, consulting firms, and small businesses. Their successes are no surprise: migrants are much more likely to start a business, file for a patent, and hire people than are native-born Americans.[78] American migrants have similar track records when they move to Mexico and Canada.

Still, easier movement remains a political nonstarter in the United States. Politicians have shown themselves more inclined to make political hay demonizing the influx of Central Americans and Mexicans to the U.S. southern border than to fix the problems of the U.S. immigration system that the exodus of men, women, and children has laid bare. Without a rules revamp, the chronic problems at the border won't end, and the United States will lose much of the demographic benefit that these migrants could bring.

COVID-19 has further strained people-to-people ties. In the darkest days of the pandemic, North American manufacturing delivered lifesaving ventilators and personal protective equipment. Yet the borders slammed and stayed shut to nonessential travel, stranding friends and families on either side. That governments were so reluctant to resume the back-and-forth shows just how separate their thinking had become.

The outline of an integrated North America is still there. Nearly thirty years of summits, agreements, and day-to-day cooperation across agencies and bureaucracies have brought the three nations much closer together. An animated private sector has done its best with the rules as they are, creating jobs and offering consumers an ever-wider range of products by building regional supply chains in cars, planes, medical equipment, machinery, and processed foods. The current fluidity of Asia's supply chains opens an opportunity for more textiles, electronics, and machinery to be made in North America in the years to come.

Yet for now, a united continent remains a distant prospect. Yes, NAFTA made trade a little easier. But no bigger social or political goals came out of what was fundamentally a commercial deal. Yes, security cooperation has brought crime-fighting agencies together. But no North American identity or continental strategy has emerged. The business-driven visions of an integrated Asia or Brussels's dream of a Europe whole and free remain decidedly missing in North America.

For a while, perhaps, that didn't matter. Armed with the world's largest consumer market and one of its strongest industrial bases, the United States could go it alone. But global forces are shifting, Asia's consumers are rising, and to be isolated is now to be vulnerable. If the United States wants to regain its momentum, it needs its neighbors.

5

Going Forward: As Supply Chains Peak, Regional Ties Deepen

From 1980 until the eve of the global financial crisis, world trade grew twice as fast as the world economy. Since then, it has struggled just to keep pace. In part, this deceleration reflects the fallout of the financial crash. Companies slashed foreign investment, banks pulled back cross-border lending, and international sales stalled. But the slowdown in trade also comes from longer-term trends that are transforming the way things are made and sold.

While some of these changes, such as better video-conferencing software and algorithms trained on big data, are making it easier to stretch international supply chains ever farther around the globe, many of them are making intercontinental production much less necessary and less advantageous. Automation is bringing down labor costs, and 3D printing is upending the logic behind big factories and their economics of scale.

Demographics are reshaping both supply and demand. Aging populations mean shrinking workforces. The next billion flush customers will be in Asia (although the factories that supply them may not be). As incomes have risen, so has demand for services; over half of the world's workers no longer make physical things.

And governments everywhere are intervening in strategically important economic sectors, many embracing protectionist measures.[1] Tariffs, subsidies, and export controls are on the rise. The United States and China have pulled back from each other, and the EU is binding closer together without Britain. COVID-19 has accelerated these shifts. Goods and parts shortages and other disruptions have pushed companies to rethink the balance between short-term profits and longer-term risks. Supply-chain bottlenecks have motivated governments to take a heavier hand in a host of industries. And vaccine production and distribution have added new political pressures and at times barriers as nations scramble for doses.

Many of these technological, demographic, environmental, and political trends are leaning in the United States' favor. High-tech manufacturing advantages the better-educated, better-paid U.S. workforce. The U.S. economy already leads the world in services. And North America is on course to avoid the demographic bust coming for much of Asia and Europe. For U.S. companies and workers, the next round of globalization does not have to look like the last one. Still, the quick recovery, resilience, and adaptability of international supply chains in the face of COVID-19 show their stamina and permanence. Companies may pull back their global footprints or lessen the number of links along their production chains, but there are too many advantages and profits to be made in international making and selling of goods and services to stop. Instead, the same trends that are giving the United States a boost in global competition are also reinforcing the benefits of regionalization. And if the United States continues to limit its international ties, especially with its neighbors, it will squander its newfound advantages.

Smart Manufacturing

There are lots of names for the coming transformation in production—the Fourth Industrial Revolution, Industry 4.0, Smart Manufacturing—and lots of theories go with them. Some analysts think that this technological revolution will be different from past ones and that machines are on their way to replacing workers for good. Others predict a happier coexistence, in which tasks are divvied up between humans and robots. Whichever side is right—and, in truth, it's too early to say—it's clear that profound changes are under way as data and automation infuse every aspect of commerce.

Computers have long been involved in making things. For decades, they have helped run payrolls, monitor assembly lines, track inventories, and forecast sales. Now they are moving from an auxiliary to a central role, in which software not only collects data and crunches numbers for human decision-makers but also increasingly makes decisions itself.

Consider the fishing industry, in which almost every step from sea to supermarket now involves automation. At plants that process and prepare seafood, algorithms assess each catch against the backlog of customer orders, automated x-rays scan every fish for bones, and specialized software calculates the most efficient cuts. Mechanical arms wielding precision water-jet cutters work alongside gloved and aproned employees to skin, gut, debone, portion, and trim fillets. On packaging lines, a technician or two watches from behind glass walls and uses a handheld tablet to control the robotic pickers inside as they measure precise quantities of fish into plastic containers and stick labels on them before they are whisked away on conveyor belts.[2] Fish and seafood aren't anomalies. Across many industries and sectors, it is machines, not humans, that flank assembly lines.

Automation is coming for the grocery store, too. Inside AmazonGo convenience stores, shelves are stocked with the usual boxes of cereals, plastic-wrapped sandwiches, fruit, snacks, and cans of beer, but the checkout lines and cashiers are missing. Instead, cameras track customers from every angle as they peruse the aisles. Weight sensors record what people pick up or put back on shelves. Machine learning lets computers figure out who took what as customers pack their own shopping bags. Once a customer leaves, the system charges their credit card, and a receipt appears in the Amazon app minutes later. Today, Amazon operates just a few dozen of these stores in a handful of U.S. cities. But with plans for three thousand more, the model could revolutionize grocery shopping.[3]

The automation revolution depends on big data. Sensors and tracking tags increasingly permeate factory floors, attached to thermostats, storage racks, assembly-line stations, and even workers themselves, transmitting troves of information every few seconds. They keep tabs on temperatures, test air quality, record vehicle speeds, check products for defects, and track shipments down to the last inch. They follow goods long after they leave the shop floor to distribution centers, store shelves, living rooms, and kitchens. Computers connect inventory, bank accounts, security, electricity, and dozens of systems to each other. Today, over half of all connections are machine to machine. Channeling terabytes, petabytes, and zettab information, they read and relay the physical world.[4]

Big data and automation start before the product even exists. Companies simulate scenarios and assembly-line runs. When Ford was redesigning its fastest sports car, the Shelby Mustang GT500, the car's brake and cooling systems were all tested virtually. Other manufacturers use software to predict the wear and tear on excavator buckets, the weight loads for video walls, or the spray range for car washer-fluid nozzles before ever prototyping, much less manufacturing, the part.[5]

Software programs study patterns, run tests, solve problems, and learn from their mistakes. They can find where seconds are wasted along an assembly line, where output tends to slow, and where machines (or humans) falter. Managers can fix gauges before they break, order parts before inventories dwindle, and switch energy sources when prices fall. Computers tell ships where to sail and warehouses what to stock. More and more, humans just oversee an automated dance.

Big data goes beyond the factory floor to give companies an edge in sales and marketing. Nike scours local social media to decide whether to send Air Force Ones or Air Maxes to Los Angeles stores. Unilever crunches real-time purchases to adjust factory runs. For all kinds of businesses, big data can guide sales teams on what to say, to send, to offer to entice new customers or keep established ones.[6]

Automation and big data are changing the types of workers companies need and the wages those workers get paid. Postings for technicians and engineers are rising; those for line workers are falling. And once the decisions about what products to make and how and where to make them are made, robots increasingly do the work, making wages matter less relative to spending on equipment. Car companies use the lion's share of industrial robots today. At Nissan's mammoth plant in Sunderland, England, just a handful of workers supervise scores of yellow robotic arms as they laser on doors and add sides and roofs to silver Infiniti frames moving along automated lines. Robots have also taken over the painting room, where their sensors mark and maintain precisely calculated distances from each car's body as they spray coat after coat of "super black" or "storm blue metallic" on each Leaf, Juke, Note, and Q30. In auto plants around the world, hundreds of thousands of mechanical arms now do much of the pressing, welding, sealing, and testing, too.[7]

Robots have moved into food processing. They debone chicken legs, rotate pizzas in hot ovens, and decorate cakes. In pharmaceutical labs, they treat and categorize cell plates and turn out thousands of pills a minute on drug production lines. And while the iPhone maker Foxconn is best known for colossal factory floors filled with hundreds of thousands of workers, technicians now labor alongside tens of thousands of robots inserting batteries and polishing cases.[8]

Asia leads the way in mechanization. China and South Korea each deploy more robots than all of North America and Germany combined. Japan is not far behind. Its machines handle everything from assisting surgeons in the operating room to welding columns and installing floors on new high-rises. For every ten thousand workers in Singapore's workforce, it now has over six hundred robots.[9]

What's known as "additive manufacturing" promises to replace some assembly lines altogether. By methodically fusing plastic powders or pulverized metals in fine layer upon fine layer, 3D printers can create everyday goods. Health care has already embraced the promise of futuristic printing tech. Dentists digitally print crowns to fit the contours of each patient's mouth. Doctors mold hearing aids to the shape of individual ears. Surgeons print copies of tumors for practice runs, and orthopedists mold custom prosthetics.

Other manufacturers are beginning to use printed parts alongside ones that have been cast, molded, forged, or machined. Carmakers and their suppliers use 3D printers to create prototypes of brakes, gear shifts, slide valves, roof brackets, and other components. Airplane suppliers use printers to make jet-engine fuel nozzles, gearbox covers, and titanium brackets. Others make specialized tools and vital but little-used parts.[10]

Easy-to-adjust computerized designs make producing small batches and one-off products possible and even affordable, with economies of scale at times trumped by flexible 3D printers. And with printers right there on factory floors, workers can tinker with different designs in real time. Engineers can churn out models in hours or days, iterating and improving as they go, rather than waiting weeks for prototypes to come back from machine shops that are states or even oceans away.

Despite the hype, much of 3D printing's promise remains just that. The process isn't yet fast, cheap, or reliable enough to go mainstream. Machines, resins, and powders are expensive. Economies of scale still matter. Adidas has found this out to its cost. In 2019, the German shoemaker scrapped a high-profile attempt to use computerized knitting, robotic cutting, and 3D printing to make sneakers in the United States and Germany. Production headed back, once again, to Vietnam.[11]

But as automation takes hold, robots proliferate, and printing tech improves, trade will change. Low wages will be less of a draw, higher skills more of one. Logistics, distance, and raw materials will weigh more heavily than workers' wages on companies' bottom lines. More blueprints and designs and fewer pieces and products will cross borders. Fewer parts will be needed. That will mean fewer links in international supply chains. For those links that do remain, and many will, they will favor regional over global locations.

Even as manufacturing begins to retreat, services are set to venture abroad. From opening bank accounts to selling insurance, caring for the elderly to building websites, entertaining tourists to enlightening students, designing office buildings to piloting planes, services provide the majority of jobs around the world.[12]

Many of these tasks already cross borders.[13] Banks, insurers, law firms, strategic consultants, electricity providers, telecoms, and dozens of others have set up branches abroad, earning trillions of dollars each year. Beaches, mountains, orchestras, and museums draw in foreigners and their cash. Airlines, shipping companies, railroads, and truckers make a living moving goods across borders and seas.

Still, trade in services lags far behind trade in goods. In part, the face-to-face nature of many of these businesses makes it hard to buy them from a distance. You have to be in the same place as your hairdresser, masseuse, or plumber, after all. Government regulations also hold back trade in services. Lawyers have to pass local bar exams, doctors must take medical-board exams, and pilots need to clock in hundreds of additional flight hours in each jurisdiction.[14] Dozens of other professions require licenses, certifications, and in-country training. Differences in accounting standards and building codes make it difficult to transfer one's knowledge from one nation to another. Some governments make this kind of trade all the harder by requiring local data storage, restricting ecommerce payments, or blocking foreign websites.[15]

Despite those hurdles, technology is making it easier to deliver more and more types of services over longer distances. Cheaper broadband, 5G networks, and satellite internet forge faster and more reliable connections. Better video software, augmented and virtual reality, and tools like Zoom, Google Docs, and Slack allow cooperation across geographical barriers. Translation software helps surmount language differences, while the internet of things reduces the need for humans to talk at all as devices communicate with one another.

Online platforms make it easier to buy and sell services at a distance. If you are looking for an editor, a designer, a social media marketer, or a sound engineer, sites like Upwork, Indeed.com, Fiverr, and Toptal can match you with freelancers across dozens of nations. From kitchen tables to full-blown workshops, makers of handmade crafts can reach customers in scores of countries on Etsy. For the more esoteric, illustrators, authors, and musicians can find international subscribers on Patreon. These transactions are made all the easier by digital ways to move money. PayPal, Square, Stripe, and other financial apps make it straightforward to get paid for your work wherever you live.

Finally, as incomes rise around the world, so does demand for services. Fuller wallets mean more money for medical and legal advice, for taking architectural chances and streaming movies, for tour groups and language courses. More and more of this demand, as well as supply, will come from abroad. True, COVID-19 set back international travel, education, and other in-person adventures. But it won't stop the transition. And the embrace of remote working is simply accelerating the possible internationalization of many jobs.

The buying and selling of services across borders is just getting started.[16] As exchanges grow, they too will lean regional as much as if not more than global. The pullback of global finance means that bankers, lawyers, accountants, and many consultants will tend to travel to and work in the nearer abroad as they venture forth. International online searches and interactions are already predominantly regional, and the geographic circumscribing of the World Wide Web is likely to become more so as it splinters geopolitically. In theory, anyone can compose, edit, calculate, or study from anywhere. Yet as we have seen in manufacturing, time zones, cultural cues, and language still stubbornly matter for managers, workers, freelancers, tourists, and students alike. Proximity will still matter.

Demographics

Shifting demographics are causing many nations to move from labor surplus to scarcity. This transformation, too, is changing international production and supply chains. Fewer new workers mean that wages and purchasing power rise in once-low-cost countries, even as new business start-ups, consumption, and overall economic growth tend to slow.

China's current population pyramid is among the most challenging, brought on by decades of strict family-planning policies. At the start of the twenty-first century, some ten million new workers were joining the Chinese labor market every year. Now, more are exiting than entering. In twenty years, China's workforce will have shrunk by more than one hundred million. And low birth rates look here to stay, as official policies have morphed into cultural norms.

The loss is already being felt in southeastern Dongguan. Home to nearly one million factories, the city thrived during China's great migration and urbanization. Now the central labor market is quiet compared to years past.[17] Villages in neighboring provinces have emptied out, forcing recruiters to go farther inland to Hubei and Jiangxi, where they have to compete with local factories for workers. As the workforce dwindles, many young people are becoming less interested in working "the 996"—9 a.m. to 9 p.m., six days a week. Even with big pay raises, factories are struggling to fill the slots.

Much of the rest of Asia is not far behind. Japan's, Singapore's, Taiwan's, and South Korea's labor forces are shrinking. And while Vietnam, Indonesia, and the Philippines remain demographic bright spots, even there, the rate of population growth is slowing, meaning that expanding workforces won't provide the GDP boosts they once did.[18]

Europe also faces worker scarcity. The working populations of Italy, Spain, and France are already on the decline, and those of Germany and Austria will soon tip that way as well.[19] Migration has boosted urban France,

Sweden, and Germany, yet those countries' gains have come in large part from emptying out eastern Europe; three million Romanians, hundreds of thousands of Hungarians, and one-fifth of Latvians are now gone from their homelands.[20] The recent influx of refugees will help buoy population figures. But even so, in twenty years, ten million fewer people will be contributing their energy, ideas, and brawn to Europe's economy.[21]

North America has the best demographic prospects of the three hubs. Instead of losing steam, its working population is expected to grow by some fifty million between now and 2050.[22] A good portion of these gains comes from the roughly one million new settlers on the continent each year. Another big boost comes from North Americans' greater penchant for having kids.[23] These new citizens will boost the continent's economic growth for years to come.

Still, notwithstanding this impending demographic shift, nowhere in the world is consumption rising as quickly as in Asia. Chinese families already purchase five million more cars every year than residents of any other country do, as well as more iPhones, sneakers, and, even with their baby bust, more infant formula.[24] This purchasing power is set to grow over the next decade as hundreds of millions of Chinese citizens join the middle and upper-middle classes.[25]

Asia's other consumers are no slouches either. South Koreans spend $10 billion a year on creams and makeup alone.[26] Japan trails only the United States in its demand for handbags, designer garb, and other luxury goods.[27] The buying power of nearly two hundred million Indonesians, Malaysians, Filipinos, Thais, and Vietnamese is expected to rise dramatically as a majority of their citizens join the global middle class over the next ten years.[28]

Much of this consumption will take place online. Asia's consumers are increasingly likely to buy not just food, clothes, and appliances but also massages, house cleaning, and cars on their smartphones rather than in a store. China's ecommerce sites take in $1.5 trillion each year, more than the next ten markets combined.[29]

North Americans, thanks to their much-higher incomes, will outshine Asians in sheer buying power for years to come.[30] Europeans have long been and will continue to be big consumers as well. But as home to nine out of every ten new entrants into the middle class, Asia is quickly moving from factory to mall. That will bring a strong commercial advantage to companies that can win those customers' attention and loyalty.

Climate Change

Climate change will affect global trade, as port cities flood, rails buckle, roads crumble, and transportation costs rise.[31] Hurricanes, tsunamis, droughts, and fires will ruin crops, scare off tourists, and ground planes. Container ships already face stronger storms, shifting currents, and changing sedimentation that are rendering heavily used shipping channels less easy and safe to navigate. Rising sea levels are forcing shipping companies and ports to make huge capital outlays raising berths, reinstalling cranes, and moving data and cargo control centers farther inland. Regulations requiring more environmentally friendly fuels with lower sulfur content add to the cost of sea voyages.[32]

Climate challenges will probably hit Asia the hardest, as the back-and-forth of parts in the region is one of the most intense and water dependent in the world. A good portion of Asia's two billion coastal dwellers will likely have to move to higher ground, disrupting not just the economy but society writ large. The more land-based North American and European border crossings are somewhat less vulnerable, although they too will suffer from warmer temperatures and more extreme weather. And Western nations, assuming they can overcome their divisive politics, have more money to spend on adaptation than many emerging markets do.

The response to climate change may batter trade even more. European proposals to tax carbon footprints would make longer supply chains more expensive, at least for companies selling to Europe's half billion citizens.[33] Calls to tax "carbon leakage"—when companies decamp for countries with lax environmental rules—have gained hearings in both Europe and the United States.[34] And many companies are doing carbon offsetting all by themselves, calculating emissions and investing in carbon-reducing projects to match.[35] As the private sector adopts these efforts more broadly, the advantages of far-flung global operations are shrinking even further.

Climate change could have modest positive effects expanding trade's footprint if melting ice opens up Arctic sea lanes between Asia and northern Europe, lowering transportation time and costs. But overall, the disruptions, uncertainty, and instability will make it harder to manufacture products across continents, leading production to stay or return closer to consumers. When combined with the continuing advantages of international specialization, the real benefits of geographic dispersion in the face of more extreme weather and policies will advantage regional production and sales over purely national operations.

The Return of Industrial Policy

Political choices are also making farther-flung supply chains relatively less attractive too. After decades of opening up, many nations are now pulling back. The Global Trade Alert, a nonprofit initiative that collates trade-policy information from official sources from around the world, finds that government economic interventions have increased nearly fourfold since 2018, with protectionist measures outpacing liberalizing ones by a ratio of nearly three to one. Active industrial policies are making a comeback in capitals across the globe.[36]

Government actions have always been necessary to take on market failures and externalities ignored by individual companies or whole industrial sectors. But now there is a rising inclination to step up the public sector's role in the economy. In part, it comes from the sense that nearly three decades of economic laissez-faire conventional wisdom—advocated by scholars, finance ministers, bankers, and multilateral institutions, including the WTO and IMF and often dubbed the "Washington Consensus"—didn't deliver. Emerging economies that opened their borders and financial systems often didn't thrive, while those that protected their markets and championed local industries tended to grow more and to progress faster up the socioeconomic and technological ladders. In advanced industrial economies, the more-hands-off approach offered few solutions to the disruptions caused by automation, technological change, labor-union decline, and trade.

Governments are now stepping in to address these perceived market failings, using at times ambitious mixes of financial carrots and sticks to expand industrial clusters and gain economic advantage. Industrial policies are also often seen as a way to create local jobs and reap political rewards.

And government industrial policy goals and ambitions now go beyond advancing economic competitiveness to enhancing national security, protecting public health, and saving the planet from overheating.

National-security hawks eye international supply chains with trepidation. The internationalization of manufacturing exposes production to far-away natural disasters and pandemics. It also can give geopolitical rivals leverage. For instance, China has effectively cornered the making of polysilicon and refining of rare earth minerals, giving it power over vital inputs into consumer electronics, cars, and a host of critical parts for U.S. fighter planes, tanks, personnel carriers, and weapons systems. The same goes for the active pharmaceutical ingredients that go into Tylenol, penicillin, and a slew of antibiotics, or the manufacturing of N95 masks and other protective equipment that keep us virus-free.

Security worries go beyond trade interruptions. Policy makers also fear that foreign-made hardware and software could expose citizens and governments to surveillance and espionage. Technological back doors into phones could steal sensitive information; car computers could be hacked and vehicles remotely hijacked; or embedded malware could bring down power plants, electricity grids, or banking systems.

Whether worried about access to critical minerals, medicines, and technologies, about vulnerable manufacturing choke points, about cyber weaknesses, or about advancing a technological and economic edge, nations the world over are calling to enhance industry at home.

China leads this pullback. Its planners no longer want the country to be the world's assembly line. The nation has long given local companies a leg up through coordinated industrial policies involving state-owned enterprises, preferential subsidies, cheap money, and tax breaks.[37] For three decades, this strategy meant binding Asia together in the making of apparel, electronics, toys, and thousands of other products to sell to the West. Now, in a drive to become more self-sufficient, China is using its support for local companies to cut back on the imports and exports that helped fuel years of double-digit growth. Over the past decade, even as economic growth has continued, its trade is down by more than half as a proportion of GDP.[38]

China's restrictive policies take many forms. Local content rules, forced technology transfers, and at times outright bans keep out or boot many foreign companies and their goods. This pullback has hit all sorts of U.S. and European businesses: social media and video sites like Facebook and YouTube, the network hardware maker Cisco, and industrial giants such as Siemens, Bayer, Boeing, and Airbus. South Korean, Japanese, and other Asian parts makers, suppliers, and brands have suffered as much as—if not more than—Western companies, as China's retreat has shut out its more embedded neighbors.[39]

The latest five-year plan continues down this path. By 2025, China aims to pour hundreds of billions of public dollars into research and development to own technological advances in quantum computing, semiconductors, artificial intelligence, and neuroscience. It will spend hundreds of billions more to build out 5G networks and install tens of millions of cameras and sensors to power a growing digital economy. And the state isn't forgetting manufacturing, throwing its weight behind electric cars, high-end medical equipment, airplane engines, industrial robots, and satellite systems and pushing factories of all stripes to upgrade and automate.[40] The government is pushing farmers to sow homegrown, genetically modified, high-yield seeds and rebuild pork herds devastated by swine flu.[41]

Still, Asia's regionalism will remain strong. China's push to get the Regional Comprehensive Economic Partnership done, and its speedy ratification to pressure others to follow suit, now tie it commercially closer to the fourteen other Asian members. Even as it reserves higher-tech manufacturing steps for itself, Chinese companies are farming out some of the more-labor-intensive parts of supply chains to its neighbors, boosting its own exports of machinery, synthetic fabrics, steel, and other intermediate parts for assembly. Meanwhile, Chinese brands are going full into Asian markets, eager to capture the growing number of Indonesian rupiahs, Thai bahts, and Malaysian ringgits spent by newly minted middle classes.

Government interventionism is rising in Europe, too. Brussels is taking an increasingly skeptical stance toward "predatory" (read: Chinese) companies buying into its telecommunications, energy, media, auto, and technology sectors. It has begun vetoing more transactions and allowing governments to take "golden shares" to keep their companies out of foreign hands.[42] It has stepped up tax, trade, and customs oversight to support regional industrial champions.[43]

Wary of being left behind, Europe has grasped onto the notion of "strategic autonomy" to help it compete technologically and economically. Here it is putting money behind constructing homegrown industries and regional supply chains in strategic areas such as cloud computing, artificial intelligence, green hydrogen, semiconductors, and satellite communications. One of its biggest bets is on electric batteries for the next generation of vehicles, electricity grids, and smart homes.[44] The EU is funding Austrian and German research, building up the Portuguese and eastern European lithium mining and refining industries, helping underwrite massive Swedish manufacturing facilities, and even backing metal-recycling and battery-repurposing companies in an effort to create a cradle-to-grave European battery-production chain.[45]

The United States has made perhaps the biggest about-face in its approach to trade and its embrace of a more active role for the federal government in the economy. Under the Trump administration, it pulled out of trade negotiations and marginalized the WTO, added layers of tariffs, reintroduced quotas, and put in place export controls. It has expanded Buy American rules and bumped up agricultural subsidies.[46]

The Biden administration hasn't been inclined to pull back or end many of these punitive steps, with the biggest shift being to add carrots in the form of tens of billions of dollars for domestic research, development, and supportive investments. It has also ordered a comprehensive review of U.S. government supply chains from defense to public health, information and communications technology to energy, transportation to agriculture.[47] Nearly every department and agency is assessing its vulnerabilities across a sweeping set of cyber, health, climate, environment, economic, geopolitical, human rights, and defense risks from international trading ties.

So far, these bipartisan U.S. actions have gone farthest when it comes to China. In the name of national security, Washington has blocked Chinese companies from buying stakes in U.S. semiconductor material makers, wind farms, and even mobile dating apps.[48] U.S. blacklists deny Huawei and a number of other Chinese tech firms access to U.S. software, technology, and equipment.[49] The United States warned companies off doing business in Hong Kong.[50] President Trump in particular browbeat U.S. companies for doing business in China and lobbied other countries and their corporations to exit China's market as well.[51] It has even threatened to end financial flows by limiting Chinese companies' stock-market listings and pension-fund investments in the United States.[52] And the U.S. government has kicked out researchers, shut down some Chinese-funded institutes, and in general made it much more difficult for Chinese students to study in the United States.[53]

China has responded in kind. Government agencies are weeding out U.S.-made laptops and software from their offices.[54] The government is spending hundreds of billions of dollars on research and development to make its own semiconductor chips, aerospace equipment, robots, and electric vehicles.[55] It has also created a list of banned U.S. companies, including Facebook and Google. It has encouraged periodic boycotts of foreign brands—Houston Rockets gear, Apple phones, Versace clothes, and Coach bags—in retaliation for political statements by their associates.[56] And it has leaned heavily on other countries to take its side and buy its technology, particularly when it comes to 5G and other telecommunications infrastructure.

The noted economist Jagdish Bhagwati presents a compelling case as to why global trade agreements, such as those forged in the WTO, are the best economically.[57] Yet as tit-for-tat tariffs and other punitive measures accelerate around the world, the WTO is essentially out of commission. Even before the U.S.-Chinese trade war kicked off, the international trading body was faltering. In 2015, it relinquished any hope of actively promoting freer trade as negotiators finally gave up on the Doha round of trade talks after years of stalemate. In 2019, it lost its ability to referee disputes when the United States refused to approve new judges to its appellate court. As trading tensions mount, the WTO's relative absence leaves the world's trading system rudderless and fragile. This encourages more regionalism, as countries fall back on less expansive arrangements that they police themselves.

COVID-19

COVID-19 has accelerated the shift toward trade regionalism and nationalism. The novel coronavirus hit international supply chains with simultaneous supply and demand shocks. As cities and countries locked down, vital goods stopped flowing. Factories quieted, container ships idled away from docks, airplanes were grounded. Consumer demands shifted as dramatically, with the world clamoring for face masks and hand sanitizer, not dress clothes or suitcases. As the coronavirus pandemic spread, many countries stopped or slowed exports, first of medical equipment and protective gear, then of rice, wheat, beans, and other basic foods.[58]

A year later, the scramble for vaccines led some nations to again slam shut. Countries that had worked together funding scientific breakthroughs to beat back the virus turned on each other when vaccine manufacturing stumbled. Italy stopped 250,000 doses of AstraZeneca from heading to Australia. India put vaccine exports to the developing world on hold as it struggled to tamp down its own rising caseloads. And the United States initially refused to part with even one of the ten million AstraZeneca doses sitting unused in an Ohio warehouse as they awaited Food and Drug Administration approval.[59]

On the whole, international supply chains held up remarkably well. Within a few months, Clorox wipes, toilet paper, aspirin, frozen vegetables, and garlic were again back on store shelves. Between March and May 2020, China went from making ten million to over one hundred million surgical masks every day. It exported three times more masks that spring than the whole world had made in 2019.[60]

Still, as the disease exposed the costs of relying on farther-away production chains and other geopolitical worries mounted, countries stepped up their efforts to bring manufacturing home.[61] Japan has allocated some $2 billion to help its companies repatriate or move out of China into other Southeast Asian locations. India is offering land to firms open to switching domiciles.[62] South Korea is subsidizing robots and machines to lessen the wage differential with its neighbors.[63] The United States is promising federal loans for medical and technology companies wanting to return home.[64]

Some nations are offering more public contracts, using the state's hefty purchasing power to create or support local supply chains and manufacturing. The Indian government is buying up locally made food and medical devices. Saudi Arabia has contracted for more Saudi-made sterilizers and face masks.[65] China, Kazakhstan, and Peru are among those increasing public procurement from small- and medium-sized companies.[66]

The United States already has local content rules written into many government contracts. It requires the use of U.S.-made steel and iron in its highways and airports. It buys only homegrown food for publicly funded school lunch programs. And the Defense Department favors U.S.-mined rare earths and other minerals in its stockpiles. After COVID-19's arrival, the Trump administration decreed that government medicines and medical equipment purchases also should be made in the United States.[67] The Biden administration is calling for the federal government to do even more, including expanding Buy American rules to energy pipelines, telecommunications equipment, and a bigger chunk of the defense budget and using federal funding to bring home semiconductor research, development, fabrication, and testing.[68]

There are real reasons for governments to step in to enhance national security, protect the environment, and better ensure the health and wealth of citizens. But beyond a finite number of critical minerals, components, and products, reshoring—relocating production back home—may be counterproductive as the geographic concentration and potential marginalization from global innovations increase vulnerabilities that policy makers hope to diminish.

And logistically, governments will find it hard to bring back companies and reshore entire industries. In most sectors, governments' political carrots and sticks are limited compared to costs of uprooting existing operations, and public agencies are ill-equipped to help companies build out trusted local supplier networks and relationships from scratch.

The changing policy landscape will, on balance, encourage not just nationalization but also regionalization. Europeans are already turning to each other. The United States pullback looks to include allies in strategic supply chains and production; many of these allies are geographically nearby. And across the world, countries are relying more on established trade partners and paths (which involve, more often than not, their neighbors).

What This All Means for the United States

On balance, the transformations in this latest round of globalization play to the United States' strengths. One of the United States' greatest assets is its stable ground rules.[69] It isn't hard to start a business, and if things don't work out, closing one down is similarly straightforward. Physical and intellectual property rights are more or less assured. Courts are seen as generally free from political meddling. Sure, there are stories of politics coming into play when companies try to get local licenses or break ground on new factory sites. And there have been worrisome cases of alleged federal-level corruption as well. But overall the United States has nowhere near the levels of insider dealing and fraud of many places. There is a reason so many international bond holders prefer to do business under New York law.

Money is abundant too. Businesses big and small can get bank loans and letters of credit or tap private equity and venture capital. The diversity of ideas and identities, the embrace of a fail-fast mentality, and a general openness to conflict and questioning received wisdom promote entrepreneurial risk taking. This culture of innovation appeals to executives and supply-chain managers deciding where to open their next office or factory.

The United States' people are another strong point. Thanks to migration, the United States faces a far less difficult demographic curve than other countries do. Every year, the nation welcomes hundreds of thousands of people on visas to work, study, and reunite with their families.[70] They bring ideas, ambition, and potential additions to the labor force. Immigrants and their kids spur innovation: they're more likely to invent new products, file patents, and hire people than native-born Americans are.[71] And they have founded half of all high-tech "unicorns"—companies valued at $1 billion or more—and one in four Main Street businesses: florists, noodle shops, delis, hotels, nail salons.[72] Contrary to the myth that immigrants take jobs from locals, when immigration to a town or city rises, employment often does, too.[73] The jobs come not only from the businesses that immigrants start but also from outside companies attracted by the dynamism that the new arrivals bring.

In the past, high wages often dissuaded companies from opening operations in the United States, but with smart manufacturing, automation, and 3D printing all gaining ground, labor costs don't matter as much as they used to, and skilled workers are more of a draw. Likewise, physical proximity is growing in importance as customers become accustomed to quicker deliveries and gratification.

The United States has a big advantage in this algorithm-run future: its companies invented, own, and run much of the technology. Amazon and Microsoft lead the pack of U.S. providers that dominate cloud computing. 3D printing is a largely U.S. enterprise. And U.S.-based scholars excel in artificial intelligence research and development.

The United States has a leg up in the logistics race as well.[74] It costs less to move things in the United States than it does almost anywhere else—about half the price of moving freight within China.[75] Sure, the United States' infrastructure needs an upgrade, but the backbone of U.S. transportation remains strong. Deep ports, protected harbors, and two oceans are linked by rivers and canals to inland lakes and waterways and connected to tens of thousands of miles of rail lines, millions of miles of roads, and tens of thousands of airports.[76] U.S. companies, distributors, and transportation specialists employ automated warehouses, software platforms, algorithms, and all sorts of tracking and tracing systems to speed shipments and last-mile deliveries.[77] And despite the vulnerabilities of U.S. infrastructure, it is more resilient to climate change than many other countries' are. The country relies less on ports than Asia does, and it has more money for adaptation (if it wants to spend it).

The United States shines in services. It already exports more movies, songs, and other entertainment every year than it does planes, chemicals, or corn. It is a top global tourism destination. Tens of millions of international visitors spend $250 billion every year walking in Central Park, gambling in Las Vegas casinos, crossing the Golden Gate Bridge, and visiting Disney World.[78] U.S. schools and universities bring in tens of billions of dollars each year educating over a million international students.[79] While these revenues have plummeted during the coronavirus pandemic, they will return.

U.S. companies lead in international accounting, consulting, legal advising, software, branding, and design sales. And they own a big global chunk of what economists call "intangible" assets: the immediate recognition and higher price customers will pay for iPhones, Starbucks, and Nikes; the digital platforms like Uber and Airbnb that bring in billions of dollars; and the intellectual property within Microsoft Office, Qualcomm's chips, and DuPont's Kevlar.

Many people worry that offices will empty out as factories once did, with new technologies forcing Americans to compete with cheaper Indian programmers, Kenyan copy editors, Filipino customer-support technicians, Turkish web developers, and other intercontinental telecommuters willing to work for less.[80] Some of this will probably happen, and it will disrupt many white-collar jobs and industries. Yet the reverse will also be true. Cleveland Clinic doctors will consult remotely; Harvard professors will lecture thousands of foreign students; Goldman Sachs and Morgan Stanley will become bankers to the world; YouTubers, content curators, recording artists, athletes, inventors, app makers, and all kinds of celebrities and consultants will find audiences and revenues from afar.

This technologically infused future will privilege the knowledge economy. This too is one of the United States' strengths (though not including as many Americans as it could or should). The United States has a deeper and broader bench of universities and colleges than anywhere else; Harvard, Yale, Stanford, MIT, and Caltech are all world-leading names, and they're matched by thousands of public universities, small liberal arts colleges, community colleges, and vocational schools. The United States spends more, often vastly more, on higher education than most any other nation does.[81] This depth and breadth attracts students from all over the world. The United States' neighbors add to these strengths: more Canadians have graduated from college than not, and Mexico is churning out tens of thousands of engineers and technicians each year.[82]

Beyond the U.S. government's spending on education, it has a long history of promoting invention.[83] Public funds spurred the science behind GPS, touch screens, solar panels, LED lights, and shale fracking. They helped build the internet, sequence the human genome, and kick off artificial intelligence and quantum computing. Hundreds of billions of dollars in federal funds have gone to programs run by the Pentagon, the Defense Advanced Research Projects Agency (DARPA), the National Aeronautics and Space Administration (NASA), the National Institutes of Health, and the National Science Foundation and have funded hundreds of university research labs, private contractors, and businesses. Those investments paid for themselves many times over in new industries, better health care, faster economic growth, and greater technological dominance. Every day, labs are building robots that can navigate tough terrain, designing solar panels fit for use in space, editing genes to cure blindness and cancer, or applying quantum computing to encryption.[84]

Years of relative openness to people, goods, ideas, and information have helped the United States become one of the most competitive global economies. It has already accumulated $4.5 trillion in foreign direct investment and is set to bring in much more as wages matter less and knowledge, services, climate resilience, and logistics more[85]—that is, assuming the country capitalizes on its new advantages, fixes its continuing vulnerabilities, and doesn't squander its edge.

There's reason to worry. These advantages aren't permanent or givens. The United States' educational prowess is uneven. Yes, its universities award more science doctorates than anywhere else in the world. Yet many recipients are immigrants, who face growing restrictions on their ability to study or to stay in the United States after earning their degree, limiting the economic and social benefits they bring and diverting their energy, ideas, and innovations elsewhere. U.S. citizens are unprepared to fill the gap. The average American high schooler's math test score lags behind not just those of northern Europe, Japan, and Korea but also Russia, the Czech Republic, and Hungary.[86]

The United States' scientific lead is also shrinking. U.S. public support for basic science has fallen to just half its 1960s levels, while China has upped its research and development outlays by hundreds of billions of dollars.[87] Yes, the private sector has surpassed public funding to buoy overall national research and development spending. But only the U.S. government has proven that it can invest in ways that ignite invention again and again, as its resources are larger and its time frame far longer than those of any start-up or corporate behemoth. Since firms focus on their bottom line, this means less blue-skies research and more customer-focused development, leading away from the quixotic quests that have historically led to the biggest breakthroughs. For the United States to keep its technological dominance far into the future, the government needs to fund invention again.

The warning signs that the United States' technological lead can slip away are already present. China now files more patents and publishes more scientific papers than the United States does (though China's are still less used and cited).[88] The Chinese government and its companies are investing huge sums in machine learning, AI, and logistics. Big data pouring in from two hundred million cameras, billions of social media posts, and hundreds of millions of purchases every day provides China an impressive reservoir to use in training the AI algorithms that go into facial recognition, navigation systems, online shopping, and all sorts of manufacturing processes.[89] In robotics and electric vehicles, some of Shenzhen's companies rival those of Silicon Valley, and upstarts are emerging in aerospace and semiconductors.[90] China's Alibaba and JD.com threaten U.S. ecommerce dominance.[91] And even as the U.S. consumer continues to reign, the next billion buyers to come online won't be in the United States. That means U.S. companies will need to adapt to grow.

Here, they face headwinds caused by Washington not looking outward. Politicians and trade negotiators have largely failed to open up Asian markets to U.S. companies. Washington has signed broad agreements with only South Korea and Singapore. A 2019 deal with Japan affects just 5 percent of bilateral trade (mostly agricultural), far from the full-fledged market opening that the Trans-Pacific Partnership (TPP) would have brought.[92] Negotiations with Europe have stalled as well, with earlier talk of a comprehensive trade agreement now replaced with tiny wins like lowering tariffs on lobster and glassware (covering less than 0.2 percent of trade) and the halt in tit-for-tat penalties tied to airplane subsidies.[93]

Even worse, the United States has taken to slapping tariffs on geopolitical friends and foes alike. Washington has hiked levies on washing machines, solar panels, steel, aluminum, champagne, cheese, and a majority of Chinese goods. Predictably, other countries have retaliated. U.S.-made motorcycles, washing machines, tobacco, and bourbon faced EU import taxes in response. U.S. apples and almonds cost more in India, as do U.S. cars, nuts, and alcohol in Turkey. For over a year, China slashed purchases of U.S. soy, pork, apples, and more.[94] Even after agreeing to big boosts in imports as part of a new trade deal at the start of 2020, China failed to ramp its purchases back up.[95]

This protectionism has created more losers than winners. Consumers lose out for sure, and the poor the most, as they spend more on basics. Farmers suffer—even with $30 billion in federal aid, farm bankruptcies are on the rise.[96] Workers across the economy have felt the pain. By hiking the cost of raw materials and parts, tariffs make U.S.-made goods more expensive. This leads to fewer international sales and dampens local purchases as American families wait, make do, and buy less. As demand and profits fall, so do jobs.

Tariffs haven't brought back manufacturing jobs. Three years of levies on selected goods from allies including Europe, Canada, and Japan and hefty charges on most everything from China did little to boost U.S. industrial employment, which has lagged opportunities in the rest of the economy both before COVID-19 and in the pandemic's wake.[97] Rather than leveling the playing field, these blunt tools ended up harming U.S. manufacturers, businesses, and consumers.

Take solar panels. In 2018 the United States levied a 30 percent duty on foreign-made solar cells and modules (at the behest, interestingly, of U.S.-based German- and Chinese-owned companies).[98] What happened? Solar panels quickly got more expensive. Electricity providers switched to wind and natural gas. Solar projects dried up, and so did manufacturing contracts for domestic equipment makers of brackets, frames, cables, and wiring.[99] Retaliatory tariffs hurt exports of U.S.-manufactured polysilicon wafers that go into panels made abroad, eliminating even more jobs. Add to this the thousands of solar-panel installers who couldn't find work. As customers disappeared, the original complainants, Suniva and SunWorld Americas, filed for bankruptcy. Today, the United States still imports most of its solar panels; it has succeeded only in replacing Chinese imports with those from South Korea, Malaysia, Vietnam, Thailand, and Mexico.[100]

The story of the 2018 steel tariffs is equally grim. Yes, they created some forty-five hundred jobs in steel foundries and mills over the next year.[101] Yet a Federal Reserve study estimates that the tariffs cost the United States seventy-five thousand manufacturing jobs during that same time period.[102] The higher price of steel reverberated through domestic industries that use metal, which employ eighty times as many people as the steel industry.[103] Ford and GM alone lost over $1 billion each in profits in just the first year, part of the reason both closed plants and laid off tens of thousands of U.S. workers.[104] Caterpillar, the engine maker Cummins, the tool maker Stanley Black & Decker, and 3M are some of the better-known names that cut jobs and production due to hundreds of millions of dollars lost to tariffs. Smaller companies also suffered as prices rose and sales fell. Car dealerships shut as Americans waited to trade in older models and builders idled as fewer high-rises broke ground. And those extra forty-five hundred steel mill jobs ended up costing $900,000 a piece in higher prices for cars, washing machines, tractors, and housing passed on to U.S. consumers.[105]

Overall, the nonpartisan Congressional Budget Office estimates that the tariffs launched under the Trump administration shaved 0.5 percent off annual GDP growth and cost the average household more than $1,200 each year.[106] For U.S. exporters, tariffs make it all the harder to reach international clients and markets as they raise input costs and invite retaliation. For some 80 percent of U.S. exporters, the tariffs acted as the equivalent of a 2 percent rise in tariffs imposed by other nations. In competitive industries, that's a significant margin—hence the slump in U.S. exports in the tariffs' wake.[107]

As the United States pulls back from global trade, others are moving ahead. The European Union has signed new agreements with Canada, Japan, New Zealand, and several South American and African countries. As a result, Europe's companies now face lower tariffs than their U.S. competitors do in many of these markets. The agreements put U.S. farms at a further disadvantage if they make one of the products designated as exclusively European in the deals, including Parmesan, Gorgonzola, feta, sauerkraut, and kielbasa.[108]

With the U.S. exit from the TPP, the new Comprehensive and Progressive Agreement for Trans-Pacific Partnership (CPTPP) rolled back provisions freeing data to cross borders. Vietnam was quick to put in place local data-storage rules and content restrictions in ways that raise costs for U.S. cloud-computing, search, and social media companies.[109] And U.S. grown or made products now cost relatively more in these markets compared to those coming from one of the eleven nations in the trading club. U.S. wheat faces Japanese levies of $14 per metric ton, whereas Canadian and Australian growers pay none.[110] U.S. steaks cost 12 percent more than similar cuts heading to Japan from Canada. The UK, South Korea, China, Taiwan, and several other nations are now eager for these insider rewards. Their entrance would further edge out U.S.-based products if the United States continues to stay away.

The unfavorable tilt to Asia's commercial playing field will grow as the Regional Comprehensive Economic Partnership, or RCEP, comes into force. Japanese-made cars and car parts won't pay the double-digit tariffs that U.S.-made alternatives do in China's lucrative market.[111] Chinese-made steel, chemicals, industrial instruments, and machines will face lower levies than U.S.-made options in factories across Asia. And the common rules of origin will make it easier and more profitable to build out and run Asian manufacturing supply chains.

More broadly, the United States is losing ground in setting the foundational rules and standards that govern whole industries. A wide set of international committees and technical organizations negotiate and define design requirements, measurements, performance indicators, and technical protocols. They even decide which words and symbols are used on the labels for a host of products.[112] For power generation, home appliances, semiconductors, fiber optics, batteries, solar energy, nanotechnology, and more, these bodies set the basic rules for functionality, interoperability, and safety. To be sure, countries often pass their own laws and regulations. But for many companies, these more widely used international standards are what matter. They influence the ability to export and expand into new markets. They define who owns essential patents and reaps licensing fees and royalties from others. And they decide which products already meet technical specifications and which will have to adjust to conform.

In the past, U.S. leadership and participation often meant that U.S. models became the global status quo, determining auto fuel-economy standards, internet protocols, high-definition television signals, and international payments systems.[113]

Yet now the U.S. government is sending fewer people to participate in these technical committees than China, Germany, Russia, and over a dozen other nations are.[114] The Trump administration tried to cut federal funding for the labs that conduct studies and produce expert opinions for standard-setting discussions.[115]

In the United States' absence, China is pushing its advantage.[116] It has taken over the leadership of the body governing most things electrical and electronic and has proposed more than a dozen new committees and competencies in which it will have outsize influence. Its experts have submitted hundreds of technical documents related to 5G mobile networks, autonomous vehicles, artificial intelligence, cloud computing, blockchain, and semiconductors, working to shape the rules to the advantage of its companies.

Europe has been formulating regional standards and approaches that have global implications, most notably on data privacy. The General Data

Protection Regulation, or GDPR, requires organizations to get permission to collect and sell the data of anyone in the EU and to better protect personal information from breaches. These rules are already forcing digital advertising giants like Google and Facebook to revamp the way they run their businesses and making other companies change the way they store customer data, send marketing emails, and manage cybersecurity.[117] Here again, the United States has abdicated its tech watchdog and standard-setting role.

If the United States remains disconnected, its businesses will increasingly become rule takers rather than rule makers. They may have to license others' patents or pay more in royalties than in the past. And they may need to rework or adjust their measurements, sizes, internal technical processes, and other specifications to fit international norms that are now more geared to others' products, raising the costs for homegrown and regional manufacturers. If U.S. companies and workers aren't at the table, they'll be on the menu.

With cutting-edge technology and entrepreneurial people, legal solidity and best-in-class scholars, favorable demographics, and a core base of consumers, the United States has real strengths in this latest iteration of globalization. The fading allure of cheap wages and the rising role of services can further advantage the U.S. economy and its people. But this edge isn't immutable. Other nations are keen to grow. The United States can still outpace the world, but only if it recognizes that global economic success requires a team effort. To push its advantage, it needs to embrace its neighbors.

6

The United States' Best Bet: More NAFTAs and Fewer America Firsts

Akron is still struggling to find a prosperous path forward. It has held onto its history with rubber through polymer chemistry, now at the center of local tech innovation. Firestone chemists work on new compounds in labs just south of downtown. Goodyear scientists fill facilities half a dozen miles to the east. Halfway in between sits the University of Akron, which houses extensive polymer laboratories and trains classrooms full of students in the sciences. Biomimicry is another growing strength on the campus, with academics and local incubators inventing glues modeled on gecko feet, pipes latticed like snake skins to stave off corrosion, and bird-friendly building glass with spider-like silk strands woven into the panes.

The downtown has spruced up. Gone are rows of blighted buildings; new apartments fill their place. The old Ohio and Erie Canal Towpath is now home to walkers and bikers, its borders decorated with flower beds planted by the Akron Garden Club. A few blocks away, the Art Museum offers free admission through its vaulted glass lobby connecting the traditional brick building on one side to a modern aluminum addition on the other.

But like so many struggling midwestern cities, too many storefronts are empty. Downtown dining options are few. The city's bids to attract new companies and industries have rarely panned out. And the academic research breakthroughs haven't scaled commercially. Jobs are still scarce, and wage raises even more so.

Immigrants have staunched the city's demographic decline. But young ambitious people still tend to leave. Others get trapped in addiction, with opioid overdoses causing more Akron deaths than car accidents.[1]

The manufacturing void has been filled in part by health care. Summa Health, the Cleveland Clinic, and Akron Children's Hospital are the three biggest local employers, with run-of-the-mill and specialty procedures being a draw for patients near and far. Still many of these positions don't provide the steady shifts or pay packages of the halcyon days of Akron's industrial past.

Some local manufacturing companies have figured out how to survive and thrive. Over one hundred employees cast and mold parts for Ford, Toyota, and industrial clients at Seco Machine's factory just outside the city limits. APV Engineered Coatings' industrial adhesives and lubricants make their way across North America's borders too, bound for vehicles, planes, buildings, and more. Other local corporations have hooked into regional supply chains and grown as a result. For Akron to recover, more need to follow their path.

Over the past forty years, a drive for efficiency and profits, combined with an information and communications revolution and a pro-trade policy consensus, produced a new form of globalization. That globalization was characterized by regionalization and the rise of three big economic hubs. The nations within each region turned to their neighbors, making things together, buying and selling among themselves, and learning from and entertaining one another. Integration fostered innovation. As companies and countries collaborated and competed, they spurred industrial competitiveness, lowered prices, brought greater variety, and boosted prosperity. This globalization and regionalization created vast wealth and lifted hundreds of millions of people out of poverty. They also disrupted industries, bankrupted companies, displaced workers, and increased inequality, especially in wealthier nations.

Now, new technologies, changing demographics, shifting political winds, and the heightened awareness of the risks of pandemics and natural disasters are again changing government and business calculations. Cheap outsourcing is being replaced by high-tech, flexible production. Just-in-time delivery is yielding to just-in-case planning. These changes in globalization favor the United States. Still, they also reinforce the benefits of regionalization over any nation, including the United States, trying to go it alone.

To take full advantage of the next phase of global commerce and improve the prospects for more workers and citizens, the United States needs domestic reforms. It needs to better train students and workers for the jobs to come and bolster support for those who will inevitably lose out. It needs to build and rebuild its infrastructure and its innovation edge.

Making the most of the United States' opportunity also means turning to our neighbors, to gain the benefits that come from combining different skills, resources, and know-how and also from creating bigger markets and better export platforms for each other and the world. The United States' competitors have regionalized to their advantage. The United States should copy them. To beat them, the United States needs to join them.

Growth through Trade

Despite the United States' leading role in setting global commercial rules, its economy remains relatively inward looking. Even with a big boost in trade in the twenty-first century, not much more than a tenth of the U.S. economy caters to people beyond its borders. Only 1 percent of U.S. companies export at all. For decades, with the world's largest market right here at home, there was little need.[2]

Still, more than 95 percent of the world's buyers live beyond our shores, and every day they have more to spend. These consumers will be the next big purchasers of cars and computers, movies and machines. As they get richer, they will eat more corn, pork, soy, and wheat, buoying farm prices. As their economies grow, they can boost our own—but only if U.S. companies and brands get a foothold in these newly booming markets. To boost U.S.-based manufacturing and jobs, boardrooms and the halls of Congress alike should foster a more export-friendly environment.

Exporting more will help American workers. Jobs in export-focused industries already pay more than average, as they can take advantage of a much bigger consumer base and the international competition they face makes these companies more productive.[3] And businesses that export tend to be more stable and employ more people than those that cater only to Americans.[4]

So how can the United States get a larger slice of the growing global market? In today's regional world, exports are more competitive when countries make them together. Germany provides a telling lesson. Over the past three decades, it became an export powerhouse. The goods and services it sends abroad have more than doubled as a share of its economy, reaching nearly half of its GDP.[5]

This success resulted in large part from Germany's decision, starting in the 1990s, to collaborate with eastern Europe. Volkswagen opened factories in the Czech Republic and Slovakia; Mercedes-Benz built new plants in Hungary and Slovenia. Germany's famed Mittelstand also made the leap. These midsized companies now make everything from gummy bears to car parts across the newer EU members. By shifting part of their production east, they took advantage of significant differences in workforces, labor costs, and industrial clusters. Yes, there were bumpy moments, as significant wage gaps between East and West spurred outsourcing.[6] Still, as regional supply chains thickened, Germany's businesses boosted overall sales, profits, and, ultimately, jobs at home.

China's export boom followed a similar pattern of relying on deep ties to other countries. More of the money, technology, and manufacturing know-how that helped China quickly scale the socioeconomic ladder came from nearby countries than from those on other continents. For years, over a quarter of what went into China's exports came from somewhere else (nearly half for tech-related goods), much of it coming from China's neighbors.[7] As China has climbed from apprentice to master, its industries and government have further seeded regional supply chains, stepping up investment and recently cementing ties with regional trade agreements.

If the United States wants to replicate these successes, it too will need a regional strategy. As Germany and China (and other Asian nations before it) have already found, countries are much more likely to be able to foster specialized manufacturing clusters and scale their production in partnership rather than alone. And while automation and technology favor the United States and other high-wage nations compared to the past, labor-costs advantages are not gone. In this world of international commerce, the way to make U.S.-made products as good, fast, and affordable as their competition is to bring in at least some parts from elsewhere. The notable size and variation within the fifty U.S. states still doesn't match the heft and diversity of Europe's 450 million citizens and twenty-seven nations, much less the heterogeneity and scale that is coming together in Asia. And looking regionally opens up whole new markets and potential customers for U.S. part and component makers, both in those nations themselves and through the reach that the United States' neighbors have throughout the world.

The regional push doesn't have to be limited to just Mexico and Canada. Central American and Caribbean countries can and should play a role, too. Already shared geography and preferential trade rules have enabled a partial revival of apparel making in the Western Hemisphere. Guatemala, Honduras, El Salvador, and the Dominican Republic have enticed big brands back by taking smaller orders with more colors spread out across more sizes, a plus for buyers dealing with the heightened uncertainty of ecommerce sales. They can get clothes to U.S. wearers faster, reducing the time from design sketch to Amazon box from Asia's six months to Central America's ten weeks. And as labor-intensive cutting, sewing, and gluing have ramped up around the Caribbean Sea, so have orders for Georgia-made zippers and North Carolinian snaps, buttons, and elastics. The expansion of regional textile supply chains has lifted exports all around.[8]

Still, for the United States, its nearest neighbors provide the most advantageous ties. Canada and Mexico are already where most U.S. exporters make their foreign sales, taking advantage of their proximity, cultural ties, legal certainties, and special access for U.S. companies through the USMCA. This familiarity can help others that are first venturing abroad. Feeding into Mexican or Canadian assembly and manufacturing provides preferential access for U.S. suppliers to over half of the world's markets through Mexican and Canadian free-trade agreements, which are much more expansive than what the United States has achieved on its own (or than Central American and Caribbean nations have gained). The size of Mexico's and Canada's workforces, their consumer purchasing power, far greater access to global markets, and the comprehensiveness of the USMCA trade agreement make them more vital for the United States' future economic competitiveness than other nearby nations are, at least to start.

These factors mean that the two countries are the best places for U.S. manufacturers to build supply chains that benefit Americans as well as Mexicans and Canadians. Yes, Mexico's lower wages draw labor-intensive sewing, machining, welding, and assembling south. But studies show that new hires in Mexico create jobs in the United States too. Apparel makers in Puebla or Tlaxcala buy U.S.-made Velcro and threads. Mexican plants buy U.S.-made machines and parts. And while assembly moves south, management and services often do not. Instead, as sales rise, corporations bring on more U.S.-based engineers, coders, designers, bankers, and marketers.[9]

Cheaper production chains help work stay on the continent rather than go farther abroad. Critics of globalization will argue that while these shifts may help U.S.-based knowledge workers, they hurt their less skilled brethren. Here, there is an element of truth, even as technological advances play a much bigger role in eroding these sorts of jobs. But given the reality of global competition, turning to geographic partners makes it much more likely that lower-skilled jobs will stick around and, in some cases, even thrive. When things are made in Mexico or Canada, U.S. suppliers are far more likely to remain in business, keeping their own assembly lines running and employing knowledge workers and less skilled laborers alike. If assembly moves to China, Vietnam, Hungary, or Romania, so do so many of the other factories and jobs that feed into the production process. Looking back at the China Shock literature and its findings, one is struck by the lack of evidence that Mexico had similar costs with regard to U.S. jobs, despite the real wage differences. This suggests that for lower-skilled workers, free-trade agreements and distance really matter, as imports from China (with which the United States has no special agreement or proximity) rarely contain much of anything made in the USA.

It won't be enough for U.S. companies to make high-quality, affordable goods for export if other countries won't let them in. U.S. companies often face higher barriers when they go abroad than when their foreign competitors come here.[10] This is in part because the United States has signed relatively few free-trade agreements, giving U.S. companies preferred access to less than 10 percent of the world's markets. The United States' problem isn't too much free trade; it's not enough free trade.[11]

History shows that when the United States does pass free-trade agreements, exports rise. During the first ten years of NAFTA, U.S. sales north and south outpaced those to the rest of the world. After deals with Israel, Colombia, South Korea, and Central America, U.S. exports to those countries grew faster too, creating hundreds of thousands of new jobs.[12]

Yet today, the United States has no trade agenda. The critical supply-chain report released during the first six months of the Biden administration called on the nation to rethink where things are made in order to enhance national security, increase domestic equity through more good-paying jobs, and spur homegrown innovation. It ambitiously recommends reshoring mining, processing, and manufacturing of critical materials and products to the United States or in some cases to its geopolitical allies.[13] The report said next to nothing about opening global markets for U.S.-made goods or services.

To help U.S.-based companies become more globally competitive and U.S.-based jobs be more secure, the United States needs more NAFTAs. A good first step would be to rejoin abandoned deals and revive stalled negotiations. The Comprehensive and Progressive Agreement for Trans-Pacific Partnership, or CPTPP, would give U.S. companies greater access to some 500 million consumers. A deal with the EU would make it easier to sell U.S. chickens, vegetables, cars, machines, and dozens of other goods and services to another 450 million potential buyers. These deals would lessen the relative costs for U.S. makers of intermediate goods wanting to sell into international supply chains, too. And the comprehensive nature of recent trade negotiations means that they bring benefits beyond just lowering tariffs. They can help U.S. businesses compete by opening up bidding for lucrative foreign government contracts, bringing other countries' labor and environmental standards more in line with our own, protecting intellectual property, and taking on state subsidies. Free-trade agreements can be designed or structured to take into account broader worker and societal interests than some of those negotiated in the past. What we have seen with China is that when the United States has no special access or arrangements, its workers are sure to lose out.

Even if the United States isn't willing to sign new agreements of its own—a tricky proposition in today's political climate—it can benefit from its neighbors. The USMCA trade accord with Mexico and Canada gives the United States a larger market than it has alone: 160 million more consumers and almost $3 trillion more every year in spending.

And, in addition to the two countries' own consumers, Mexico and Canada already have much-better access to world markets. Mexico has preferred trading arrangements with fifty nations, representing over 60 percent of the globe's GDP. Canada has a similarly wide reach, encompassing some one and a half billion consumers. By supplying Mexican and Canadian exporters, U.S.-based operations can grow beyond North America. And honing products for Mexico's consumers can provide insight into customers in other emerging markets.[14]

Today, foreign inputs represent roughly a tenth of the overall value of U.S. exports. On that measure, the United States lags behind Germany, France, the United Kingdom, Canada, South Korea, and most other industrialized nations. Compared with those countries, the United States isn't all that integrated into global or regional supply chains. That means that it is losing some of the competitive advantages that come with international diversification.[15]

There is a trade-off here. The United States' relative economic isolation means that more of each appliance, machine, and drug made here is made by American workers. But isolation also makes many U.S.-based businesses less nimble, efficient, and globally competitive. Their higher costs and prices dampen both domestic and international sales. At home, American families choose to repair rather than replace the washing machine that keeps breaking down, or they delay home renovations when the costs of building materials rise.[16] This dampens local sales and retail jobs and leads to fewer factory orders and worker shifts. Internationally, U.S.-made products become priced out. The U.S. labor force gains a larger slice of a smaller domestic pie and a shrinking slice of the growing international one as the world's consumers buy from others. By shying away from, rather than championing, freer trade, the United States is squandering its edge.

Making North America Economically Stronger

The United States won't compete effectively on the world stage if it doesn't embrace its neighbors. Regional supply chains mean that the fates of Americans, Canadians, and Mexicans are linked. The policies to support them should be linked too.

The United States' physical ties to the world could use an upgrade. The country's infrastructure is more geared toward moving things around the country than in and out of it. U.S. ports host fewer trips and smaller ships than Asian ones do. U.S. highways too often fail to link up to those ports, slowing goods and parts headed in or out.

Connections with the United States' neighbors are particularly shoddy. A new train bridge linking Brownsville, Texas, and Matamoros, Mexico, in 2015 was the first built between the United States and Mexico in over a century. Many other rail lines stop before they reach the border. Interstates often don't hook up with thoroughfares in Canada and Mexico. And the U.S. government hasn't been willing to spend money to fix things. For example, a new bridge between Detroit and Windsor, Ontario, North America's busiest crossing, only happened when Canada agreed to pick up the whole $2 billion tab, including a $250 million customs plaza on the U.S. side.

This penny-wise, pound-foolish strategy slows goods and raises logistical costs, making North American products more expensive. As the United States looks in the coming years to invest over $1 trillion in infrastructure, it should prioritize regional connections to speed the movement of goods and services across the country and over its borders. It should encourage and work with its neighbors to do the same to create more seamless North American connections.

The U.S. workforce is one of its advantages. But in a regional-supply-chain world, U.S. jobs will continue to depend on the performance and productivity of workers and factories next door. If one part fails, the whole production chain falls apart. As a result, the benefits of better education and training and safer work environments in one place will help workers and companies in all.

Across the three countries, there are already big skills gaps. Companies increasingly say that they can't find workers able to do what they now need: too few are able to analyze data, create software, or oversee high-tech manufacturing. There are too few welders, teachers, renewable-energy technicians, and people to professionally care for others.[17] These disparities between job needs and worker qualifications in the region's labor force will just grow as the nature of work transforms. By facing these workforce challenges at least in part together, the three nations will have a larger and more diverse working-age population to draw on to help ease the mismatches. And together, a larger complementary labor pool can make North America more attractive for future investments than any one nation alone is.

Many of these new openings will be in what people call the "knowledge economy." Educating more engineers, programmers, and technical designers means continuing the expansion of science, technology, engineering, and mathematics (STEM) course offerings across the three nations. Yet tomorrow's workforce will have to move beyond statistics, computer science, and engineering as machines and programs take over calculations and coding. Liberal arts education needs to make a comeback as well, as the most valued (and best paid) workers will be those skilled in creative thinking, problem solving, and drawing connections among issues, operations, and departments. Writers, managers, deal makers, and experts in guiding and protecting information flows will be in high demand too in each of North America's countries.

The opportunities won't only be for people with higher degrees. Automated factories still need machinists, boilermakers, and electricians. Vocational training and apprenticeships can offer solid paths to millions of jobs that will open up over the next decade.[18] In other areas, algorithms can make advanced degrees less necessary: with big data, nurse practitioners can diagnose thousands of diseases as accurately as doctors with years more training, and workers restocking shelves could potentially expand to filling online orders and managing inventories.[19]

The United States, Canada, and Mexico must rethink the tools their citizens need and reinvent the ways they get them. There is much to gain from doing at least part of this together, as designing programs and policies for the region's workforce is another way to up North America's competitive edge. Stronger language skills, cultural ties, and enhanced cross-border knowledge and understanding will allow people to work more effectively with their counterparts across the continent. And this integration, through regionally oriented education and professional training, can offer a bigger and more seamless potential workforce and industrial ecosystem to entice companies with multistep production needs to come or to stay.

Yet today North America's students tend to look farther away than next door. Americans who study abroad are more likely to head to Europe, South Africa, Japan, and even Costa Rica than to Mexico or Canada. Only around forty thousand Canadians and Mexicans make their way into U.S.

classrooms each year, far fewer than Chinese, South Korean, and Vietnamese undergraduates and graduate students.

There have been fitful efforts to boost North America's educational connections. As NAFTA began, higher-education institutions joined together too. Yet the new cross-border associations and umbrella organizations never grew much beyond databases of interested schools and small exchange programs. In 2011, the U.S. State Department launched the 100,000 Strong in the Americas initiative to bring Latin American students to schools across dozens of states. Mexico responded with a plan to fill a similar number of slots all on its own. Yet these programs soon foundered, left underfunded and underutilized. More often, U.S. educational outreach has ignored its neighbors. For instance, neither Mexicans nor Canadians are eligible for the State Department program that recruits international students to community colleges.[20]

Efforts to educate the continent's citizens and future workforce need to be revived and, this time, sustained. From high school exchanges to cross-border college instruction, internships to vocational programs, regional education and exchange will enhance the business advantages of proximity. Joint research too can bring regional gains, as inventions, innovations, and new knowledge are likely to stay and prosper here.

Education outside the classroom is just as important. Learning won't end in your twenties anymore. People are living and working longer; changes in the job market are happening faster. Apprenticeships and other hands-on experiences need to be a bigger part of the mix to help people pick up new skills, supplementing, or even substituting for, classrooms. These too should span borders, strengthening each of the fast-evolving steps along regional supply chains and border-crossing industries.

To bolster the continent's workforce, the three nations need to recognize skills acquired elsewhere in North America. This requires creating common professional credentials with set minimum standards, criteria, and evaluations, ensuring that the holders have similar mastery of their chosen trade. These qualifications then need to be more transferable, not just across states but also among North America's nations. This will help to alleviate workforce mismatches and provide a larger and more stable base of employees.

In a world of more remote work and online learning, movement becomes less important. But it will still be necessary. Production lines cross borders; so too should workers. Temporary visas enable workers to do internships or complete short-term assignments, gaining knowledge and keeping regional supply chains efficiently running. Longer-term migration paths allow workers to follow jobs and fill labor-market gaps.

International scholars are the lifeblood of U.S. science, medicine, and engineering. So are the millions of other migrants who contribute to our economy and society. Migrants are even more important to the North. Nearly a quarter of Canada's population was born abroad, and these newer entrants are on average more highly educated than the general citizenry is. Migrants are a much smaller part of Mexico's social and economic fabric, though there many individuals from abroad play prominent roles in business, finance, and academia. In each of North America's nations, migrants tend to bring desirable skills and add dynamism to the economic fortunes of the communities where they settle.[21]

The United States in particular is throwing away its demographic and entrepreneurial advantages by undercutting the ability of people with skills and gumption, from PhDs and engineers to construction workers and caregivers, to come and prosper. Shutting people out makes it much more likely that innovation will happen elsewhere. Foreign companies will be the ones to bring new or better products to market. Foreign workers will be the ones to make them. Today the United States has too few pathways for regional migrants, especially those from Mexico and Central America, to come either temporarily or permanently. These tough immigration laws make it harder to keep jobs at home, as studies show that in the face of restrictions, companies send more operations abroad. By hampering the pooling of talent across North America, the United States makes it less likely that some jobs will stay here. The cost of this xenophobia reverberates in Mexico and Canada as well, as their suppliers and assemblers close too when firms go farther abroad. Migration has long been fundamental to North America's demographic advantage; it is not the time to lose it.

Infrastructure, education, and migration policies will always have a national and even local tilt. And they should. Still, better cross-border connections; transferrable credentials, licenses, and diplomas; more business visas; and longer-term migration avenues would make the region as a whole more productive. And that will make it easier for companies to keep operations on the continent as they cater to markets and consumers at home and around the world.

North America's Industrial Strategy

Industrial policy is making a comeback. COVID-19 has made hot topics out of risk, resilience, and national security in supply chains. Here too a North American strategy will be more effective and secure than a national one. To be sure, some products and sectors will be deemed too vital to be allowed to go abroad. Governments will simply pay to support solely domestic production. In U.S. discussions, these may in the end include a set of vital medicines, the mining and refining of critical minerals such as rare earths, and particular advanced technologies such as semiconductors and high-capacity batteries. But in most sectors and for most nations, governments will find that they can't keep entire industries effectively, efficiently, and safely at home.

Regionalization gives companies and nations a leg up by diversifying risk. Moving a company's factories back from Wuhan to Wichita won't make them any less vulnerable to natural disasters and pandemics, as long as they're still concentrated in one place. Just look at what happened in the months after Hurricane Maria hit Puerto Rico in 2017. Hospitals across the United States ran low on IV bags, surgical scalpels, and a number of common drugs as dozens of factories on the island struggled to reopen.[22] Had drug companies distributed their production across the continent, no one disaster would have threatened supplies all that much.

Stockpiles too will benefit from greater geographic dispersion. For energy, rare earth minerals, medical equipment, and other products deemed necessary for national security, bringing in nearby allies can lessen risk. This goes for both stashing actual inventories and ramping up potential capacity. Supplies and supply chains are more resilient to unforeseen shocks when they are spread out.

Hurricane Maria and other disruptions have taught businesses that whatever the flaws of global supply chains, fully reshoring production to the United States brings its own problems. Governments need to learn this lesson as well. To truly strengthen U.S.-centered supply chains, the United

States needs more, not less, international collaboration. And a big part of the answer should be to turn to Mexico and Canada to develop diversified, but still relatively local, production systems. As the United States maps out and tries to rejigger its critical supply chains, it should enlist its neighbors to the cause. This means spreading strategic reserves and government stockpiles across the three nations. It means including Mexico and Canada in new schematics and contracts for critical goods such as personal protective equipment, medicines, minerals, and semiconductors. It means shifting Washington's mindset from "Buy American" to "Buy North American."

By building better infrastructure, upping investment, streamlining customs and regulations, expanding regional educational opportunities and credentials, and enabling the freer movement of people and professionals between nations, the United States, Mexico, and Canada can use their differences to their advantage. By throwing in together, each country will be safer, sounder, and more competitive.

Even as globalization is changing to the United States' benefit, the country faces fierce competition from a fast-growing China and a host of other developing countries eager to follow it. One option is to try to keep others down. But blocking the advancement of other countries will never be as effective as outpacing them. Trying to preserve the past through protectionism only weighs down the future. Yet that seems to be a road the United States is considering. Just when the country is poised to come again into its economic own, it is closing itself off, fighting the last, somewhat-misunderstood round of globalization.

We need a bolder strategy—and one that understands and takes into account the regionalization that has been the heart of globalization, particularly in the underlying latticework of supply chains, and that has upped the competitive ante around the world. This won't change. Today's and tomorrow's upheavals are making regional economic hubs all the more important. Their closeness in miles, time zones, legal ground rules, and cultural references complements their differences in labor, finance, natural resources, and market access to provide competitive advantages that no nation can achieve by itself.

The United States remains the envy of much of the world. It has abun-

dant land, water, natural resources, advanced technologies, and an educated and growing population. As we move deeper into the twenty-first
century, many of the United States' challenges will be easier to overcome
than those of Europe or Asia.

Luckily, our system not only allows reinvention but reveres it. Americans already know that trade is helpful—polls show that three out of four
see it as an opportunity, not a threat.[23] Still, for supporters and skeptics
alike, U.S. leaders need to lay out a compelling vision that goes beyond
trade to explain why links to the world, and above all to U.S. neighbors,
are vital for a more competitive and inclusive U.S. future. They need to
show how the United States gains strength from geographic diversity.

If the United States wants to remain a manufacturing powerhouse, a
services leader, and a bustling economy, we can't do it alone. Our best
path to growth and prosperity lies with the countries closest to us. Looking outward together is the best way for the Akrons of the United States
to prosper once again.

Acknowledgments

The Council on Foreign Relations has been my professional home now for fifteen years. Richard Haass and Jim Lindsay have achieved the feat of creating a work environment that is intellectually curious and rigorous and personally warm and collegial. It thrives too due to my Senior Fellow colleagues, so many of whom have been generous with their time, scholarly insights, and many a laugh over the years. Thanks too to those throughout CFR for their support for my work and for their friendship: Amy Baker, Nancy Bodurtha, Patrick Costello, Trish Dorff, Irina Faskianos, Doug Halsey, Stacey LaFollete, Bob McMahon, Jean-Michel Oriol, Shira Schwartz, Anya Schmemann, Lisa Shields, and Iva Zoric among them.

This book wouldn't have been as well researched or visually appealing without the Research Associates and interns that helped me along the way. From fleshing out the initial idea for the book with research memos and literature reviews to the final copyediting, a deep thanks go to Chloé Mauvais, Sofia Ramirez, Natalia Cote-Muñoz, Brian Harper, Aysar Gharaibeh, Sara Torres, Harold Cárdenas, Sean Silbert, Jessie Wall, Hannah To, Isak Jones, Sannan Dhillon, Cecília Godoy Albuquerque de Almeida, Sophia Campbell, and Erin Straight.

I am deeply grateful to the dozens of policy makers, scholars, business leaders, and thinkers who generously offered their time, analyses, and connections in interviews across the three continents, enriching the book.

I am thankful too to the many readers of various drafts. The region-specific chapters are all the better due to the feedback from Mark Copelovitch, Nils aus dem Moore, and Katrin Suder on Europe; Brad Sester and Miles Kahler on Asia; Christopher Wilson and Nate Parish Flannery on North America. Ted Alden, Stephanie Junger Moat, Matthias Matthijs, Jamie Trowbridge, Alasdair Philips-Robins, and James Gibney read most and often all of the manuscript. Richard Haass, Jim Lindsay, and two anonymous reviewers read it more than once. Their critiques, queries, and suggestions have made the final book all the stronger.

Thanks to Lisa Adams at Garamond Agency for her help from idea to book proposal to final manuscript draft. And I appreciate the dedication of Jaya Chatterjee, Eva Skewes, and the many others at Yale University Press who have brought the book to fruition.

The biggest thanks go to my family. Jamie, Lillias, and Beatrice Trowbridge took my weekend absences and copious time in front of the computer in stride and with good humor, offering support and sympathy when I most needed it. They are as excited as I am to see it published. I dedicate it to them.

Notes

Introduction

1. Rajan, Raghuram, Paolo Volpin, and Luigi Zingales. "The Eclipse of the U.S. Tire Industry." In *Mergers and Productivity,* edited by Steven N. Kaplan, 51–92. Chicago: University of Chicago Press, 2000. http://www.nber.org/chapters/c8649.

2. Weiner, Richard. "Industrial Leagues Put Akron on Hoops Map." *Crain's Cleveland Business,* February 19, 2017. https://www.crainscleveland.com/article /20170219/NEWS/170219808/industrial-leagues-put-akron-on-basketball-map; "Truckers Set Back Tapers, 103 to 101." *New York Times,* February 4, 1961. http:// timesmachine.nytimes.com/timesmachine/1961/02/04/118897628.html.

3. Krisetya, Markus, Larry Lairson, and Alan Mauldin. "Global Internet Map 2021." TeleGeography, 2021. https://global-internet-map-2021.telegeography.com/.

4. Neubert, Jonas. "Exploring the Supply Chain of the Pfizer/BioNtech and Moderna COVID-19 Vaccines." *JonasNeubert.com* (blog), January 10, 2021. https:// blog.jonasneubert.com/2021/01/10/exploring-the-supply-chain-of-the-pfizer-biontech -and-moderna-covid-19-vaccines; Johnson, Carolyn Y. "A Vial, a Vaccine and Hopes for Slowing a Pandemic—How a Shot Comes to Be." *Washington Post,* November 17, 2020. https://www.washingtonpost.com/health/2020/11/17/coronavirus-vaccine -manufacturing; Hope, Michael J., Barbara Mui, Paulo Jia Ching Lin, Christopher Barbosa, Thomas Madden, Steven M. Ansell, and Xinyao Du. "Lipid Nanoparticle Formulations." WO2018081480A1, issued May 3, 2018. https://patents.google .com/patent/WO2018081480A1/en; Thermo Fisher Scientific. "Site ISO Certifications." Accessed May 18, 2021, https://www.thermofisher.com/us/en/home/tech nical-resources/manufacturing-site-iso-certifications.html; Geiger, Marion. "Corona-Impfstoffe in Produktion: Eine Logistische Herausforderung." *ZDF Heute,* February 11, 2020. https://www.zdf.de/uri/bfd22bdd-a846-49a8-ba02-c3d0057f643c; SCHOTT: Glass Made of Ideas. "SCHOTT Inaugurates New Production Facility at Its Gujarat

Plant, Production Capacity to Increase by 50%." November 28, 2019. https://www
.schott.com/brazil/portuguese/news/press.html?NID=com5707&freturl=%2Fbrazil
%2Fportuguese%2Fcompany%2Fbusiness_units.html.

5. Friedman, Thomas L. *The World Is Flat: A Brief History of the Twenty-First Century*. New York: Farrar, Straus and Giroux, 2005.

6. World Bank. "World Integrated Trade Solution," 2019. https://wits.worldbank
.org/. Author's calculations based on World Bank data.

7. United Nations Conference on Trade and Development (UNCTAD). "Trade Structure by Partner." In *e-Handbook of Statistics 2020*. Geneva: UNCTAD, December 7, 2020. https://stats.unctad.org/handbook/MerchandiseTrade/ByPartner.html. Author's calculations based on UNCTAD trade data.

8. World Bank. "Trade (% of GDP)—United States, East Asia & Pacific, European Union, World, North America," 2021. https://data.worldbank.org/indicator
/NE.TRD.GNFS.ZS?locations=US-Z4-EU-1W-XU. The World Bank calculates this measure as the sum of exports and imports of goods and services measured as a share of gross domestic product. World average is 60 percent of GDP, U.S. trade is 26 percent of GDP, North America's trade is 30 percent of GDP, East Asia and the Pacific's trade is 57 percent, and Europe's is 91 percent.

9. U.S. Census Bureau. "Trade in Goods with World, Seasonally Adjusted," July 2, 2021. https://www.census.gov/foreign-trade/balance/c0004.html#2000. Author's calculations based on U.S. Census Bureau data on U.S. trade in goods with the rest of the world.

10. Statista. "U.S. Exports of Trade Goods, by End-Use Commodity Category 2019," February 2020. https://www.statista.com/statistics/258796/volume-of-us
-exports-of-trade-goods-in-by-end-use-commodity-category/.

11. Hufbauer, Gary Clyde. "Why Globalization Pays." Peterson Institute for International Economics, June 28, 2016. https://www.piie.com/blogs/realtime-economic
-issues-watch/why-globalization-pays; Bergsten, C. Fred, ed. *The United States and the World Economy: Foreign Economic Policy for the next Decade*. Washington, DC: Peterson Institute for International Economics, 2005. The Peterson Institute's calculations cover the post–World War II era household incomes.

12. Slaughter, Matthew J. "The 'Exporting Jobs' Canard." *Wall Street Journal,* June 14, 2017. https://www.wsj.com/articles/the-exporting-jobs-canard-1497482039.

13. Desai, Mihir A., C. Fritz Foley, and James R. Hines. "Domestic Effects of the Foreign Activities of U.S. Multinationals." *American Economic Journal: Economic Policy* 1, no. 1 (February 2009): 181–203. https://doi.org/10.1257/pol.1.1.181.

14. Matthew J. Slaughter, unpublished paper.

15. Riker, David. "Export-Intensive Industries Pay More on Average: An Update." U.S. International Trade Commission, April 2015. https://www.usitc.gov
/publications/332/ec201504a.pdf.

16. Goldin, Claudia, and Lawrence Katz. *The Race between Education and Technology*. Cambridge, MA: National Bureau of Economic Research, 2007. https://doi

.org/10.3386/w12984; Acemoglu, Daron, and Pascual Restrepo. "The Race between Man and Machine: Implications of Technology for Growth, Factor Shares, and Employment." *American Economic Review* 108, no. 6 (June 2018): 1488–1542. https://doi.org/10.1257/aer.20160696; Western, Bruce, and Jake Rosenfeld. "Unions, Norms, and the Rise in U.S. Wage Inequality." *American Sociological Review* 76, no. 4 (August 2011): 513–37. https://doi.org/10.1177/0003122411414817.

17. Saad, Lydia. "Americans' Views on Trade in the Trump Era." Gallup, October 25, 2019. https://news.gallup.com/opinion/gallup/267770/americans-views -trade-trump-era.aspx.

18. Autor, David H., David Dorn, and Gordon H. Hanson. "The China Shock: Learning from Labor-Market Adjustment to Large Changes in Trade." *Annual Review of Economics* 8, no. 1 (October 31, 2016): 205–40. https://doi.org/10.1146 /annurev-economics-080315-015041; Reynolds, Alan. "Little-Known Facts about U.S. Trade with China." Cato Institute, March 30, 2016. https://www.cato.org/blog /little-known-facts-about-us-trade-china. Autor, Dorn, and Hanson in their paper do not quantify the jobs in other sectors those imports create, for instance, the many engineers, coders, and marketers at Apple who work on the iPhone. For a critique of their methodology, see Reynolds, "Little-Known Facts."

19. McLaren, John, and Shushanik Hakobyan. "Looking for Local Labor Market Effects of NAFTA." NBER Working Paper Series, no. 16535. National Bureau of Economic Research, November 2010, 49. https://doi.org/10.3386/w16535. McLaren and Hakobyan find no discernible effect on employment levels. They do find that wage growth was limited for people in exposed industries such as apparel and footwear and in factory towns, particularly for people who did not finish high school.

20. Koopman, Robert, William Powers, Zhi Wang, and Shang-Jin Wei. "Give Credit Where Credit Is Due: Tracing Value Added in Global Production Chains." National Bureau of Economic Research, September 2010. https://doi.org/10.3386 /w16426.

21. Trade Partnership Worldwide, "Trade and American Jobs: The Impact of Trade on U.S. and State-Level Employment: 2019 Update." March 2019. https:// tradepartnership.com/wp-content/uploads/2019/03/Trade-and-American-2019 -FINAL.pdf. Quoted in Wilson, Christopher. "Growing Together: Economic Ties between the United States and Mexico." Development Bank of Latin America, 2017, 61–65. https://www.wilsoncenter.org/sites/default/files/media/documents/publica tion/growing_together_economic_ties_between_the_united_states_and_mexico.pdf.

22. Koopman et al., "Give Credit."

23. World Bank, "World Integrated." Author's calculations based on World Bank data.

24. Larson, Greg, Norman Loayza, and Michael Woolcock. "The Middle-Income Trap: Myth or Reality?" Research & Policy Briefs. World Bank, March 1, 2016. https:// documents.worldbank.org/en/publication/documents-reports/documentdetail /965511468194956837/the-middle-income-trap-myth-or-reality.

25. Rodrik, Dani. "Premature Deindustrialization." National Bureau of Economic Research, February 2015. https://doi.org/10.3386/w20935.

26. Engel, Jakob, and Daria Taglioni. "The Middle-Income Trap and Upgrading along Global Value Chains." In *Global Value Chain Development Report 2017: Measuring and Analyzing the Impact of GVCs on Economic Development*, 119–34. Washington, DC: World Bank, 2017. https://www.wto.org/english/res_e/booksp_e/gvcs_report_2017.pdf.

27. While Richard Baldwin in his 2016 book *The Great Convergence* depicts the new round of globalization, what he calls the "second unbundling," beginning in roughly 1990 with the information and communications technology revolution, many of the underlying factors discussed here that encouraged regionalization, particularly in Europe and Asia, began accelerating in the 1970s and 1980s.

1. The Rise of Regional Supply Chains

1. Broner, Fernando, Tatiana Didier, Aitor Erce, and Sergio L. Schmukler. "Gross Capital Flows: Dynamics and Crises." *Journal of Monetary Economics* (Carnegie-NYU-Rochester Conference) 60, no. 1 (January 1, 2013): 113–33. https://doi.org/10.1016/j.jmoneco.2012.12.004; López, Gerardo García, and Livio Stracca. "Changing Patterns of Capital Flows." CGFS Papers, no. 66. Committee on the Global Financial System and the Bank for International Settlements, May 2021. https://www.bis.org/publ/cgfs66.htm; World Bank. "GDP (Constant 2010 US$)," 2020. https://data.worldbank.org/indicator/NY.GDP.MKTP.KD?end=2020&start=1961&view=chart. Gross capital flows include direct investment, portfolio investment, and other investments—primarily bank flows. These flows reached a peak in the middle of the first decade of the twenty-first century of $20 trillion, then plummeted with the 2008 global financial crisis. They never recovered the highs, in good part because European banks pulled back from global (as opposed to domestic and regional) lending. Author's calculations based on data from the Committee on the Global Financial System and the World Bank.

2. Roser, Max. "Tourism." Our World in Data, 2017. https://ourworldindata.org/tourism#citation.

3. UNCTAD. "Global Value Chains and Development," 2013. https://unctad.org/en/PublicationsLibrary/diae2013d1_en.pdf.

4. Gereffi, Gary. *Global Value Chains and Development: Redefining the Contours of 21st Century Capitalism*. New York: Cambridge University Press, 2019. A vast literature on global value chains has developed a typology of varying types of corporate governance and the role of lead firms with regard to their relations and power over outside suppliers.

5. Nike, Inc. "Where Nike Products Are Made," February 2021. http://manufacturingmap.nikeinc.com/.

6. Gereffi, *Global Value Chains*. These ranges of buyer and supplier relationships illustrate those conceptualized in the global value chain literature. Luxottica and Ikea are examples of hierarchical and integrated firms, Apple has created what is called a

"captive governance structure" (with a lead firm and captive suppliers), and Nike uses a relational structure with suppliers that then contract out component and material inputs themselves.

7. Broner et al., "Gross Capital Flows." Author's calculations based on data collected.

8. Ghemawat, Pankaj, and Steven A. Altman. *DHL Global Connectedness Index 2014*. Deutsche Post, DHL, October 2014, 292, https://web.archive.org/web/2021 0429002224/https://www.dhl.com/content/dam/Campaigns/gci2014/down loads/dhl_gci_2014_study_high.pdf. Author's calculations based on data.

9. World Bank. *World Development Report 2020: Trading for Development in the Age of Global Value Chains*. Washington, DC: World Bank, 2020. https://doi.org /10.1596/978-1-4648-1457-0.

10. Levinson, Marc. *The Box: How the Shipping Container Made the World Smaller and the World Economy Bigger*. Princeton, NJ: Princeton University Press, 2008. https:// doi.org/10.2307/j.ctvcszztg.

11. DHL. "History from 1960 to Present," 2002. http://wap.dhl.com/info/history .html.

12. "Rates on Overseas Phone Calls Decline." *New York Times*, May 19, 1981. https://www.nytimes.com/1982/05/19/garden/rates-on-overseas-phone-calls -decline.html; California Cable & Telecommunications Association. "History of Cable," 2020. https://calcable.org/learn/history-of-cable/. Author's calculations based on the U.S. population in 1981 and the number of annual overseas calls.

13. Roy, Isabel. "This Is the Best-Selling Phone of All Time (It's Not iPhone)." *Reader's Digest*, April 5, 2020. https://www.rd.com/article/nokia-all-time-best-selling -phone/.

14. Raz, Guy. "Compaq Computers: Rod Canion." *How I Built This with Guy Raz*, NPR, March 25, 2019. https://www.npr.org/2019/03/22/705892242/compaq -computers-rod-canion.

15. Comen, Evan. "Check Out How Much a Computer Cost the Year You Were Born." *USA Today*, June 22, 2018. https://www.usatoday.com/story/tech/2018/06 /22/cost-of-a-computer-the-year-you-were-born/36156373/.

16. Kulkarni, Rahul. "Evolution of CAD—From Light Pens to Synchronous Technology!" *Technical Illustration* (blog), March 4, 2017. https://medium.com/technical -illustration/evolution-of-cad-from-light-pens-to-synchronous-technology-549cc8eef5d0.

17. Grand View Research. "Customer Relationship Management Market Report, 2021–2028." May 2021. https://www.grandviewresearch.com/industry-analysis/cus tomer-relationship-management-crm-market.

18. Bank of England. "CHAPS," July 19, 2021. http://www.bankofengland.co .uk/payment-and-settlement/chaps; OFX. "What Is CHIPS: Clearing House Interbank Payments System?" Accessed July 27, 2021. https://www.ofx.com/en-us/faqs /what-is-chips/; EBA Clearing. "Single Payments: EURO1." Accessed March 26, 2021. https://www.ebaclearing.eu/services/euro1/overview/. In 1970, CHIPS (Clearing House Interbank Payment System) began moving dollars electronically inter-

nationally. This was followed by other currency-specific systems: CHAPS (Clearing House Automated Payment System) for pound sterling transactions started in 1984, and the EURO1 platform began with the start of the euro in 1999. In 2002, a platform called CLS began clearing trades across eighteen different foreign currencies and between its sixty-six members. This system now handles over half of all foreign exchange transactions.

19. "Credit Card." *Encyclopedia Britannica Online,* March 4, 2021. https://www .britannica.com/topic/credit-card.

20. UNCTAD. *World Investment Report 2020: International Production beyond the Pandemic.* 30th ed. Geneva: United Nations, 2020. https://unctad.org/system/files /official-document/wir2020_en.pdf; Lund, Susan, Toos Daruvala, Richard Dobbs, Philipp Härle, Ju-Hon Kwek, and Ricardo Falcón. "Financial Globalization: Retreat or Reset?" McKinsey Global Institute, March 1, 2013. https://www.mckinsey.com /featured-insights/employment-and-growth/financial-globalization.

21. WTO. "Principles of the Trading System." November 2020. https://www .wto.org/english/thewto_e/whatis_e/tif_e/fact2_e.htm.

22. World Bank. "The Tokyo Round: Results and Implications for Developing Countries." Working Paper No. 372. World Bank, 1980. http://documents1.world bank.org/curated/en/927621468764703995/pdf/multiopage.pdf.

23. World Bank. "Trade (% of GDP)," 2020. https://data.worldbank.org/indi cator/NE.TRD.GNFS.ZS?locations=US-Z4-EU-1W-XU. Author's calculations based on World Bank data.

24. Ghemawat and Altman, *DHL Global,* 16.

25. Ghemawat and Altman, *DHL Global,* 322.

26. Isil, Erel, Rose C. Liao, and Michael S. Weisbach. "Determinants of Cross-Border Mergers and Acquisitions." *Journal of Finance* 67, no. 3 (2012): 1045–82. http://citeseerx.ist.psu.edu/viewdoc/download?doi=10.1.1.377.4529&rep=rep1 &type=pdf.

27. Sunesen, Eva Rytter, Tine Jeppesen, and Jonas Juul Henriksen. "The World in Europe, Global FDI Flows towards Europe." *ESPON EGTC,* 2018, 2. https:// www.copenhageneconomics.com/dyn/resources/Publication/publicationPDF/0 /440/1525770844/espon-fdi-08-main-report-intra-european-fdi.pdf.

28. Ghemawat and Altman, *DHL Global,* 83; Oh, Chang Hoon, Timo Sohl, and Alan Rugman. "Regional and Product Diversification and the Performance of Retail Multinationals." *Journal of International Management* 21, no. 3 (2015): 220–34.

29. Rugman, Alan. *The Regional Multinationals: MNEs and "Global" Strategic Management.* Cambridge: Cambridge University Press, 2005.

30. Rugman, Alan M., and Alain Verbeke. "A Perspective on Regional and Global Strategies of Multinational Enterprises." *Journal of International Business Studies* 35, no. 1 (2004): 3–18. Quoted in Ghemawat, Pankaj. *Redefining Global Strategy: Crossing Borders in a World Where Differences Still Matter.* Cambridge, MA: Harvard Business School Press, 2007. The ten companies found in the study to be truly "tri-

regional," in decreasing order of total sales revenues, are IBM, Sony, Philips, Nokia, Intel, Canon, Coca-Cola, Flextronics, Christian Dior, and LVMH.

31. Deutsche Bank. *Deutsche Bank Annual Report 2019,* 2020. https://www.db .com/ir/en/download/Deutsche_Bank_Annual_Report_2019.pdf; Barclays PLC. *Barclays PLC Annual Report 2019,* 2020. https://home.barclays/content/dam/home -barclays/documents/investor-relations/reports-and-events/annual-reports/2019 /Barclays%20PLC%20Annual%20Report%202019.pdf; Bank of America. *Bank of America Annual Report 2019,* 2020. http://investor.bankofamerica.com/static-files/898007fd -033d-4f32-8470-c1f316c73b24; JPMorgan Chase & Co. *JPMorgan Chase & Co. Annual Report 2019,* 2020. https://www.jpmorganchase.com/corporate/investor-relations /document/annualreport-2019.pdf. European net revenues represent 67 percent of total for Deutsche Bank, and European income represents 63 percent of total for Barclays. Over 89 percent of Bank of America's net income and 78 percent of JP Morgan's revenue comes from North America.

32. Rugman, *Regional Multinationals,* 97.

33. Ghemawat and Altman, *DHL Global,* 12.

34. Ghemawat and Altman, *DHL Global,* 92.

35. "Sometimes It Just Gets Lost in Translation." *ProLingo,* March 16, 2016. https://www.prolingo.com/blog/sometimes-it-just-gets-lost-in-translation/; James, Geoffrey. "20 Epic Fails in Global Branding." *Inc.,* October 29, 2014. https://www .inc.com/geoffrey-james/the-20-worst-brand-translations-of-all-time.html.

36. Walmart. *Walmart Annual Report 2019,* 2020. https://s2.q4cdn.com/0565 32643/files/doc_financials/2019/annual/Walmart-2019-AR-Final.pdf.

37. Vodafone Group PLC. *Annual Report 2019,* 2019, 111, 125, 244. https://www .vodafone.com/content/dam/vodcom/Vodafone-annual-report-2019.pdf; Vodafone. "Results, Reports & Presentations." Accessed October 14, 2020. https://investors .vodafone.com/reports-information/results-reports-presentations. Based on earnings before interest, taxes, depreciation, and amortization (EBITDA), a measure of profitability that equals operating profit in addition to depreciation expenses and amortization expenses. The total adjusted EBITDA is €13.9 billion; €10.3 billion of those come from Europe. For reference, gross profit is €13.5 billion.

38. Dewhurst, Martin, Jonathan Harris, and Suzanne Heywood. "Understanding Your Globalization Penalty." McKinsey & Company, 2011. https://www.mckinsey .com/business-functions/organization/our-insights/understanding-your-globalization -penalty.

39. Qian, Gongmin, Theodore A. Khoury, Mike W. Peng, and Zhengming Qian. "The Performance Implications of Intra- and Inter-Regional Geographic Diversification." *Strategic Management Journal* 31, no. 9 (2010): 1018–30.

40. Ghemawat, *Redefining Global Strategy,* 109, figure 4-1.

41. Hurrell, Andrew. "Explaining the Resurgence of Regionalism in World Politics." *Review of International Studies* 21, no. 4 (1995): 331–58; Milner, Helen. *The Political Economy of Regionalism.* New York: Columbia University Press, 1997.

42. Ohmae, Kenichi. *Triad Power: The Coming Shape of Global Competition.* New York: Free Press, 1985.

43. O'Neill, Jim. "Building Better Global Economic BRICs." Goldman Sachs, 2001. https://www.goldmansachs.com/insights/archive/archive-pdfs/build-better -brics.pdf.

44. Zakaria, Fareed. *The Post-American World.* New York: Norton, 2008.

2. Europe

1. Tolliday, Steven. "Enterprise and the State in the West German Wirtschafts-wunder: Volkswagen and the Automobile Industry, 1939–1962." *Business History Review* 69, no. 3 (1995): 273–350, 326–27. https://doi.org/10.2307/3117336; Daimler. "1961–1983. Growth in All Areas," 2021. https://www.daimler.com/company /tradition/company-history/1960-1980.html.

2. Simmie, James, Corinne Siino, Jean Mark Zuliani, Guy Jalabert, and Simone Strambach. "Local Innovation System Governance and Performance: A Comparative Analysis of Oxfordshire, Stuttgart and Toulouse." *International Journal of Technology Management* 28, nos. 3–6 (2004): 534. https://doi.org/10.1504/ijtm.2004.005308; German Convention Bureau. "The Stuttgart Region—Europe's Leading Location for Innovation and High-Technology." Accessed March 26, 2021. https://www.gcb.de /case-stories/kompetenzfelder/the-stuttgart-region-europes-leading-location-for -innovation-and-high-technology.html.

3. 4motors. "About." October 2020. http://www.4motors.eu/en/about.

4. Region Stuttgart. "High-Tech Economy Meets International Corporations," May 4, 2020. https://www.region-stuttgart.de/englisch/economy.html.

5. WTO. "World Trade Statistical Review 2018," 2018. https://www.wto.org /english/res_e/statis_e/wts2018_e/wts2018_e.pdf; European Commission. "EU Positions in World Trade," February 18, 2019. https://ec.europa.eu/trade/policy /eu-position-in-world-trade/.

6. European Commission. "Winston Churchill: Calling for a United States of Europe." Accessed March 29, 2021. https://europa.eu/european-union/sites/default /files/docs/body/winston_churchill_en.pdf.

7. Levi, Lucio, Richard Corbett, Ortensio Zecchino, Roland Bieber, John Pinder, Paolo Ponzano, Jean-Louis Quermonne, and Philippe de Schoutheete. *Altiero Spinelli—European Federalist.* Brussels, Belgium: European Parliament, 2009. https:// www.europarl.europa.eu/cmsdata/174892/20090316ATT51977EN.pdf. The Italian politician and political theorist Altiero Spinelli called for a federalist Europe in his Manifesto of Ventotene (1941), written while imprisoned by the Fascist government. He was a founder of the European Federalist Movement, formed in 1943.

8. European Commission. "Jean Monnet: The Unifying Force behind the Birth of the European Union." Accessed July 15, 2021. https://europa.eu/european-union /sites/europaeu/files/docs/body/jean_monnet_en.pdf.

9. Hitchcock, William H. *The Struggle for Europe: The Turbulent History of a Divided Continent, 1945 to the Present.* New York: Anchor Books, 2003.

10. Eichengreen, Barry. "Lessons from the Marshall Plan." World Development Report Background Papers. World Bank, 2010. https://doi.org/10.1596/27506; OECD. "OECD 60th Anniversary," October 2020. https://www.oecd.org/60-years/.

11. Haas, Ernst B. *The Uniting of Europe: Political, Social, and Economic Forces, 1950–1957.* Contemporary European Politics and Society. Notre Dame, IN: University of Notre Dame Press, 2004, 63.

12. Gilbert, Mark. *European Integration: A Concise History.* Rev. ed. Lanham, MD: Rowman and Littlefield, 2011, 53–54; Gethard, Gregory. "The German Economic Miracle: The Story behind Germany's Economic Rebirth after World War II." Investopedia, February 12, 2020. https://www.investopedia.com/articles/economics/09/german-economic-miracle.asp; CVCE. "Treaty Establishing the European Economic Community (Rome, 25 March 1957)," September 11, 2015, 35. https://www.cvce.eu/content/publication/1999/1/1/cca6ba28-0bf3-4ce6-8a76-6b0b3252696e/publishable_en.pdf.

13. Maddison, Angus. *The World Economy.* Paris: OECD, 2006, 362. https://www.stat.berkeley.edu/~aldous/157/Papers/world_economy.pdf; Commission of the European Communities and the Canadian Department of External Affairs. "European Community: The Facts." 1976. http://aei.pitt.edu/56989/1/A7224-CRcanada.delete.pdf. Between 1950 and 1973, the weight of trade in these economies also grew faster than it did for the United States and the world average. For instance, French, German, and Dutch exports in proportion to GDP grew 7.6 percent, 17.6 percent, and 28.5 percent, respectively, while U.S. exports increased by 1.9 percent and global aggregate exports grew 5.0 percent in relation to aggregate GDP. Author's calculations.

14. Braun, Hans-Joachim. *The German Economy in the 20th Century.* London: Routledge, 1990, 7; Baily, Neil Martin, and Jacob Funk Kirkegaard. "Europe's Postwar Success and Subsequent Problems." In *Transforming the European Economy.* Washington, DC: Peterson Institute for International Economics, 2004. In the period spanning 1947–75, GDP per capita grew by 250 percent, compared to 225 percent between 1800 and 1948.

15. Lütticken, Sven. *History in Motion: Time in the Age of the Moving Image.* Berlin: Sternberg, 2013, 99.

16. ZF Friedrichshafen AG. *1986 Annual Report Abridged Version,* 5; ZF Friedrichshafen AG. *Excerpts from the 1981 Annual Report,* 10.

17. Homola, Peter. "German Luxury Brands Investing in Eastern Europe." WardsAuto, August 18, 2016. https://www.wardsauto.com/industry/german-luxury-brands-investing-eastern-europe; ZF Friedrichshafen AG. *Annual Report, 2004,* 45; ZF Friedrichshafen AG. *Annual Report, 2007,* 17.

18. EUR-Lex. "Judgement of the Court of 5 February 1963," December 2020. https://eur-lex.europa.eu/legal-content/EN/TXT/?uri=CELEX%3A61962CJ0026; Purnhagen, Kai P. "The Virtue of Cassis De Dijon 25 Years Later—It Is Not Dead, It Just Smells Funny." SSRN Scholarly Paper. Social Science Research Network, January 22, 2014. https://doi.org/10.2139/ssrn.2383202.

19. Individual member states nominate a number of potential commissioners from which the president chooses to form a team.

20. Tudor, Jarrod. "Consumer Protection and the Free Movement of Goods in the European Union: The Ability of Member-States to Block the Entry of Goods across Borders." *Houston Journal of International Law* 39, no. 3 (2017): 567, 568. http://www.hjil.org/wp-content/uploads/Tudor-FINAL.pdf.

21. Egan, Michelle P. *Constructing a European Market: Standards, Regulation, and Governance.* Oxford: Oxford University Press, 2001, 74.

22. Chase, Kerry A. *Trading Blocs: States, Firms, and Regions in the World Economy.* Michigan Studies in International Political Economy. Ann Arbor: University of Michigan Press, 2005, 145. https://doi.org/10.3998/mpub.133506.

23. Lastra, Rosa M., and Jean-Victor Louis. "European Economic and Monetary Union: History, Trends, and Prospects." SSRN Scholarly Paper. Social Science Research Network, April 4, 2013. https://papers.ssrn.com/abstract=2244764.

24. Tagliabue, John. "Extra Vitamins? A Great Idea, Except in Denmark." *New York Times,* June 17, 2011, sec. World. https://www.nytimes.com/2011/06/17/world/europe/17copenhagen.html; Rytz, Benita Kidmose, James Sylvest, Julia Culver, Thomas Teichler, Kristin Kosk, and Katrin Mannik. "Evaluation of the Application of the Mutual Recognition Principle in the Field of Goods." European Commission, June 2015. http://ec.europa.eu/DocsRoom/documents/13381/attachments/1/translations/en/renditions/native.

25. Electrolux Group. "1990–2000s: Refocusing, Stronger Brands and New Markets." Accessed March 29, 2021. https://www.electroluxgroup.com/en/1990-2000s-refocusing-stronger-brands-and-new-markets-26789.

26. Daneshkhu, Scheherazade, Robert Cookson, Kevin Brown, and Elizabeth Rigby. "Carrefour to Slim Down in Asia." *Financial Times,* July 13 2020. https://www.ft.com/content/odf317ca-8e99-11df-8a67-00144feab49a.

27. Carrefour, *2001 Annual Report,* 2001. https://ddd.uab.cat/pub/infanu/29485/iaCARREFOURa2001ieng.pdf; Investegate. "Carrefour: 2004 Q4 Sales," January 11, 2005. https://www.investegate.co.uk/carrefour/rns/2004-q4-sales/200501111737552672H/; United Press International. "Carrefour Owns 107 Stores Worldwide, with Locations in Argentina . . . ," June 26, 1989. https://www.upi.com/Archives/1989/06/26/Carrefour-owns-107-stores-worldwide-with-locations-in-Argentina/3448614836800/.

28. World Tourism Organization (UNWTO). *European Union Tourism Trends.* Madrid: UNWTO, 2018. https://doi.org/10.18111/9789284419470.

29. Grasland, Emmanuel. "Robotisation: Une étude nuance les retards de la France par rapport à l'Allemagne." *Les Echos,* July 11, 2014. https://www.lesechos.fr/2014/07/robotisation-une-etude-nuance-les-retards-de-la-france-par-rapport-a-lallemagne-306660; Ipmark. "Distribuidores y exhibidores van de la mano en la campaña #YoVoyAlCine," June 16, 2020. https://ipmark.com/distribuidores-y-exhibidores-van-de-la-mano-en-la-campana-yovoyalcine/; AFRY. "AFRY Helps the Flying Tiger Copenhagen Develop Sustainable Packaging Solutions," March 17, 2020. https://

afry.com/en/newsroom/news/afry-helps-flying-tiger-copenhagen-develop-sustain able-packaging-solutions; AFRY. "€9bn Could Be Saved by Using Gas Infrastructure to Decarbonise Portugal," March 12, 2020. https://afry.com/en/newsroom/news /eu9bn-could-be-saved-using-gas-infrastructure-decarbonise-portugal.

30. European Commission. "Single Market Scoreboard." 2020. https://ec.eu ropa.eu/internal_market/scoreboard/integration_market_openness/trade_goods _services/index_en.htm. Roughly 56 percent of services sold abroad occur between EU nations. Another 23 percent is with the recent EU member the UK.

31. Jolley, David. "E-Car and Component Map of Europe." *Automotive News Europe,* September 4, 2019. https://europe.autonews.com/e-car-and-component -map-europe.

32. Stehrer, Robert, Sandra Leitner, Manuel Marcias, Daniel Mirza, Olga Pindyuk, Iulia Siedschlag, Roman Stöllinger, and Zuzanna Studnicka. "The Evolving Composition of Intra-EU Trade." Vienna Institute for International Economic Studies, November 2016. https://wiiw.ac.at/the-evolving-composition-of-intra-eu-trade-dlp-4059.pdf. From 1992 to 2012, intra-EU trade jumped from 12 percent to 22 percent of GDP on average.

33. World Bank. "Trade (% of GDP)." Accessed March 26, 2021. https://data .worldbank.org/indicator/NE.TRD.GNFS.ZS?end=2018&start=1990. Trade as a percentage of GDP went from 52 percent to 86 percent between 1992 and 2012, compared to the world averages of 41 percent to 60 percent.

34. CVCE.EU. "The Difficulties of the Monetary Snake and the EMCF," July 7, 2016. https://www.cvce.eu/en/collections/unit-content/-/unit/56d70f17-5054-49fc -bb9b-5d90735167d0/2d84f078-672e-4ae9-92d5-b49699ll442a.

35. Lastra and Louis, "European Economic and Monetary Union," 10.

36. Angerer, Jost. "The EU Framework for Fiscal Policies | Fact Sheets on the European Union | European Parliament." European Parliament, April 2021. https:// www.europarl.europa.eu/factsheets/en/sheet/89/the-eu-framework-for-fiscal-policies. These guidelines require that the deficit not exceed 3 percent of GDP and sovereign debt remain below 60 percent of a country's GDP.

37. Lastra and Louis, "European Economic and Monetary Union," 50, 113–14.

38. Berend, Iván T. *An Economic History of Twentieth-Century Europe from Laissez- Faire to Globalization.* Cambridge: Cambridge University Press, 2006.

39. Carril-Caccia, Federico, and Elena Pavlova. "Foreign Direct Investment and Its Drivers: A Global and EU Perspective." *ECB Economic Bulletin,* no. 5 (2018). https://www.ecb.europa.eu/pub/economic-bulletin/articles/2018/html/ecb.ebart 201804_01.en.html.

40. Suneson, Eva Rytter, Tine Jeppesen, Jonas Juul Hendrikson, and Julien Grun- felder. "The World in Europe, Global FDI Flows towards Europe: Intra-European FDI." ESPON, March 2018. https://www.copenhageneconomics.com/dyn/resources /Publication/publicationPDF/0/440/1525770844/espon-fdi-08-main-report-intra -european-fdi.pdf.

41. PharmaBoardroom. "Top 10 Global Pharma Companies 2020." June 23, 2020. https://pharmaboardroom.com/facts/top-10-global-pharma-companies-2020/.

42. Decressin, Jörg, Wim Fonteyne, and Hamid Faruqee. "Toward a Single Financial Market." In *Integrating Europe's Financial Markets*. Washington, DC: International Monetary Fund, 2007. https://www.elibrary.imf.org/view/books/071/03624 -9781589066236-en/03624-9781589066236-en-book.xml. The Single Banking License allowed a bank licensed in one EU (then EC) country to operate in any other EU country and—most notably—to be subject only to the regulation of the home country that had issued its license. It was enacted under the Second Banking Directive of 1989.

43. Allen, Franklin, Thorsten Beck, Elena Carletti, Philip R. Lane, Dirk Schoenmaker, and Wolf Wagner. *Cross-Border Banking in Europe: Implications for Financial Stability and Macroeconomic Policies*. London: Centre for Economic Policy Research, 2011, 2. https://voxeu.org/sites/default/files/file/cross-border_banking.pdf.

44. BanksDaily.com. "The World's 10 Largest Banks by Total Assets (2007)." Accessed March 29, 2021. https://banksdaily.com/topbanks/World/2007.html; Berend, *Economic History;* Allen et al., *Cross-Border Banking in Europe,* 24.

45. Teixeira, Pedro Gustavo. "The Legal History of the Banking Union." *European Business Organization Law Review* 18, no. 3 (2017): 535–65. https://doi.org /10.1007/s40804-017-0074-2.

46. European Commission. "Motorway Axis Gdansk-Brno/Bratislava-Vienna." 2005. https://ec.europa.eu/ten/transport/priority_projects_minisite/PP25EN.pdf; Berend, *Economic History,* 167.

47. Michael Dooms, associate professor at Vrije Universiteit Brussels (VUB), in discussion with the author, November 13, 2019.

48. Mobility and Transport, European Commission. "EU Aviation: 25 Years of Reaching New Heights." June 21, 2017. https://ec.europa.eu/transport/modes/air /25years-eu-aviation_en.

49. Berend, *Economic History,* 286.

50. European Commission. "Regional Policy: France Resider II Picardy." March 9, 2015. https://ec.europa.eu/regional_policy/archive/reg_prog/po/prog_181.htm.

51. Gruševaja, Marina, Gerhard Heimpold, Oliver Schwab, and Kristin Schwarze. "Evaluation of the Main Achievements of Cohesion Policy Programmes over the Longer Term in 15 Selected Regions (From 1989–1993 Programming Period to the Present): Case Study Sachen-Anhalt." University of Strathclyde European Policies Research Centre, July 10, 2013, 3. https://ec.europa.eu/regional_policy/sources /docgener/evaluation/pdf/eval2007/cohesion_achievements/sachsen_anhalt.pdf.

52. Rollings, Neil. *British Business in the Formative Years of European Integration 1945–1973.* Cambridge Studies in the Emergence of Global Enterprise. New York: Cambridge University Press, 2007, 60–61; Renato Mazzolini. "Creating Europe's Multinationals: The International Merger Route." *Journal of Business* (Chicago) 48, no. 1 (1975): 39–51. https://doi.org/10.1086/295710.

53. European Trade Union Institute for Research. "Total Number of Registered European Companies (SEs) by Year of Establishment (2004–2014)." 2014. http://

www.worker-participation.eu/var/ezwebin_site/storage/images/media/images/folie0216/97022-1-eng-GB/Folie02.png.

54. Inditex. "Our Story." October 2020. https://www.inditex.com/about-us/our-story.

55. Quickbooks Commerce. "Zara Supply Chain Analysis—the Secret behind Zara's Retail Success," June 25, 2018. https://www.tradegecko.com/blog/supply-chain-management/zara-supply-chain-its-secret-to-retail-success.

56. Aftab, Md Afzalul, Qin Yuanjian, Nadia Kabir, and Zapan Barua. "Super Responsive Supply Chain: The Case of Spanish Fast Fashion Retailer Inditex-Zara." *International Journal of Business and Management* 13, no. 5 (April 22, 2018): 212. https://doi.org/10.5539/ijbm.v13n5p212.

57. mhugos. "Zara Clothing Company Supply Chain." SCM Globe. January 4, 2020. https://www.scmglobe.com/zara-clothing-company-supply-chain/.

58. Hansen, Suzy. "How Zara Grew into the World's Largest Fashion Retailer." *New York Times Magazine,* November 9, 2012. https://www.nytimes.com/2012/11/11/magazine/how-zara-grew-into-the-worlds-largest-fashion-retailer.html.

59. Ismaili, Uran, Matus Samel, Elena Solomon, Emilka Valentova, and Etjen Xhafaj. "Microeconomics of Competitiveness." Harvard Business School, May 5, 2016. https://www.isc.hbs.edu/Documents/resources/courses/moc-course-at-harvard/pdf/student-projects/Slovakia%20Automobiles%202016.pdf.

60. Willetts, David. "How Thatcher's Bruges Speech Put Britain on the Road to Brexit," *Financial Times,* August 31, 2018. https://www.ft.com/content/0b0afe92-ac40-11e8-8253-48106866cd8a; Weissmann, Jordan. "Watch Margaret Thatcher Explain Why the Euro Is a Terrible Idea in 1990." *Atlantic,* April 8, 2013. https://www.theatlantic.com/business/archive/2013/04/watch-margaret-thatcher-explain-why-the-euro-is-a-terrible-idea-in-1990/274768/.

61. Rytz, Benita Kidmose, James Sylvest, Julia Culver, Thomas Teichler, Kristin Kosk, and Katrin Mannik. "Evaluation of the Application of the Mutual Recognition Principle in the Field of Goods." European Commission, June 2015, 57–58, 98. https://ec.europa.eu; Jervelund, Christian, Svend Torp Jesperson, Daniel Mekonnen, Miguel Nieto Arias, Jacques Pelkmans, and Anabela Correia de Brito. "Delivering a Stronger Single Market." Nordic Innovation, June 2012, 34, 45–46. http://www.diva-portal.org/smash/get/diva2:707233/FULLTEXT01.pdf.

62. OECD. "Services Trade," 2020. http://www.oecd.org/trade/topics/services-trade/; Barry, Olga, and Valérie Guigue-Koeppen. "Integration and Performance of Services in the EU." In *Single Market Integration and Competitiveness Report: 2016.* Brussels: European Commission, 2016. https://ec.europa.eu/growth/content/single-market-integration-and-competitiveness-eu-and-its-member-states-2016_en.

63. European Commission, Directorate-General for Economic and Financial Affairs and Ipsos European Public Affairs. "Flash Eurobarometer 488: The Euro Area." European Commission, Directorate-General for Communication, March 2021. https://data.europa.eu/doi/10.2765/995591; European Commission, Directorate-General for

Communication. "The EU and the Coronavirus Pandemic." Standard Eurobarometer. European Commission, May 2021. https://europa.eu/eurobarometer/surveys/detail/2355.

64. Willetts, "Thatcher's Bruges Speech"; D'alfonso, Alessandro. "The UK 'Rebate' on the EU Budget: An Explanation of the Abatement and Other Correction Mechanisms." European Parliament Think Tank, February 18, 2016. https://www.europarl.europa.eu/thinktank/en/document.html?reference=EPRS_BRI(2016)577973.

65. Sommerlad, Joe, and Ben Chapman. "Which Companies Are Leaving UK, Downsizing or Cutting Jobs ahead of Brexit?" *Independent,* February 26, 2019, sec. News. https://www.independent.co.uk/news/business/news/brexit-companies-leaving-uk-list-job-cuts-eu-no-deal-customs-union-a8792296.html; Tidey, Alice. "Brexit: Number of Companies Relocating to the Netherlands 'Is Accelerating.'" *Euronews,* February 19, 2020. https://www.euronews.com/2020/02/19/brexit-number-of-companies-relocating-to-the-netherlands-is-accelerating.

66. World Bank. "GDP (Current US$)—United States, Canada, Mexico," 2020. https://data.worldbank.org/indicator/NY.GDP.MKTP.CD?end=2003&locations=US-CA-MX&start=1993; Parker, George, Jim Brunsden, and Laura Hughes. "Economic Cost of Brexit Laid Bare in OBR Forecasts." *Financial Times,* March 11, 2020. https://www.ft.com/content/72938c66-638f-11ea-a6cd-df28cc3c6a68; UK Office for Budget Responsibility. "Economic and Fiscal Outlook: March 2020." March 11, 2020. https://obr.uk/efo/economic-and-fiscal-outlook-march-2020/.

67. Castle, Stephen. "Brexit Border Bureaucracy Looms for Truckers, Pet Owners and Travelers." *New York Times,* July 13, 2020, sec. World. https://www.nytimes.com/2020/07/13/world/europe/brexit-border-bureaucracy.html.

68. Federation of Small Businesses. "One in Four Small Exporters Halt EU Sales, Three Months On from Transition End, New Study Finds." March 29, 2021. https://www.fsb.org.uk/resources-page/one-in-four-small-exporters-halt-eu-sales-three-months-on-from-transition-end-new-study-finds.html.

69. Schulmeister, Philipp, Elise Defourny, Luisa Maggio, Said Hallaouy, Matthias Büttner, Alice Chiesa, and Bart Van Gasse. "Parlemeter 2018: Taking Up the Challenge: From (Silent) Support to Actual Vote." Eurobarometer Survey. European Parliament, October 2018. https://www.europarl.europa.eu/at-your-service/en/be-heard/eurobarometer/parlemeter-2018-taking-up-the-challenge.

70. Eurostat. "Intra-EU Trade in Goods—Main Features." April 2021. https://ec.europa.eu/eurostat/statistics-explained/index.php?title=Intra-EU_trade_in_goods_-_main_features&oldid=452727#Evolution_of_intra-EU_trade_in_goods:_2002-2019.

71. Lund, Susan, James Manyika, Jonathan Woetzel, Jacques Bughin, Mekala Krishnan, and Mac Muir. "Globalization in Transition: The Future of Trade and Global Value Chains." McKinsey & Company, January 16, 2019. https://www.mckinsey.com/featured-insights/innovation-and-growth/globalization-in-transition-the-future-of-trade-and-value-chains.

72. Stehrer et al., "Evolving Composition"; Eurostat. "Trade in Services in the EU." 2017. https://ec.europa.eu/eurostat/news/themes-in-the-spotlight/trade-in-services.

3. Asia

1. "The Future of Factory Asia: A Tightening Grip." *Economist,* March 12, 2015. https://www.economist.com/briefing/2015/03/12/a-tightening-grip.

2. World Bank. "DataBank | World Development Indicators." Database, 2021. https://databank.worldbank.org/source/world-development-indicators.

3. Ishimaru, Yasuzo. "The Korean War and Japanese Ports: Support for the UN Forces and Its Influences." *NIDS Security Reports,* no. 8 (December 2007): 55–70. http://www.nids.mod.go.jp/english/publication/kiyo/pdf/2007/bulletin_e2007_5.pdf.

4. In 1953, the United States granted Japan most favored nation status and helped bring the country into the GATT in 1955.

5. Erstling, Jay, and Ryan E. Strom. "Korea's Patent Policy and Its Impact on Economic Development: A Model for Emerging Countries?" *San Diego International Law Journal* 441, no. 11 (Spring 2010): 441–80. https://open.mitchellhamline .edu/facsch/138/; Chang, Ha-Joon. *The East Asian Development Experience: The Miracle, the Crisis and the Future.* New York: Zed Books, 2007.

6. World Bank. *Belt and Road Economics: Opportunities and Risks of Transport Corridors.* Washington, DC: World Bank, 2019. https://openknowledge.worldbank .org/handle/10986/31878; Hatch, Walter, and Kozo Yamamura. *Asia in Japan's Embrace: Building a Regional Production Alliance.* Cambridge: Cambridge University Press, 1996.

7. Hatch and Yamamura, *Asia in Japan's Embrace,* 123.

8. A *keiretsu* is a family of companies with interlocking business relations and shareholdings.

9. Hatch and Yamamura, *Asia in Japan's Embrace,* 122, 144; AGC. "AGC Group," 2016. https://www.agc-flatglass.co.th/en/aboutus; MCIS. "Operation Management," 2011. http://creativemcis.blogspot.com/p/operation-management.html.

10. Glass Online Archive. "Asahi Indonesia Restructures Its Forex Loans." July 2, 1998. http://archive.glassonline.com/site/news/topic/Sector-trends/id/3830/Asahi -Indonesia-restructures-its-forex-loans; Picken, Stuart D. B. *Historical Dictionary of Japanese Business.* Lanham, MD: Rowman and Littlefield, 2017; Bitting, Robert K. "Observations from Japan: Lessons in Research and Technology Transfer." *Journal of the Society of Research Administrators* 19, no. 4 (March 22, 1988): 17–23. https:// search.proquest.com/docview/214811936?pq-origsite=gscholar&fromopenview =true.

11. AGC Inc. "Company Overview." PowerPoint presentation, August 2020. https://www.agc.com/en/ir/library/outline/pdf/c_overview.pdf; "AGC Inc." Yahoo! Finance, December 2020. https://finance.yahoo.com/quote/asgly/.

12. Lau, Lawrence J. "Taiwan as a Model for Economic Development." Depart-

ment of Economics, Stanford University, Stanford, CA, October 2002. https://web
.stanford.edu/~ljlau/Presentations/Presentations/021004.PDF.

13. Kenton, Will. "Chaebol Structure." Investopedia, September 29, 2019. https://
www.investopedia.com/terms/c/chaebol-structure.asp. South Korea's *chaebols* are
similar to Japan's *keiretsu* system but with some differences. *Chaebols* are generally
controlled by their founding families, while *keiretsu* businesses are run by professional
managers. *Chaebol* ownership is also centralized, while *keiretsu* businesses are de-
centralized.

14. Studwell, Joe. *How Asia Works: Success and Failure in the World's Most Dynamic Region*. New York: Grove, 2014.

15. Krause, Lawrence B. "Hong Kong and Singapore: Twins or Kissing Cousins?"
Economic Development and Cultural Change 36, no. S3 (April 1988): 45–66. https://
doi.org/10.1086/edcc.36.s3.1566538.

16. Krause, 52–53.

17. Soon, Teck-Wong, and William A. Stoever. "Foreign Investment and Economic Development in Singapore: A Policy-Oriented Approach." *Journal of Developing Areas* 30, no. 3 (April 1996): 317–40. https://www.jstor.org/stable/4192566.

18. Hwa, Cheng Siok. "Economic Change in Singapore, 1945–1977." *Southeast
Asian Journal of Social Science* 7, nos. 1–2 (1979): 81–113. https://doi.org/10.1163
/080382479X00054.

19. Cai, Kevin G. *The Political Economy of East Asia: Regional and National
Dimensions*. Basingstoke, UK: Palgrave Macmillan UK, 2008. http://public.ebook
central.proquest.com/choice/publicfullrecord.aspx?p=4720207. Japanese FDI grew
from 5.9 percent of total FDI in Taiwan in 1965 to 39.7 percent in 1990.

20. Permporn, Sangiam. "Japan's Foreign Direct Investment in Thailand: Trends,
Patterns and Determinants." DBA thesis, Victoria University Graduate School of
Business, 2006. https://citeseerx.ist.psu.edu/viewdoc/download?doi=10.1.1.665.3869
&rep=rep1&type=pdf; Encarnation, Dennis J. "Asia and the Global Operations of
Multinational Corporations." In *Japanese Multinationals in Asia: Regional Opera-
tions in Comparative Perspective*, 49. Japan Business and Economics Series. New York:
Oxford University Press, 1999.

21. World Bank, "Japan Exports, Imports and Trade Balance by Country and Region 2002." World Integrated Trade Solution, October 2020. https://wits.worldbank
.org/CountryProfile/en/Country/JPN/Year/2002/TradeFlow/EXPIMP. Combined
exports and imports from Japan to East Asia and the Pacific surpassed the combined exports and imports of the United States, Europe, and Central Asia in 2002.

22. Japan's auto companies also assemble nearly ten million motor vehicles a year
in Japan itself (many parts brought in from around the region). Of these, roughly half
were sold to Japanese consumers, 18 percent exported to the United States, and another 7 percent sold around Asia. Author's calculations based on data from Japan
Automobile Manufacturers Association. "JAMA," 2020. http://www.jama.org; and
Dent, Christopher M. "East Asian Integration: Towards an East Asian Economic Com-

munity." Asian Development Bank, February 2017. https://www.adb.org/sites/default/files/publication/228896/adbi-wp665.pdf.

23. Yeung, Henry Wai-Chung. "The Political Economy of Transnational Corporations: A Study of the Regionalization of Singaporean Firms." *Political Geography* 17 (May 1998): 389–416. https://doi.org/10.1016/S0962-6298(97)00021-8.

24. Weiping, Tan. "China's Approach to Reduce Poverty: Taking Targeted Measures to Lift People out of Poverty." International Poverty Reduction Center in China. April 18, 2018. https://www.un.org/development/desa/dspd/wp-content/uploads/sites/22/2018/05/31.pdf; World Bank. "GDP Growth—China," 2020. https://data.worldbank.org/indicator/NY.GDP.MKTP.KD.ZG?locations=CN.

25. Stoltenberg, Clyde D. "China's Special Economic Zones: Their Development and Prospects." *Asian Survey* 24, no. 6 (June 1, 1984): 637–54. https://doi.org/10.2307/2644396.

26. Alvis, James H. "Developments in Korea's Overseas Foreign Direct Investments." Korea Economic Institute, 2006. http://www.keia.org/sites/default/files/publications/december%2006.pdf.

27. Yu, Howard H., and Willy C. Shih. "Taiwan's PC Industry, 1976–2010: The Evolution of Organizational Capabilities." *Business History Review* 88, no. 2 (2014): 339–42. https://doi.org/10.1017/S0007680514000051.

28. Wang, Shuguang. "Foreign Retailers in Post-WTO China: Stories of Success and Setbacks." *Asia Pacific Business Review* 15, no. 1 (2009): 59–77. https://doi.org/10.1080/13602380802399353.

29. Loeys, Jan, and Joyce Chang. "JPMorgan Perspectives: Made in China 2025: A New World Order?" JPMorgan, 2019. https://markets.jpmorgan.com/research/email/-qieqbmn/Lse9sLxumTweg_M-msjKbw/GPS2900159-0; Mahabir, Aruneema, and Chris Milner. "Has China Displaced Other Asian Countries' Exports?" In *China and the World Economy*, edited by David Greenaway, Chris Milner, and Shujie Yao, 60–90. Basingstoke, UK: Palgrave Macmillan, 2010. https://doi.org/10.1057/9781137059864_4.

30. Magretta, Joan. "Fast, Global, and Entrepreneurial: Supply Chain Management, Hong Kong Style." *Harvard Business Review*, October 1998. https://hbr.org/1998/09/fast-global-and-entrepreneurial-supply-chain-management-hong-kong-style.

31. Ohio State University. "Raw Materials | Nike Shoes." 2015. https://u.osu.edu/nikeshoes/raw-materials/.

32. Samsung. "Eight Major Steps to Semiconductor Fabrication, Part 1: Creating the Wafer." Samsung Newsroom, 2015. https://news.samsung.com/global/eight-major-steps-to-semiconductor-fabrication-part-1-creating-the-wafer. Samsung. "Eight Major Steps to Semiconductor Fabrication, Part 6: The Addition of Electrical Properties." Samsung Newsroom, 2015. https://news.samsung.com/global/eight-major-steps-to-semiconductor-fabrication-part-6-the-addition-of-electrical-properties; Nikkei Asia. "Taiyo Nippon Sanso Plans Chinese Plant for Chipmaking Gases." June

29, 2017. https://asia.nikkei.com/Business/Taiyo-Nippon-Sanso-plans-Chinese-plant-for-chipmaking-gases; Deguchi, Toshihisa. "Business Strategy for IT-Related Chemicals Sector." PowerPoint presented at Sumitomo Chemical, Tokyo, Japan, September 2016; OLED-Info. "Mobile Phones and Smartphones with OLED Screens." Accessed March 30, 2021. https://www.oled-info.com/oled-devices/mobile-phones; Gordon, Scott. "Why Samsung Is Building the Biggest OLED Factory in the World." Android Authority, July 3, 2017. https://www.androidauthority.com/why-samsung-building-biggest-oled-factory-784228/.

33. Han, Jy. "Samsung Electronics to Open Third Factory in Vietnam. . . Hunger for De-Sinicization." *Thelec,* November 14, 2018. http://www.thelec.net/news/articleView.html?idxno=13; Kang, Hansoo. "Global Cooperation and Corporate Internationalization Strategy—Samsung Electronics' Manufacturing Complex in Vietnam." Presentation at the eighteenth TCI Global Conference, "Clusters in a Creative Economy: New Agendas for Companies and Policymakers," November 5, 2015. https://es.slideshare.net/TCINetwork/tci-2015-samsung-electronics-manufacturing-complex-in-vietnam.

34. Asian Development Bank. "Trade and the Global Value Chain." In *Asian Economic Integration Report 2018*. Manila, Philippines: Asian Development Bank, October 2018, 23–24, 33. https://aric.adb.org/pdf/aeir/AEIR2018_2_trade-and-the-global-value-chain.pdf.

35. Asian Development Bank. *Institutions for Regional Integration: Toward an Asian Economic Community.* Manila, Philippines: Asian Development Bank, 2010, 33. https://aric.adb.org/pdf/Institutions_for_Regionalization_Web.pdf; UNCTAD. "Trade Structure by Partner." In *UNCTAD Handbook of Statistics.* Geneva: UNCTAD, 2019. https://stats.unctad.org/handbook/MerchandiseTrade/ByPartner.html.

36. Tonby, Oliver, Jonathan Woetzel, Wonsik Choi, Karel Eloot, Rajat Dhawan, Jeongmin Seong, and Patti Wang. "Asia's Future Is Now." McKinsey Global Institute, July 2019, 4. https://www.mckinsey.com/~/media/McKinsey/Featured%20Insights/Asia%20Pacific/Asias%20future%20is%20now/Asias-future-is-now-final.pdf.

37. Tonby, Oliver, Jonathan Woetzel, Wonsik Choi, Karel Eloot, Rajat Dhawan, Jeongmin Seong, and Patti Wang. *The Future of Asia.* McKinsey Global Institute, September 2019, 16. https://www.mckinsey.com/~/media/McKinsey/Featured%20Insights/Asia%20Pacific/The%20future%20of%20Asia%20Asian%20flows%20and%20networks%20are%20defining%20the%20next%20phase%20of%20globalization/MGI-Future-of-Asia-Flows-and-Trade-Discussion-paper-Sep-2019.pdf.

38. McCawley, Peter. *Banking on the Future of Asia and the Pacific: 50 Years of the Asian Development Bank.* Manila, Philippines: Asian Development Bank, 2017, 348–49. https://www.adb.org/sites/default/files/publication/235061/adb-history-book-second-edition.pdf; Asian Infrastructure Investment Bank. "Approved Projects," 2020. https://www.aiib.org/en/projects/approved/index.html; Mercator Institute for China Studies. "Mapping the Belt and Road Initiative: This Is Where We Stand." June 7, 2018. https://www.merics.org/sites/default/files/2018-06/MERICS_Silk_Road_v8.jpg.

39. Llovet Montanes, Ruth, and Sergio L. Schmukler. "Financial Integration in East Asia and Pacific: Regional and Interregional Linkages." *World Bank Research and Policy Briefs*, no. 15 (2018): 3.

40. Asian Development Bank. *Asian Economic Integration Report 2019/2020*. Manila, Philippines: Asian Development Bank, November 2019, 63–64. https://www.adb.org/sites/default/files/publication/536691/aeir-2019-2020.pdf.

41. Regional Cooperation and Integration Division of the Economic Research and Regional Cooperation Department of the Asian Development Bank. *Asian Economic Integration Report 2018: Toward Optimal Provision of Regional Public Goods in Asia and the Pacific*. Manila, Philippines: Asian Development Bank, October 2018. https://doi.org/10.22617/TCS189599-2.

42. Testaverde, Mauro, Harry Moroz, and Claire H. Hollweg. *Migrating to Opportunity: Overcoming Barriers to Labor Mobility in Southeast Asia*. Washington, DC: World Bank, 2017. https://doi.org/10.1596/978-1-4648-1106-7; Human Rights Watch. "'They Deceived Us at Every Step.'" October 31, 2011. https://www.hrw.org/report/2011/10/31/they-deceived-us-every-step/abuse-cambodian-domestic-workers-migrating-malaysia; Hickey, Maureen, Pitra Narendra, and Katie Rainwater. "A Review of Internal and Regional Migration Policy in Southeast Asia." Asia Research Institute, National University of Singapore, September 2013, 47. http://www.migratingoutofpoverty.org/files/file.php?name=wp8-hickey-review-of-internal-and-regional-migration-policy-in-sea.pdf&site=354; World Bank. "Managing Migration Better Can Help Boost Welfare and Growth in ASEAN," October 9, 2017. https://www.worldbank.org/en/news/press-release/2017/10/09/managing-migration-better-can-help-boost-welfare-and-growth-in-asean-world-bank. Indonesia and Cambodia discourage young women from migrating to Malaysia or Singapore due to widespread abuses.

43. Asian Development Bank, *Asian Economic Integration Report 2018*, 82; Sawitta Lefevre, Amy, and Panarat Thepgumpanat. "Thailand Cracks Down on Migrant Workers as Anti-immigration Feelings Rise." *Reuters*, September 28, 2016. https://www.reuters.com/article/us-thailand-migrants/thailand-cracks-down-on-migrant-workers-as-anti-immigration-feelings-rise-idUSKCN11Z0C3.

44. Xing, Yuqing. "How the iPhone Widens the U.S. Trade Deficit with China: The Case of the iPhone X." *VOXEU*, November 11, 2019. https://voxeu.org/article/how-iphone-widens-us-trade-deficit-china-0.

45. OECD-WTO. "Trade in Value Added: China," October 2015, 2. https://www.oecd.org/sti/ind/tiva/CN_2015_China.pdf; OECD. "Trade in Value Added: China 2018." December 2018, fig. 1. https://www.oecd.org/industry/ind/TIVA-2018-China.pdf.

46. Li, Yun. "More than 50 Companies Reportedly Pull Production out of China Due to Trade War." *CNBC*, July 18, 2019. https://www.cnbc.com/2019/07/18/more-than-50-companies-reportedly-pull-production-out-of-china-due-to-trade-war.html; Hufford, Austen, and Bob Tita. "Manufacturers Move Supply Chains out of China." *Wall Street Journal*, July 14, 2019. https://www.wsj.com/articles/manu

facturers-move-supply-chains-out-of-china-11563096601; Nikkei Staff Writers. "Trade War Drives Asian Manufacturing Out of China." *Nikkei Asia,* October 24, 2018. https://asia.nikkei.com/Economy/Trade-war/Trade-war-drives-Asian-manufacturing -out-of-China.

47. Kynge, James. "China Triples Investment in Emerging Asia on Trade War." *Financial Times,* April 2, 2020. https://www.ft.com/content/b9b44cd6-55b0-11e9 -91f9-b6515a54c5b1.

48. World Bank. "China Intermediate Goods Exports by Country in US$ Thousand 1992–2018." World Integrated Trade Solutions, 2018. https://wits.worldbank .org/CountryProfile/en/Country/CHN/StartYear/1992/EndYear/2018/Trade Flow/Export/Indicator/XPRT-TRD-VL/Partner/BY-COUNTRY/Product /UNCTAD-SoP2.

49. Kurlantzick, Joshua. "ASEAN's Future and Asian Integration." Working paper. Council on Foreign Relations, 2012, 2. https://www.cfr.org/sites/default/files/pdf /2012/10/IIGG_WorkingPaper10_Kurlantzick.pdf.

50. Soesastro, Hadi. "The ASEAN Free Trade Area: A Critical Assessment." *Journal of East Asian Affairs* 16, no. 1 (2002): 20–53. http://www.jstor.org/stable /23255936.

51. Kawai, Mashiro, and Ganeshan Wignaraja. "Main Findings and Policy Implications." In *Asia's Free Trade Agreements: How Is Business Responding?,* edited by Mashiro Kawai and Ganeshan Wignaraja. Northampton, MA: Asian Development Bank, 2011, 59. https://www.adb.org/sites/default/files/publication/28013/asias -free-trade-agreements.pdf.

52. Sally, Razeen. *Regional Economic Integration in Asia: The Track Record and Prospects.* Brussels: ECIPE, 2010. https://ecipe.org/wp-content/uploads/2014/12 /regional-economic-integration-in-asia-the-track-record-and-prospects.pdf. Currency swaps were part of the Chiang Mai Initiative started in 2000 in the wake of the 1997 Asian financial crisis. ASEAN nations, China, Japan, and South Korea created a fund for the central banks to draw on during currency and financial crises. The initiative never got beyond the uncoordinated voluntary stage and was not used in the wake of the 2008 financial crisis.

53. Asian Development Bank. *Infrastructure for a Seamless Asia.* Tokyo: Asian Development Bank Institute, 2009, 65. https://www.adb.org/sites/default/files /publication/159348/adbi-infrastructure-seamless-asia.pdf.

54. UNESCAP. "Single Window for Trade Facilitation: Regional Best Practices and Future Development." 2020. https://www.unescap.org/resources/single-window -trade-facilitation-regional-best-practices-and-future-development.

55. UNCTAD. *Review of Maritime Transport 2018.* New York: United Nations Publications, 2018, 14, 46. https://unctad.org/en/PublicationsLibrary/rmt2018 _en.pdf.

56. Rosen, Eric. "The 2019 List of Busiest Airline Routes in The World." *Forbes,* April 2, 2019. https://www.forbes.com/sites/ericrosen/2019/04/02/the-2019-list -of-busiest-airline-routes-in-the-world/#244a1fa01d48.

57. China Power Team. "How Web-Connected Is China?" ChinaPower Project, April 18, 2019. http://chinapower.csis.org/web-connectedness/; IDG Connect. "Five Reasons South Korea Has the Fastest Internet," July 31, 2017. https://www.idgconnect.com/idgconnect/opinion/1027153/reasons-south-korea-fastest-internet; Web FX. "Who Has the Fastest Internet Connection in the World?," April 1, 2020. https://www.webfx.com/blog/internet/fastest-internet-connection-infographic/; OECD. *Southeast Asia Going Digital: Connecting SMEs.* Paris: OECD, 2019, 33. https://www.oecd.org/going-digital/southeast-asia-connecting-SMEs.pdf.

58. Fujimura, Manabu, and Ramesh Adhikari. "Critical Evaluation of Cross-Border Infrastructure Projects in Asia." *SSRN Electronic Journal,* 2010, 15. https://doi.org/10.2139/ssrn.1653699. For instance, the main highway in the Lao People's Democratic Republic stops seven kilometers from the Cambodian border, forcing cargo to shift to boats.

59. "Vietnam Pulls Abominable Film over South China Sea Map." *BBC News,* October 14, 2019. https://www.bbc.com/news/world-asia-50040667.

60. Hosokawa, Kotaro. "Samsung Races to Guard Its Secrets as China Rivals Close In." Nikkei Asia, February 12, 2021. https://asia.nikkei.com/Business/Business-Spotlight/Samsung-races-to-guard-its-secrets-as-China-rivals-close-in; "South Korea Indicts Group for Leaking Samsung Display Tech to Chinese Firm." *Reuters,* November 29, 2018. https://www.reuters.com/article/us-china-samsung-elec/south-korea-indicts-group-for-leaking-samsung-display-tech-to-chinese-firm-idUSKCN1NY17K.

61. Schneider, Jordan. "The View from Chengdu: Freelance Reporting Outside First-Tier Cities." *China EconTalk* (podcast), August 21, 2019. https://supchina.com/podcast/the-view-from-chengdu-freelance-reporting-outside-first-tier-cities/; Teixeira, Laura. "K-Pop's Big China Problem." *Foreign Policy,* July 30, 2019. https://foreignpolicy.com/2019/07/30/k-pops-big-china-problem/.

62. Kopf, Dan. "ASEAN Is Now a Bigger Trading Partner for China than the US." *Quartz,* May 27, 2020. https://qz.com/1861047/asean-is-now-a-bigger-trading-partner-for-china-than-the-us/.

4. North America

1. Petraeus, David H., Robert B. Zoellick, and Shannon K. O'Neil. "North America: Time for a New Focus." Council on Foreign Relations, 2014, 29, 32. https://cdn.cfr.org/sites/default/files/report_pdf/TFR71_North_America.pdf.

2. Aspinwall, Mark. "Learning from the Experience of NAFTA Labor and Environmental Governance." *Forbes,* August 10, 2017. https://www.forbes.com/sites/themexicoinstitute/2017/08/10/learning-from-the-experience-of-nafta-labor-and-environmental-governance/; Secretariat of the Commission for Environmental Cooperation. "North American Agreement on Environmental Cooperation: Between the Government of Canada, the Government of the United Mexican States and the Government of the United States of America." 1993. https://ustr.gov/sites/default/files/naaec.pdf.

3. WorldTradeLaw.net. "NAFTA Chapter 19 Binational Panel Decisions." Ac-

cessed March 29, 2021. https://www.worldtradelaw.net/databases/nafta19.php; May, Rachel. "The Dispute over Dispute Settlement in NAFTA." *Bipartisan Policy Center Blog,* October 30, 2017. https://bipartisanpolicy.org/blog/the-dispute-over-dispute -settlement-in-nafta/. Two separate sets of arbitration panels were set up. One enabled investors to sue the government of another country if they believe they have been treated differently from their domestic counterparts or believe government regulations harm their investments, what are now called "investor-state dispute" solutions. The second set of panels deals with antidumping and countervailing tariffs claims, which look into price dumping and unfair state subsidies, respectively.

4. Brown, Catherine, and Christine Manolakas. "Corporate Reorganizations and Treaty Relief from Double Taxation within the NAFTA Block." *Louisiana Law Review* 59, no. 1 (1998): 253–300. https://digitalcommons.law.lsu.edu/cgi/viewcontent .cgi?article=5755&context=lalrev. While some limits and inconsistencies continued, these agreements ensured overall lower taxes for those working throughout the NAFTA region.

5. Martin, Michael F. "U.S. Clothing and Textile Trade with China and the World: Trends since the End of Quotas." Congressional Research Service, July 10, 2007, 4. https://fas.org/sgp/crs/row/RL34106.pdf; Platzer, Michaela D. "Renegotiating NAFTA and U.S. Textile Manufacturing." Congressional Research Service, October 30, 2017. https://fas.org/sgp/crs/row/R44998.pdf. These protections lasted until 2005, when the Multi-Fiber Arrangement ended and WTO members gained quota-free access to the U.S. market.

6. Cadot, Olivier, Jaime De Melo, Antoni Estevadeordal, Akiko Suwa-Eisenmann, and Bolormaa Tumurchudur. "Assessing the Effect of NAFTA's Rules of Origin." Research Unit Working Papers. Laboratoire d'Economie Appliquée, INRA, June 2002. https://www.researchgate.net/publication/5162601_Assessing_the_effect_of _NAFTA%27s_rules_of_origin. Other studies find even greater costs. Alex Jameson Appiah estimates the cost to consumers at over $400 billion, using applied general equilibrium analysis of North American integration with rules of origin. Appiah, Alex Jameson. "Applied General Equilibrium Model of North American Integration with Rules of Origin." Simon Fraser University, 1999. https://www.nlc-bnc.ca/obj/s4/f2 /dsk1/tape7/PQDD_0014/NQ52704.pdf?is_thesis=1&oclc_number=1006832924. See Pastor, Robert A. *The North American Idea: A Vision of a Continental Future.* New York: Oxford University Press, 2011, 134.

7. World Bank. "GDP (Current US$)—United States, Canada, Mexico," 2020. https://data.worldbank.org/indicator/NY.GDP.MKTP.CD?end=2003&locations =US-CA-MX&start=1993; Villarreal, M. Angeles. "CRS Report for Congress: NAFTA and the Mexican Economy." Congressional Research Service, June 3, 2010. https:// crsreports.congress.gov/product/details?prodcode=RL34733. In 1994, Mexico's GDP per capita in current U.S. dollars was $5,854, Canada's was $19,935, and the United States' was $27,695.

8. Hillberry, Russell H., and Christine A. McDaniel. "A Decomposition of North

American Trade Growth since NAFTA." Working Paper No. 2002-12-A. U.S. International Trade Commission, July 1, 2002. http://dx.doi.org/10.2139/ssrn.366320.

9. OECD. "Measuring Globalisation: OECD Economic Globalisation Indicators." 2010.   https://www.oecd-ilibrary.org/docserver/9789264084360-en.pdf?expires =1626810811&id=id&accname=guest&checksum=91EDCD01AF266121A73599 FA57BFE53B; Knowledge at Wharton. "NAFTA, 20 Years Later: Do the Benefits Outweigh the Costs?" February 19, 2014. https://knowledge.wharton.upenn.edu /article/nafta-20-years-later-benefits-outweigh-costs/; Office of the United States Trade Representative. "Mexico." Accessed March 10, 2021. https://ustr.gov/countries -regions/americas/mexico. In contrast, Mexican- and Canadian-made inputs constitute a much smaller 3.4 percent on average of U.S. exports.

10. Cruikshank, Jeffrey L., and David B. Sicilia. *The Engine That Could: Seventy-Five Years of Values-Driven Change at Cummins Engine Company.* Cambridge, MA: Harvard Business School Press, 1997, 397.

11. Wagner, I. "North American Vehicle Production from 1990 to 2020," Statista, March 29, 2021. https://www.statista.com/statistics/204208/north-america-vehicle -production-since-1990/.

12. Parilla, Joseph, and Mark Muro. "U.S. Metros Most Exposed to a Trump Trade Shock." *Brookings Blog,* November 30, 2001. https://www.brookings.edu/blog /the-avenue/2017/01/27/u-s-metros-most-dependent-on-trade/.

13. Miller, Dan, and Dan Nied. "American Journey: Gaining Traction (1970–1988)." *Toyota Today,* October 2017. https://www.toyotatoday.com/news/american -journey-gaining-traction-1970-1988.htm.

14. Miller and Nied.

15. Hoopfer, Evan. "Toyota Announces Big Changes to Its Texas Plant Lineup." *Dallas Business Journal,* January 17, 2020. https://www.bizjournals.com/dallas/news /2020/01/17/toyota-texas.html.

16. Shepardson, David. "Toyota, Mazda Joint Venture Alabama Plant Will Now Cost $2.3 Billion." *Reuters,* August 13, 2020. https://www.reuters.com/article/us -toyota-mazda-plant-idUSKCN2592V0.

17. National Highway Traffic Safety Administration. "Part 583 American Automobile Labeling Act Reports." January 30, 2017. https://www.nhtsa.gov/part-583 -american-automobile-labeling-act-reports. Quoted in Johnson, David. "How American Is Your Car?" *Time,* March 2, 2017. https://time.com/4681166/car-made-american/. The Toyota Camry outranks comparable midsize sedans in U.S. and Canadian parts. Camry has 75 percent, Ford Fusion 25 percent, Chevrolet Malibu 56 percent, Honda Accord 70 percent.

18. Klier, Thomas H., and James M. Rubenstein. "Who Really Made Your Car? Restructuring and Geographic Change in the Auto Industry." W. E. Upjohn Institute for Employment Research, 2008, 206, 217. https://doi.org/10.17848/9781435678552; Larrick, Don. "The Ohio Motor Vehicle Report." Ohio Development Services Agency, February 2019. https://development.ohio.gov/files/research/B1002.pdf.

19. Lamar, Steve. "How to Keep NAFTA Dressed for Success." U.S. Chamber of Commerce, November 28, 2017. https://www.uschamber.com/series/modernizing-nafta/how-keep-nafta-dressed-success.

20. HSBC Global Connections. "How Canada's Bombardier Makes NAFTA Work." January 12, 2015. https://web.archive.org/web/20150419032849/https://globalconnections.hsbc.com/canada/en/articles/how-canadas-bombardier-makes-nafta-work; "Ready to Take Off Again?" *Economist,* January 4, 2014. https://www.economist.com/briefing/2014/01/04/ready-to-take-off-again; Trimble, Steven. "In Focus: Bombardier Reveals Queretaro Plant for Learjet 85." FlightGlobal, October 22, 2012. https://www.flightglobal.com/in-focus-bombardier-reveals-queretaro-plant-for-learjet-85/107420.article.

21. Desjardins, Jeff. "Great Lakes Economy: Examining the Cross-Border Supply Chain." Visual Capitalist, October 19, 2017. https://www.visualcapitalist.com/great-lakes-economy-cross-border-supply-chain/; Taylor, Guy. "Aerospace: An Emerging Mexican Industry." *Americas Quarterly,* January 13, 2017. https://www.americasquarterly.org/fulltextarticle/aerospace-an-emerging-mexican-industry/; Mecham, Michael. "Mexico's Welcome Mat Attracts Aerospace Manufacturers." *Aviation Week,* April 1, 2013. https://aviationweek.com/mexicos-welcome-mat-attracts-aerospace-manufacturers; Safran. "Safran in Mexico," January 9, 2015. https://www.safran-group.com/country/safran-mexico.

22. Grupo Herdez. "100 Years Creating Our Story: 2014 Annual Report." 2014, 4. https://search.proquest.com/docview/1910449268/abstract/86E514A537DA4CDFPQ/1.

23. Pastor, *North American Idea,* 215.

24. OECD. "Inward FDI Flows by Partner Country." Accessed March 31, 2021. http://data.oecd.org/fdi/inward-fdi-flows-by-partner-country.htm. Author's calculations from OECD. Santander Trade. "Mexico: Foreign Investment." July 2021. https://santandertrade.com/en/portal/establish-overseas/mexico/foreign-investment.

25. Lessard, Donald R., and Rafael Lucea. "Mexican Multinationals: Insights from CEMEX." SSRN Scholarly Paper. *Social Science Research Network,* October 24, 2008, 290. https://doi.org/10.2139/ssrn.1289439.

26. Gazcón, Fernando. "Prevén cementeras producción récord." Grupo Reforma, 1993. https://busquedas.gruporeforma.com/reforma/Documento/Impresa.aspx?id=1079763%7CInfodexTextos&url=https://hemerotecalibre.reforma.com/19931123/interactiva/RNEG19931123-024.JPG&text=cemex+abastece&tit=.

27. Case, Brendan M. "World's No. 3 Cement Maker Pays $2.8 Billion for Southdown." *Journal Times,* October 1, 2000. https://journaltimes.com/business/worlds-no-3-cement-maker-pays-2-8-billion-for-southdown/article_bfb20593-452b-5efb-9356-c58763fb4boe.html; Leal, Juan David. "CEMEX se afianza con compra Rinker en EEUU pero asume riesgos inmobiliarios." *El Economista.* Accessed March 31, 2021. https://www.eleconomista.es/empresas-finanzas/noticias/195754/04/07/Cemex-se-afianza-con-compra-Rinker-en-EEUU-pero-asume-riesgos-inmobiliarios.html;

"Update 1: U.S. Would Require Cemex Asset Sales in Rinker Deal." *Reuters*, April 4, 2007. https://www.reuters.com/article/rinker-cemex-usa-idUSN0439779420070404.

28. Lessard and Lucca, "Mexican Multinationals," 291; Henneberry, Brittany. "Top Cement Companies and Suppliers in the USA." ThomasNet. Accessed March 31, 2021. https://www.thomasnet.com/articles/top-suppliers/cement-companies-suppliers.

29. Lederman, Daniel, William F. Maloney, and Luis Servén. "Lessons from NAFTA: For Latin America and the Caribbean." Stanford University and the World Bank, 2005, 182. https://publications.iadb.org/publications/english/document/Lessons-from-NAFTA-For-Latin-America-and-the-Caribbean.pdf.

30. U.S. Senate, *Modernization of the North American Free Trade Agreement (NAFTA): Hearing Before the Subcommittee on International Trade, Customs, and Global Competitiveness of the Committee on Finance of the United States Senate.* U.S. Government Publishing Office, November 20, 2017. https://www.finance.senate.gov/imo/media/doc/33622.pdf.

31. BLS Beta Labs. "BLS Data Viewer." Accessed March 31, 2021. https://beta.bls.gov/dataViewer/view/timeseries/CEU0000000001; Statistics Canada. "Labour Force Characteristics by Industry, Annual (x 1,000)," January 25, 2021. https://www150.statcan.gc.ca/t1/tbl1/en/tv.action?pid=1410002301. OECD. "National Accounts," 2020. https://www.oecd.org/sdd/na/. Author's calculations based on data.

32. Hufbauer, Gary Clyde, Cathleen Cimino, and Tyler Moran. "NAFTA at 20: Misleading Charges and Positive Achievements." Peterson Institute for International Economics, May 2014, 2. https://www.piie.com/sites/default/files/publications/pb/pb14-13.pdf.

33. World Bank. "GDP (Constant 2010 US$)—United States, Canada, Mexico." Accessed March 31, 2021. https://data.worldbank.org/indicator/NY.GDP.MKTP.KD?end=2003&locations=US-CA-MX&start=1993; World Bank, "GDP (Current US$)." In real terms, the U.S. economy grew by 40 percent, the Canadian by 39 percent, and the Mexican by 28 percent. Author's calculations based on data from the World Bank.

34. United States Trade Representative. "Canada." Accessed March 31, 2021. https://ustr.gov/countries-regions/americas/canada; International Trade Administration. "Canada Country Commercial Guide." Accessed March 31, 2021. https://www.trade.gov/knowledge-product/canada-market-overview?section-nav=4608. In 2018, U.S. exports to Canada accounted for 18 percent of all U.S. exports.

35. James E. Risch, U.S. Senator for Idaho. "Risch, Crapo, Gardner Call for Increased Access for Fresh Potato Exports to Mexico." August 19, 2020. https://www.risch.senate.gov/public/index.cfm/2020/8/risch-crapo-gardner-call-for-increased-access-for-fresh-potato-exports-to-mexico; "Mexican Hass Avocado Import Program." *Federal Register*, May 27, 2016. https://www.federalregister.gov/documents/2016/05/27/2016-12586/mexican-hass-avocado-import-program; California Fresh Fruit Association. "International." Accessed December 2020. https://cafreshfruit.com/international-relations/.

36. Cadman, Brie. "Tell the FDA to Regulate Bogus Health Claims on Food Labels." Change.org, 2011. https://www.change.org/p/tell-the-fda-to-regulate-bogus

-health-claims-on-food-labels; Scrinis, Gyorgy. "That's Not Natural or Organic: How Big Food Misleads." Cornucopia Institute, July 25, 2013. https://www.cornucopia .org/2013/07/thats-not-natural-or-organic-how-big-food-misleads/; CerealFacts.org. "Cereal Box Claims," June 2012. http://www.cerealfacts.org/media/Parents/Cereal _Box_Claims.pdf.

37. Powell, Jennifer. "Services in the NAFTA." U.S. International Trade Commission, Office of Industries, September 2018, 13. http://usitc.gov/publications/332 /working_papers/services_in_the_nafta_compiled_version_91818_ss_tc.pdf.

38. American Petroleum Institute, Asociación mexicana de empresas de hirdocarburos, and Canada's Oil and Natural Gas Producers. "North American Oil & Natural Gas Industry Positions on NAFTA." 2. Accessed April 12, 2021. https://www.api .org/~/media/Files/Policy/Trade/API-AMEXHI-CAPP-1st-Position-Paper-on -NAFTA.pdf; Ahmed, Azam, Matt Richtel, and Andrew Jacobs. "In NAFTA Talks, U.S. Tries to Limit Junk Food Warning Labels." *New York Times,* March 20, 2018, sec. World. https://www.nytimes.com/2018/03/20/world/americas/nafta-food-labels -obesity.html.

39. Studer-Noguez, Isabel, and Carol Wise. *Requiem or Revival? The Promise of North American Integration.* Washington, DC: Brookings Institution Press, 2007, 47; Pastor, *North American Idea.*

40. Blank, Stephen, Stephanie Globb, and Guy Stanley. "A North American Transportation Infrastructure Strategy." *Canadian Transportation Research Forum,* August 2014, 15. https://ctrf.ca/wp-content/uploads/2014/08/A-North-American -Transportation-Infrastructure-Strategy.pdf.

41. U.S. Government Accountability Office (GAO). "U.S. Ports of Entry: CBP Public-Private Partnership Programs Have Benefits, but CBP Could Strengthen Evaluation Efforts." March 2018, 1. https://www.gao.gov/assets/gao-18-268.pdf; U.S. GAO. "Border Infrastructure: Actions Needed to Improve Information on Facilities and Capital Planning at Land Border Crossings." July 2019. https://www.gao.gov /assets/gao-19-534.pdf.

42. Infrastructure Report Card. "America's Infrastructure Scores a C–," 2021. https://infrastructurereportcard.org/.

43. U.S. Department of Homeland Security. "Border Infrastructure Investment Plan 3.0: Canada–United States," August 2016. https://www.dhs.gov/sites/default /files/publications/BIIP%203%200o%20-%20FINAL.PDF.

44. U.S. Border Patrol. "Border Patrol Agent Nationwide Staffing by Fiscal Year." 2019. https://www.cbp.gov/sites/default/files/assets/documents/2019-Mar/Staffing %20FY1992-FY2018.pdf; American Immigration Council. "The Cost of Immigration Enforcement and Border Security." September 23, 2013. https://www.american immigrationcouncil.org/research/the-cost-of-immigration-enforcement-and-border -security. 3; National Treasury Employees Union. "CBP FY 2019 Budget Request." April 12, 2018. https://www.nteu.org/legislative-action/congressional-testimony/cbp -fy-2019-budget-request; U.S. Department of Homeland Security. "DHS Budget." May 10, 2011. https://www.dhs.gov/dhs-budget.

45. Archibold, Randal C. "Hired by Customs, but Working for Mexican Cartels." *New York Times,* December 18, 2009, sec. U.S. https://www.nytimes.com/2009/12/18/us/18corrupt.html.

46. U.S. GAO, "U.S. Ports of Entry," 1; U.S. Customs and Border Protection. "Trusted Traveler Programs," January 2018. https://www.cbp.gov/sites/default/files/assets/documents/2018-Jan/fieldops-trusted-traveler-fact-sheet-201510.pdf. Author's calculations based on data.

47. New Mexico Border Authority. "Santa Teresa: Modern! Convenient! Fast!" Accessed June 18, 2021. http://www.nmborder.com/Santa_Teresa.aspx.

48. USTradeNumbers. "El Paso Border Crossing, Texas." Accessed March 31, 2021. https://www.ustradenumbers.com/port/el-paso-border-crossing-texas/.

49. U.S. Census Bureau. "Place of Birth for the Foreign-Born Population in the United States," 2019. https://data.census.gov/cedsci/table?t=Place%20of%20Birth&tid=ACSDT1Y2018.B05006&hidePreview=false. Author's calculations based on data.

50. U.S. Department of State, Bureau of Consular Affairs. "Worldwide NIV Workload by Visa Category FY 2013." 2013. https://travel.state.gov/content/dam/visas/Statistics/Non-Immigrant-Statistics/NIVWorkload/FY2013NIVWorkloadbyVisaCategory.pdf. The limited use of this program is due in part to the uncertainty of receiving the visa (the categories are ill defined) and in part to its very temporary nature (one year, though renewable). These issues encourage skilled individuals to pursue other visa categories and green cards.

51. OpenDoors Data. "Fast Facts 2020." 2020. https://opendoorsdata.org/fast_facts/fast-facts-2020/; Canadian Bureau for International Education. "530, 540 International Students in Canada at All Levels of Study in 2020," 2020. https://cbie.ca/infographic/.

52. Tonby, Oliver, Jonathan Woetzel, Wonsik Choi, Karel Eloot, Rajat Dhawan, Jeongmin Seong, and Patti Wang. "The Future of Asia: Asian Flows and Networks Are Defining the Next Phase of Globalization." McKinsey Global Institute, September 2019, 18. https://www.mckinsey.com/~/media/McKinsey/Featured%20Insights/Asia%20Pacific/The%20future%20of%20Asia%20Asian%20flows%20and%20networks%20are%20defining%20the%20next%20phase%20of%20globalization/MGI-Future-of-Asia-Flows-and-Trade-Discussion-paper-Sep-2019.ashx; Lock, S. "Number of United States Residents Travelling Overseas from 2002 to 2020 (in Millions)." Statista, June 3, 2021. https://www.statista.com/statistics/214774/number-of-outbound-tourists-from-the-us/.

53. Schmitt, Eric. "Bush Aides Weigh Legalizing Status of Mexicans in U.S." *New York Times,* July 15, 2001, sec. U.S. https://www.nytimes.com/2001/07/15/us/bush-aides-weigh-legalizing-status-of-mexicans-in-us.html.

54. Author's calculations using Comtrade data.

55. Peters, Enrique Dussel, and Kevin P. Gallagher. "NAFTA's Uninvited Guest: China and the Disintegration of North American Trade." *Cepal Review* 110 (August 2013): 26. https://repositorio.cepal.org/bitstream/handle/11362/37000/1/RVI110

DusselGallagher_en.pdf. U.S. exports to Mexico of women's coats and underwear reduced 66 and 72 percent, respectively, between 2000 and 2009.

56. Rodriguez, Laura V. "Footwear." United States International Trade Commission, 2015. https://www.usitc.gov/research_and_analysis/trade_shifts_2015/footwear.htm. Data from 2011 to 2015.

57. Nike. "Nike Sustainability—Interactive Map." February 2021. http://manufacturingmap.nikeinc.com/; Mexico Footwear Agency. "How to Take Advantage on Footwear Manufacturing in Mexico." May 6, 2014. https://mexicofootwear.com/blog/advantage-footwear-manufacturing-in-mexico/.

58. Peters and Gallagher, "NAFTA's Uninvited Guest."

59. Dussel Peters, Enrique. "The New Triangular Relationship between Mexico, the United States, and China: Challenges for NAFTA." In *The Renegotiation of NAFTA. And China?,* edited by Enrique Dussel Peters. México: Universidad Nacional Autónoma de México, 2018, 91. https://dusselpeters.com/CECHIMEX/20181210_Renegotiation_of_NAFTA_and_China.pdf; Canis, Bill, and Wayne M Morrison. "U.S.-Chinese Motor Vehicle Trade: Overview and Issues." Congressional Research Service, August 16, 2013, 7. https://fas.org/sgp/crs/row/R43071.pdf.

60. Dussel Peters, "New Triangular Relationship." Since China entered the WTO, intraregional trade has decreased from 56.2 percent in 2000 to under 50 percent in 2014.

61. Acemoglu, Daron, David Autor, David Dorn, Gordon H. Hanson, and Brendan Price. "Import Competition and the Great U.S. Employment Sag of the 2000s." *Journal of Labor Economics* 34, no. S1 (2016): S141–98. https://doi.org/10.1086/682384; Sargent, John, and Linda Matthews. "China versus Mexico in the Global EPZ Industry: Maquiladoras, FDI Quality, and Plant Mortality—ScienceDirect." *World Development* 37, no. 6 (December 31, 2008): 1069–82. https://doi.org/10.1016/j.worlddev.2008.10.002.

62. Atlas of Economic Complexity. "What Did United States of America Export in 2017?" Accessed March 31, 2021. https://atlas.cid.harvard.edu/explore?country=231&product=undefined&year=2017&productClass=HS&target=Product&partner=undefined&startYear=1995.

63. Fikes, Bradley J. "San Diego's Hybritech Still Influences Local Biotech, 40 Years Later." *San Diego Union-Tribune,* May 9, 2018. https://www.sandiegouniontribune.com/business/biotech/sd-me-hybritech-20180509-story.html.

64. San Diego Regional EDC. "Tijuana Regional Profile." 2017, 3. https://usmex.ucsd.edu/_files/events/frontera-fridays/tijuana-regional-profile-2017.pdf.

65. San Diego Regional EDC, 5; Committee on Binational Regional Opportunities. "2018 San Diego-Baja California Border Crossing and Trade Highlights," May 7, 2019, 32–33. https://www.otaymesa.org/wp-content/uploads/2020/01/Border-Wait-Times.pdf. The document from the Committee on Binational Regional Opportunities only includes northbound traffic, estimated at nearly seventy thousand per day in 2018. Southbound traffic is estimated to be a similar number.

66. Observatory of Economic Complexity. "Where Does Mexico Export Instru-

ments To? (2018)." Accessed March 31, 2021. https://oec.world/en/visualize/geo map/hs92/export/mex/show/18/2018/.

67. Bennett, Darryn. "How San Diego Biotech Started and Where It's Going." *Voice of San Diego,* August 4, 2008, sec. News. https://www.voiceofsandiego.org /topics/news/how-san-diego-biotech-started-and-where-its-going/.

68. Ryan, Sarah. "Vast Majority of Alberta's Masks for Schoolchildren Made in China and Mexico." *Global News,* August 10, 2020. https://globalnews.ca/news /7264331/alberta-masks-school-children-made-in-china-mexico/.

69. Faux, Jeff. "How NAFTA Failed Mexico." *American Prospect,* June 16, 2003. https://prospect.org/api/content/768d2a1e-bd1b-544f-bc49-a16e7a5533d6/; Blatchford, Andy. "Five Key NAFTA Issues Bound to Spark Friction between Canada, U.S." *Toronto Star,* July 21, 2017, sec. Canada. https://www.thestar.com/news /canada/2017/07/21/five-key-nafta-issues-bound-to-spark-friction-between-canada -us.html.

70. Desai, Mihir A., C. Fritz Foley, and James R. Hines. "Domestic Effects of the Foreign Activities of U.S. Multinationals." *American Economic Journal: Economic Policy* 1, no. 1 (February 2009): 181–203. https://doi.org/10.1257/pol.1.1.181; Hufbauer, Cimino, and Moran, "NAFTA at 20."

71. Cooney, Steven. "U.S. Automotive Industry: Recent History and Issues." Congressional Research Service, April 5, 2005. https://www.everycrsreport.com/reports /RL32883.html. Trucking figures for 1993: 10.9 million; trucking figures for 2003: 12.1 million; employment figures for 1990: 1.0 million; employment figures for 2000: 1.3 million; employment figures for 2004: 1.1 million.

72. U.S. Senate, *Modernization of the North American Free Trade,* 9, 35. The United States has had fourteen plant openings, Mexico eleven, and Canada one as of the end of 2017. Shepardson, "Toyota, Mazda Joint Venture"; Shama, Elijah. "Jaguar, BMW and Mercedes Have Most to Lose among Automakers in U.S. Tariff War." CNBC, July 10, 2019. https://www.cnbc.com/2019/07/10/automakers-jaguar-bmw -and-mercedes-have-most-to-lose-in-us-tariff-war.html.

73. Sanchez, Edward A. "General Motors' Janesville Assembly to Be Closed Permanently." *Truck Trend,* October 29, 2015. http://www.trucktrend.com/news/1510 -general-motors-janesville-assembly-to-be-closed-permanently/; Goldstein, Amy. "Janesville: An American Story." *Washington Post,* April 15, 2017. https://www.washington post.com/sf/national/2017/04/15/janesville/.

74. Reliable Plant. "Ford Ceases Production at Norfolk Assembly Plant." Accessed March 31, 2021. https://www.reliableplant.com/Read/7124/ford-ceases-production -at-norfolk-assembly-plant.

75. Muro, Mark. "Where the Robots Are." *The Avenue* (blog), Brookings, August 14, 2017. https://www.brookings.edu/blog/the-avenue/2017/08/14/where -the-robots-are/.

76. Wagner, I. "Light Vehicle Retail Sales in the United States from 1976 to 2020." Statista, February 5, 2021. https://www.statista.com/statistics/199983/us-vehicle -sales-since-1951/. By 2000, U.S.-market vehicle sales had plateaued.

77. U.S. Senate, *Modernization of the North American Free Trade*, 9, 35. See U.S. Department of Commerce, International Trade Administration, Office of Industry Policy. "NAFTA 10 Years Later." June 2004. https://legacy.trade.gov/mas/ian/build /groups/public/@tg_ian/documents/webcontent/tg_ian_001987.pdf.

78. Semuels, Alana. "How Immigrants Have Contributed to American Inventiveness." *Atlantic*, February 7, 2017. https://www.theatlantic.com/business/archive /2017/02/immigrants-american-inventiveness/515928/; Cowen, Tyler. "How Immigrants Create More Jobs." *New York Times*, October 30, 2010, sec. Economy. https:// www.nytimes.com/2010/10/31/business/economy/31view.html.

5. Going Forward

1. Global Trade Alert. "Global Dynamics." 2020. https://www.globaltradealert .org/global_dynamics.

2. Marel. "Secondary Processing." Accessed October 2, 2020. https://marel.com /fish/processes/whitefish/secondary-processing/; Marel. "RoboBatcher Thermoformer." Accessed October 2, 2020. https://marel.com/en/products/robobatcher -thermoformer/fish/salmon; Marel. "Primex Norway: The Future of Fish Processing." July 5, 2019. https://marel.com/customer-stories/primex-norway-the-future -of-fish-processing/.

3. Tillman, Maggie. "What Is AmazonGo, Where Is It, and How Does It Work?" *Pocket Lint*, February 25, 2020. https://www.pocket-lint.com/phones/news/amazon /139650-what-is-amazon-go-where-is-it-and-how-does-it-work; Gross, Ryan. "How the AmazonGo Store's AI Works." Towards Data Science, *Medium*, June 6, 2019. https://towardsdatascience.com/how-the-amazon-go-store-works-a-deep-dive -3fde9d9939e9.

4. Lund, Susan, James Manyika, Jonathan Woetzel, Jacques Bughin, Mekala Krishnan, Jeongmin Seong, and Mac Muir. "Globalization in Transition: The Future of Trade and Value Chains." McKinsey Global Institute, 2019, 75–76. https://www .mckinsey.com/featured-insights/innovation-and-growth/globalization-in-transition -the-future-of-trade-and-value-chains#.

5. AMFG. "7 Exciting Examples of 3D Printing in the Automotive Industry," May 28, 2019. https://amfg.ai/2019/05/28/7-exciting-examples-of-3d-printing-in -the-automotive-industry/; Spaulding, Beverly. "4 Companies That Use Simulation Software to Speed Design." PTC, May 30, 2018. https://www.ptc.com/en/cad-soft ware-blog/four-companies-that-use-simulation-software-to-speed-design.

6. Grill-Goodman, Jamie. "How Nike's Digital Transformation Is Personalizing Retail." *Rise News*, September 28, 2018. https://risnews.com/how-nikes-digital -transformation-personalizing-retail; Taylor, Paul. "Demand Sensing Software Helps Unilever." *Financial Times*, March 18, 2011. https://www.ft.com/content/9fab4aee -50e4-11e0-8931-00144feab49a.

7. Moody, Steve. "Two Born Every Minute: Inside Nissan's Sunderland Factory." *Car Magazine UK*, November 3, 2016. https://www.carmagazine.co.uk/features/car -culture/two-born-every-minute-inside-nissans-sunderland-factory-car-february-2016/.

8. Kuo, Lily. "A Legion of Robots from China Could Change the Future of Manufacturing." *Quartz*, November 29, 2012. https://qz.com/32117/a-legion-of -robots-from-china-could-change-the-future-of-manufacturing/.

9. Asian Development Bank. *Leveraging Services for Development: Prospects and Policies*. Tokyo: Asian Development Bank, 2019. https://www.adb.org/publications /leveraging-services-development-prospects-policies; University of Tokyo. "Japan: The Land of Rising Robotics." Accessed October 9, 2020. https://www.u-tokyo.ac.jp/en /whyutokyo/wj_003.html. Robots add roughly 5 percent to both Singapore's and South Korea's workforces. Asian Development Bank. *Asian Economic Integration Report 2019/2020*. Manila, Philippines: Asian Development Bank, November 2019, 151, 159–60. https://www.adb.org/sites/default/files/publication/536691/aeir-2019-2020.pdf.

10. AMFG, "7 Exciting Examples of 3D Printing"; Symes, Steven. "3D Printing and the Automotive Industry: What You Need to Know." *Grab Cad Blog*, June 4, 2019. https://blog.grabcad.com/blog/2019/06/04/3d-printing-and-the-automotive -industry/; CASTOR. "The Best Applications of 3D Printing in the Automotive In- dustry." January 20, 2020. https://www.3dcastor.com/post/the-best-applications-of -3d-printing-in-the-automotive-industry; Kellner, Thomas. "The 3D-Printed Age: Why This Futuristic Ohio Factory Is Proving Mark Twain Wrong." General Electric, November 30, 2018. https://www.ge.com/reports/3d-printed-age-futuristic-ohio -factory-proving-mark-twain-wrong/; Hitch, John. "State of 3D Printing 2019: All Grown Up & Ready to Work." *IndustryWeek*, February 1, 2019. https://www.industry week.com/technology-and-iiot/article/22027080/state-of-3d-printing-2019-all -grown-up-ready-to-work.

11. Adidas Group. "Adidas Deploys Speedfactory Technology at Asian Suppliers by End of 2019." November 11, 2019. https://www.adidas-group.com/en/media /news-archive/press-releases/2019/adidas-deploys-speedfactory-technology-at -asian-suppliers-by-end-2019/.

12. World Bank, "Employment in Services (% of Total Employment) (Modeled ILO Estimate)." Database, 2021. https://data.worldbank.org/indicator/SL.SRV .EMPL.ZS.

13. WTO. *World Trade Report 2019*. Geneva: WTO, 2019, 25, 27. https://www .wto.org/english/res_e/booksp_e/00_wtr19_e.pdf.

14. Gleim Aviation. "How to Convert a Foreign Pilot License to an FAA Certifi- cate." Accessed October 9, 2020. https://www.gleimaviation.com/2019/05/03/how -to-convert-a-foreign-pilot-license-to-an-faa-certificate/.

15. Ferencz, Janos. "The OECD Digital Services Trade Restrictiveness Index." OECD, 2020. https://www.sipotra.it/old/wp-content/uploads/2019/01/The-OECD -Digital-Services-Trade-Restrictiveness-Index.pdf.

16. UNCTAD. "Total Trade in Services." In *e-Handbook of Statistics 2019*. Geneva: UNCTAD, 2019. https://stats.unctad.org/handbook/Services/Total.html; World Bank. "Trade % of GDP," 2020. https://data.worldbank.org/indicator/NE.TRD .GNFS.ZS. Trade in services today is just 7 percent of global GDP, compared to that of goods, which comprise roughly 53 percent of global GDP.

17. Shen, Weiduo. "China's Coastal Manufacturing Bases Face Labor Shortage amid Upgrading." *Global Times,* February 24, 2019. http://www.globaltimes.cn/content/1139971.shtml.

18. Gnanasagaran, Angaindrankumar. "Weak Labour Productivity a Threat to ASEAN's Potential." *ASEAN Post,* June 7, 2018. https://theaseanpost.com/article/weak-labour-productivity-threat-aseans-potential; Asian Productivity Organization. *APO Productivity Databook 2018.* Tokyo: Asian Productivity Organization, 2018. http://www.apo-tokyo.org/publications/wp-content/uploads/sites/5/APO-Productivity-Databook-2018.pdf.

19. World Bank. "Labor Force Participation Rate, Total (% of Total Population Ages 15+) (Modeled ILO Estimate)—European Union, Spain, Italy, France, Germany, Sweden, Austria," 2020. https://data.worldbank.org/indicator/SL.TLF.CACT.ZS?locations=EU-ES-IT-FR-DE-SE-AT.

20. Adams, Josh. "Eastern Europe's Emigration Crisis." *Quillette,* June 29, 2019. https://quillette.com/2019/06/29/eastern-europes-emigration-crisis/; OECD. *International Migration Outlook 2018.* Paris: OECD, 2018, 239. https://read.oecd-ilibrary.org/social-issues-migration-health/international-migration-outlook-2018_migr_outlook-2018-en.

21. WTO, *World Trade Report 2019,* 239.

22. Toossi, Mitra. "A Look at the Future of the U.S. Labor Force to 2060." U.S. Bureau of Labor Statistics, September 2016, 5. https://www.bls.gov/spotlight/2016/a-look-at-the-future-of-the-us-labor-force-to-2060/pdf/a-look-at-the-future-of-the-us-labor-force-to-2060.pdf; Statistics Canada. "Section 3: Analysis of the Results of the Long-Term Projections." Accessed on October 9, 2020. https://www150.statcan.gc.ca/n1/pub/91-520-x/2010001/part-partie3-eng.htm; Lam, David. "Demographic Change and Human Capital in Mexico and Texas." Federal Reserve Bank of Dallas, 2016. https://www.dallasfed.org/~/media/Documents/research/events/2016/16texlam.pdf.

23. World Bank. "Fertility Rate, Total (Births per Woman)—North America, Mexico," 2019. https://data.worldbank.org/indicator/SP.DYN.TFRT.IN?locations=XU-MX. North American families average around 1.95 children, not too far from what demographers call the "replacement rate" of just over 2 children per family. Europe and China average 1.5 and 1.7, respectively. Author's calculations based on World Bank, "Fertility Rate, Total."

24. Horwitz, Josh. "It's Official—China Is the Largest iPhone Market in the World." *Quartz,* May 18, 2016. https://qz.com/687017/its-official-china-is-the-largest-iphone-market-in-the-world/; Research and Markets. "China Athletic Footwear Market Outlook 2018," February 2014. http://www.researchandmarkets.com/reports/2763980/china_athletic_footwear_market_outlook_2018; Chen, Yi. "Estimations and Forecasts of Global Infant Formula Production." Gira Food, July 2018. https://www.girafood.com/wp-content/uploads/2018/09/GIRA_ChinaDairy_GlobalInfantFormulaProductsMarketEN_June2018.pdf; Car Sales Base. "China Cars

Sales Analysis 2018." Accessed October 9, 2020. http://carsalesbase.com/china-car-sales-analysis-2018-brands/.

25. Hamel, Kristofer. "Look East Instead of West for the Future Global Middle Class." OECD, May 7, 2010. https://oecd-development-matters.org/2019/05/07/look-east-instead-of-west-for-the-future-global-middle-class/.

26. International Trade Administration. "Korea Country Commercial Guide." Accessed October 9, 2020. https://www.export.gov/apex/article2?id=Korea-Cosmetics.

27. Gustafson, Krystina. "The World's Biggest Luxury Markets in 2015." *CNBC*, December 31, 2015. https://www.cnbc.com/2015/12/31/the-worlds-biggest-luxury-markets-in-2015.html.

28. US-ASEAN Business Council, Inc. "Growth Projections." Last updated July 22, 2019. https://www.usasean.org/why-asean/growth.

29. Bu, Lambert, Jacob Wang, Kevin Wei Wang, and Daniel Zipser. "China Digital Consumer Trends 2019: Discovering the Next Wave of Growth." McKinsey Digital, September 2019. https://www.mckinsey.com/featured-insights/china/china-digital-consumer-trends-in-2019; International Trade Administration. "China Commercial Guide." Accessed October 15, 2020. https://www.export.gov/article?id=China-ecommerce.

30. Dobbs, Richard, James Manyika, Jonathan Woetzel, Jaana Remes, Jesko Perrey, Greg Kelly, Kanaka Pattabiraman, and Hemant Sharma. *Urban World: The Global Consumers to Watch.* McKinsey & Company, March 30, 2016, 66. https://www.mckinsey.com/featured-insights/urbanization/urban-world-the-global-consumers-to-watch.

31. Curtin, Joseph. "Climate Change Is Coming for Global Trade." *Foreign Policy,* November 16, 2019. https://foreignpolicy.com/2019/11/16/climate-change-disrupt-global-container-shipping-trade-policymakers-take-note/.

32. Costas, Paris. "Smooth Sailing for Ships after Historic Fuel Switch." *Wall Street Journal,* January 14, 2020. https://www.wsj.com/articles/smooth-sailing-for-ships-after-historic-fuel-switch-11579019829.

33. Guarascio, Francesco, and Jonas Ekblom. "Explainer: What an EU Carbon Border Tax Might Look Like and Who Would Be Hit." *Reuters,* December 10, 2019. https://www.reuters.com/article/us-climate-change-eu-carbontax-explainer/explainer-what-an-eu-carbon-border-tax-might-look-like-and-who-would-be-hit-idUSKBN1YE1C4.

34. Curtin, "Climate Change."

35. Maersk. "Maersk to Offer Customers Carbon-Neutral Transport." June 20, 2019. https://www.maersk.com/news/articles/2019/06/20/maersk-to-offer-customers-carbon-neutral-transport.

36. Global Trade Alert. "Global Dynamics," 2020. https://www.globaltradealert.org/global_dynamics. The ratio is 2.6 to 1, precisely.

37. McBride, James, and Andrew Chatzky. "Is Made in China 2025 a Threat to Global Trade?" Council on Foreign Relations. Last updated May 13, 2019. https://www.cfr.org/backgrounder/made-china-2025-threat-global-trade.

38. World Bank, "Trade (% of GDP)."

39. Wübbeke, Jost, Mirjam Meissner, Max J. Zenglein, Jaqueline Ives, and Björn Conrad. *Made in China 2025*. Berlin: Merics, 2018, 6. https://www.merics.org/sites /default/files/2018-07/MPOC_No.2_MadeinChina2025_web.pdf. South Korea will be by far the hardest hit by Made in China 2025.

40. Institute for Security and Development Policy. "Made in China 2025— Modernizing China's Industrial Capability." Accessed March 26, 2021. https://isdp .eu/publication/made-china-2025/.

41. Sutter, Karen M., and Michael D. Sutherland. "China's 14th Five-Year Plan: A First Look." Congressional Research Service, January 5, 2021, 3. https://crsreports .congress.gov/product/pdf/IF/IF11684. "China's Pork Consumption Set to Be Double That for the EU, While Interest in Meat Alternatives Grows." *Global Times*. Accessed March 15, 2021. https://www.globaltimes.cn/content/1206331.shtml.

42. Batchelor, Bill, Frederic Depoortere, Scott C. Hopkins, Giorgio Motta, and Ingrid Vandenborre. "Europe and the UK Race to Protect Businesses Impacted by the Coronavirus Pandemic: Foreign Investment, State Aid and Antitrust Rules Adjusted." Skadden, March 27, 2020. https://www.skadden.com/insights/publications /2020/03/europe-and-the-uk-race-to-protect-businesses; Dhir, Rajiv. "Golden Share." Investopedia. Last updated May 6, 2020. https://www.investopedia.com/terms/g /goldenshare.asp.

43. Chee, Foo Yun. "EU Plans More Protectionist Antitrust Rules, Data Sharing in Policy Shake Up." *Reuters*, January 25, 2020. https://www.reuters.com/article /us-eu-industrialpolicy/eu-plans-more-protectionist-antitrust-rules-data-sharing -in-policy-shake-up-idUSKBN1ZO0NC; Commission to the European Parliament. "A New Industrial Strategy for Europe." European Commission, October 3, 2020. https://ec.europa.eu/info/sites/info/files/communication-eu-industrial-strategy -march-2020_en.pdf.

44. Spaes, Joel. "EU Greenlights Aid for European Battery Alliance." *PV Magazine*, December 11, 2019. https://www.pv-magazine.com/2019/12/11/eu-green-lights -aid-for-european-battery-alliance/.

45. European Battery Alliance. "Launch of LiPlanet Project." Accessed October 15, 2020. https://www.eba250.com/launch-of-liplanet-project/; Hall, Ben, and Richard Milne. "Europe First: How Brussels Is Retooling Industrial Policy." *Financial Times*, December 2, 2019. https://www.ft.com/content/140e560e-0ba0-11ea-bb52 -34c8d9dc6d84; Simon, Frédéric. "Race for Lithium Illustrates EU Drive for Strategic Raw Materials." Euractiv, November 21, 2019. https://www.euractiv.com/section /circular-economy/news/race-for-lithium-illustrates-eu-drive-for-strategic-raw -materials/.

46. Charles, Dan. "Farmers Got Billions from Taxpayers in 2019, and Hardly Anyone Objected." NPR, December 31, 2019. https://www.npr.org/sections/thesalt /2019/12/31/790261705/farmers-got-billions-from-taxpayers-in-2019-and-hardly -anyone-objected; Global Trade Alert. "Number of New Interventions." 2020. https:// www.globaltradealert.org/country/222/period-from_20170101/period-to_20200116.

47. Biden, Joseph R. "Executive Order on America's Supply Chains." White House,

February 24, 2021. https://www.whitehouse.gov/briefing-room/presidential-actions/2021/02/24/executive-order-on-americas-supply-chains/.

48. Zhang, Jinsong, Wei Kao, and Zhengyi Pan. "Trump Blocks His First CFIUS Deal—What Can We Learn from It?" King & Wood Mallesons, October 11, 2017. https://www.kwm.com/en/us/knowledge/insights/trump-blocks-his-first-cfius-deal-what-can-we-learn-from-it-20171011; Leiter, Michael, Ivan Schlager, and Donald Vieira. "Broadcom Blocked Acquisition of Qualcomm." *Harvard Law School Forum on Corporate Governance,* April 3, 2018. https://corpgov.law.harvard.edu/2018/04/03/broadcoms-blocked-acquisition-of-qualcomm/; "The Committee on Foreign Investment in the United States (CFIUS)." Congressional Research Service, February 14, 2020. https://fas.org/sgp/crs/natsec/RL33388.pdf; Hamilton, Isobel Asher. "The Trump Administration Failed to Convince the UK to Ditch Huawei and Its Other Allies Aren't Listening Either." *Business Insider,* March 11, 2020. https://www.businessinsider.com/huawei-how-allies-are-reacting-to-us-calls-to-avoid-the-tech-firm-2019-2; Woo, Stu. "Facing Pushback from Allies, U.S. Set for Broader Huawei Effort." *Wall Street Journal,* January 23, 2020. https://www.wsj.com/articles/facing-pushback-from-allies-u-s-set-for-broader-huawei-effort-11579775403; Wayland, Michael. "Trump Attacks General Motors over China, U.S. Employment." *CNBC,* August 30, 2019. https://www.cnbc.com/2019/08/30/trump-attacks-general-motors-over-china-us-employment.html.

49. Kennedy, Scott. "Made in China 2025." *CSIS,* June 1, 2015. https://www.csis.org/analysis/made-china-2025; Atkinson, Robert. "Huawei Export Ban Shoots U.S. Tech Manufacturers in the Foot." *Industry Week,* January 30, 2020. https://www.industryweek.com/the-economy/public-policy/article/21121812/huawei-export-ban-shoots-us-tech-manufacturers-in-the-foot.

50. U.S. Department of the Treasury. "Publication of Hong Kong Business Advisory; Hong Kong-Related Designations." Accessed August 5, 2021. https://home.treasury.gov/policy-issues/financial-sanctions/recent-actions/20210716.

51. Wayland, "Trump Attacks General Motors"; Hamilton, "Trump Administration Failed"; Woo, "Facing Pushback from Allies."

52. Alper, Alexandra. "Trump Pressures Federal Pensions to Halt Planned Chinese Stock Purchases." *Reuters,* May 12, 2020. https://www.reuters.com/article/us-usa-china-investment/trump-pressures-federal-pension-to-halt-planned-chinese-stock-purchases-idUSKBN22O1XZ.

53. Wong, Edward, and Julian E. Barnes. "U.S. to Expel Chinese Graduate Students with Ties to China's Military Schools." *New York Times,* May 28, 2020. https://www.nytimes.com/2020/05/28/us/politics/china-hong-kong-trump-student-visas.html; Redden, Elizabeth. "Fewer Chinese Students at Many Campuses." *Inside Higher Ed,* October 17, 2019. https://www.insidehighered.com/news/2019/10/17/colleges-see-declines-chinese-student-enrollments.

54. Yang, Yuan, and Nian Liu. "Beijing Orders State Offices to Replace Foreign PC's and Software." *Financial Times,* December 8, 2019. https://www.ft.com/content/b55fc6ee-1787-11ea-8d73-6303645ac406.

55. Cheng, Ting-Fang. "China's No. 2 Player to Launch 5G Chip in 2020 to Rival Qualcomm." Nikkei, August 7, 2019. https://asia.nikkei.com/Business/China-tech/China-s-No.-2-player-to-launch-5G-chip-in-2020-to-rival-Qualcomm; Laskai, Lorand. "Why Does Everyone Hate Made in China 2025?" Council on Foreign Relations, March 28, 2018. https://www.cfr.org/blog/why-does-everyone-hate-made-china-2025; "'Made in China 2025' Industrial Policies: Issue for Congress." Congressional Research Service, August 11, 2020. https://fas.org/sgp/crs/row/IF10964.pdf.

56. Mei, Yan, Tim Payne, Robert Morgan, Bob Christie and Peter Zysk. "New Insight Research on Business Risks of US-China Trade Tensions." Brunswick Group, June 26, 2019. https://www.brunswickgroup.com/us-china-trade-tracker-i11293/; Wernau, Julie. "America Is Losing the Chinese Shopper." Wall Street Journal, October 12, 2019. https://www.wsj.com/articles/america-is-losing-the-chinese-shopper-11570852805.

57. Bhagwati, Jagdish N. *Termites in the Trading System: How Preferential Agreements Undermine Free Trade*. Oxford: Oxford University Press, 2008.

58. Food and Agriculture Organization of the United States. "El Salvador and Honduras Take Measures to Ensure Supplies of Staple Foods amid COVID-19 Pandemic," April 24, 2020. http://www.fao.org/giews/food-prices/food-policies/detail/en/c/1272631/.

59. Wingrove, Josh, and Suzi Ring. "Biden Rebuffs EU, AstraZeneca and Says U.S. Will Keep Its Doses." *Bloomberg*, March 12, 2021. https://www.bloomberg.com/news/articles/2021-03-12/astrazeneca-asks-biden-to-consider-shipping-u-s-doses-to-eu.

60. Gary Gereffi. "What Does the COVID-19 Pandemic Teach Us about Global Value Chains? The Case of Medical Supplies." *Journal of International Business Policy* 3, no. 3 (July 15, 2020): 287–301. https://doi.org/10.1057/s42214-020-00062-w. Gereffi argues that the supply challenges that the United States faced in the early months of COVID-19 were not market failures of global value chains but policy failures by the Trump administration.

61. Evenett, Simon J. "Chinese Whispers: COVID-19, Global Supply Chains in Essential Goods, and Public Policy." *Journal of International Business Policy* 3, no. 4 (December 2020): 408–29. https://doi.org/10.1057/s42214-020-00075-5.

62. Srivastava, Shruti. "India Offers Land Twice Luxembourg's Size to Firms Leaving China." *Economic Times*, May 5, 2020. https://economictimes.indiatimes.com/news/economy/policy/india-offers-land-twice-luxembourgs-size-to-firms-leaving-china/articleshow/75534412.cms.

63. Song, Jung-a. "South Korea Struggles to Lure Factories Home from China." *Financial Times*, September 7, 2020. https://www.ft.com/content/9e6fe3e3-7121-4f35-80d5-013bdda3bf3d?emailId=5f586d2e0da543000457a21c&segmentId=1315b184-f9a7-4265-3689-bcf707fc0d68.

64. Vergun, David. "DOD Partners with DFC to Protect Industrial Base from Economic Effects of Pandemic." U.S. Department of Defense, June 22, 2020. https://www.defense.gov/Explore/News/Article/Article/2227560/dod-partners-with-dfc

-to-protect-industrial-base-from-economic-effect-of-pandem/; Lawder, David. "New U.S. Development Agency Could Loan Billion for Reshoring." *Reuters,* June 23, 2020. https://www.reuters.com/article/us-usa-trade-reshoring-exclusive/exclusive-u-s-development-agency-could-loan-billions-for-reshoring-official-says-idUSKBN23U31F; U.S. Department of Health and Human Services. "HHS, Industry Partners Expand U.S.-Based Pharmaceutical Manufacturing for COVID19 Response." May 19, 2020. https://www.hhs.gov/about/news/2020/05/19/hhs-industry-partners-expand-us-based-pharmaceutical-manufacturing-covid-19-response.html; Hufford, Austen. "N95 Face Mask Makers Ramp Up Production to Meet U.S. Covid-19 Demand." *Wall Street Journal,* July 17, 2020. https://www.wsj.com/articles/n95-mask-makers-ramp-up-production-to-meet-u-s-covid-19-demand-11594987201.

65. Global Trade Alert. "Saudi Arabia Local Content and Government Procurement Authority Issues Mandatory List of Medical Supplies," 2020. https://www.globaltradealert.org/state-act/45098/saudi-arabia-local-content-and-government-procurement-authority-issues-mandatory-list-of-medical-supplies.

66. Global Trade Alert. "Kazakhstan Announces New Measures of State Support in Context of COVID-19." March 31, 2020. https://www.globaltradealert.org/state-act/43652/kazakhstan-president-announces-new-measures-of-state-support-in-the-context-of-covid-19; Global Trade Alert. "Peru: USD 209 Million Funds in Public Procurement from National SMEs (COVID-19)." June 27, 2020. https://www.globaltradealert.org/state-act/45130/peru-usd-209-million-funds-in-public-pro curement-from-national-smes-covid-19. Global Trade Alert. "China (Beijing): City Government Announces 10% State Procurement Preference Margin When Purchasing from Local SMEs." February 7, 2020. https://www.globaltradealert.org/state-act/43677/china-beijing-city-government-announces-10-state-procurement-preference-margin-when-purchasing-from-local-smes.

67. Morse, Susan. "Trump Orders Agencies to Purchase U.S. Made Drugs and Medical Supplies." *Healthcare Finance,* August 6, 2020. https://www.healthcare financenews.com/news/trump-orders-agencies-purchase-us-made-drugs-and-medical-supplies.

68. Lee, Don. "Why Trump's 'Buy American' Campaign Went Nowhere." *LA Times,* August 31, 2020. https://www.latimes.com/politics/story/2020-08-31/trumps-buy-american-campaign-went-nowhere; Bloomberg. "Biden Expected to Unveil Economic Plan Pushing to Buy American and Create Manufacturing Jobs." *Fortune,* July 9, 2020. https://fortune.com/2020/07/09/joe-biden-economic-plan-buy-american-made-manufacturing-jobs/; Senate Republican Policy Committee. "Update on the Coronavirus Response: Heals Act," 2020. https://www.rpc.senate.gov/policy-papers/update-on-the-coronavirus-response-heals-act.

69. World Economic Forum. "The Global Competitiveness Report 2019." 2019. http://www3.weforum.org/docs/WEF_TheGlobalCompetitivenessReport2019.pdf.

70. Batalova, Jeanne, Brittany Blizzard, and Jessica Bolter. "Frequently Requested Statistics on Immigrants and Immigration in the United States." Migration Informa-

tion Source, February 14, 2020. https://www.migrationpolicy.org/article/frequently
-requested-statistics-immigrants-and-immigration-united-states-2020; Budiman, Abby.
"Key Findings about U.S. Immigrants." Pew Research Center, August 20, 2020.
https://www.pewresearch.org/fact-tank/2020/08/20/key-findings-about-u-s
-immigrants/; U.S. Department of State. "Non-Immigrant Visas Issued by Classifi-
cation, Fiscal Years 2015–2019." Accessed August 23, 2021. https://travel.state.gov
/content/dam/visas/Statistics/AnnualReports/FY2019AnnualReport/FY19Annual
Report-TableXVI-B.pdf.

71. Kosten, Dan. "Immigrants as Economic Contributors: Immigrant Entrepreneurs." *Immigration Forum,* July 11, 2018. https://immigrationforum.org/article
/immigrants-as-economic-contributors-immigrant-entrepreneurs/.

72. Anderson, Stuart. "Immigrants and Million Dollar Startups." Policy brief. National Foundation for American Policy, March 2016. http://nfap.com/wp-content
/uploads/2016/03/Immigrants-and-Billion-Dollar-Startups.NFAP-Policy-Brief
.March-2016.pdf.

73. National Academies of Science, Engineering, and Medicine. *The Economic and
Fiscal Consequences of Immigration.* Washington, DC: National Academies Press, 2016.
https://doi.org/10.17226/23550.

74. World Bank. "International LPI," 2018. https://lpi.worldbank.org/inter
national/global.

75. Comet Labs Research Team. "AI and Robotics to Achieve China's Retail Logistics Revolution." *Comet Labs Blog,* February 5, 2019. https://blog.cometlabs.io
/ai-and-robotics-to-achieve-chinas-retail-logistics-revolution-ab98b9ee7d9a?gi
=5c3989f35168; Gilmore, Dan. "State of the Logistics Union 2019." *Supply Chain
Digest,* June 20, 2019. http://www.scdigest.com/firstthoughts/19-06-20.php?cid
=15592&ctype=content.

76. Bureau of Transportation Statistics, U.S. Department of Transportation. "System Mileage within the United States," October 2020. https://www.bts.gov/content
/system-mileage-within-united-states; World Airport Codes. "U.S. Top 40 Airports,"
2020. https://www.world-airport-codes.com/us-top-40-airports.html.

77. Arvis, Jean-François, Lauri Ojala, Christina Wiederer, Ben Shepherd, Anasuya
Raj, Karlygash Dairabayeva, and Tuomas Kiiski. *Connecting to Compete 2018: Trade
Logistics in the Global Economy.* Washington, DC: World Bank, 2018. https://open
knowledge.worldbank.org/bitstream/handle/10986/29971/LPI2018.pdf.

78. International Trade Administration. "United States Travel and Tourism Industry." 2018. https://travel.trade.gov/outreachpages/download_data_table/Fast
_Facts_2018.pdf; Orcutt, April. "America's Most-Visited Tourist Attractions." *Travel and
Leisure,* December 5, 2012. https://www.travelandleisure.com/slideshows/americas
-most-visited-tourist-attractions.

79. Study International Staff. "Which Country Is Home to the Largest International Student Population?" *Study International,* May 2, 2018. https://www.study
international.com/news/country-home-largest-international-student-population/;
NAFSA. "Benefits from International Students." 2019. https://www.nafsa.org/sites

/default/files/media/document/isev-2019.pdf; U.S. Bureau of Labor Statistics. "Employment, Hours, and Earnings from the Current Employment Statistics Survey (National): All Employees, Thousands, Manufacturing, Seasonally Adjusted." Accessed March 31, 2021. https://data.bls.gov/timeseries/CES3000000001?amp%253bdata_tool=XGtable&output_view=data&include_graphs=true.

80. Baldwin, Richard. *The Globotics Upheaval: Globalization, Robotics, and the Future of Work*. Oxford: Oxford University Press, 2019. Richard Baldwin lays out a compelling argument of the challenges to come.

81. American Institute of Physics. "Rapid Rise of China's STEM Workforce Charted by National Science Board Report," January 31, 2018. https://www.aip.org/fyi/2018/rapid-rise-china%E2%80%99s-stem-workforce-charted-national-science-board-report.

82. World Population Review. "Most Educated Countries 2020," 2019. http://worldpopulationreview.com/countries/most-educated-countries/; O'Neil, Shannon K. "China's Manufacturing Loss Should Be Mexico's Gain." *Bloomberg*, September 17, 2019. https://www.bloomberg.com/opinion/articles/2019-09-17/china-s-manufacturing-loss-should-be-mexico-s-gain; Monroy, Carlos, and Stefan Trines. "Education in Mexico." *WENR*, May 25, 2019, https://wenr.wes.org/2019/05/education-in-mexico-2.

83. UNESCO. "How Much Does Your Country Invest in R&D?," 2020. http://uis.unesco.org/apps/visualisations/research-and-development-spending/.

84. Snowden, Scott. "Solar Power Stations in Space Could Supply the World with Limitless Energy." *Forbes*, March 12, 2019. https://www.forbes.com/sites/scottsnowden/2019/03/12/solar-power-stations-in-space-could-supply-the-world-with-limitless-energy/#4d3688034386; Kessler, Sarah. "A Problem That Keeps Warehouse Word from Being Fully Automated Has Just Been Solved." *Quartz*, April 7, 2017. https://qz.com/952240/righthand-robotics-has-automated-a-new-type-of-warehouse-work-that-could-help-amazon-amzn/; Yndurain, Elena, Stefan Woerner, and Daniel J. Egger. "Exploring Quantum Computing Use Cases for Financial Services." IBM, September 2019. https://www.ibm.com/downloads/cas/2YPRZPB3; Bates Ramirez, Vanessa. "First Human CRISPR Trial in the U.S. Aims to Cure Inherited Blindness." *SingularityHub*, July 28, 2019. https://singularityhub.com/2019/07/28/first-human-crispr-trial-in-the-us-aims-to-cure-inherited-blindness/.

85. UNCTAD. "World Investment Report 2020: International Production beyond the Pandemic," 2020. https://unctad.org/system/files/official-document/wir2020_en.pdf.

86. Schleicher, Andreas. "PISA 2018: Insights and Interpretations." OECD, 2019. http://www.oecd.org/pisa/PISA%202018%20Insights%20and%20Interpretations%20FINAL%20PDF.pdf.

87. Sargent, John. "Global Research and Development Expenditures: Fact Sheet." Congressional Research Service, June 27, 2018. http://fas.org/sgp/crs/misc/R44283.pdf, quoted in Segal, Adam, James Manyika, and William H. McRaven. "Innovation and National Security Task Force Report: Keeping Our Edge." Council on Foreign

Relations, September 18, 2019, 36. https://www.cfr.org/report/keeping-our-edge/pdf/TFR_Innovation_Strategy.pdf.

88. American Institute of Physics, "Rapid Rise of China's STEM Workforce"; Schwab, Klaus. "The Global Competitiveness Report 2019." World Economic Forum, 2019. http://reports.weforum.org/global-competitiveness-report-2019/.

89. Lucas, Louise, and Richard Waters. "China and U.S. Compete to Dominate Big Data." *Financial Times,* April 30, 2018. https://www.ft.com/content/e33a6994-447e-11e8-93cf-67ac3a6482fd; Sheehan, Matt. "Much Ado about Data: How America and China Stack Up." MacroPolo, July 16, 2019. https://macropolo.org/ai-data-us-china/.

90. Rathi, Akshat. "Five Things to Know about China's Electric-Car Boom." *Quartz,* January 8, 2019. https://qz.com/1517557/five-things-to-know-about-chinas-electric-car-boom/; Lawder, David. "China Trade Steps Seen as Good Start but Leave Core U.S. Demands Untouched." *Reuters,* December 16, 2018. https://www.reuters.com/article/us-usa-trade-china-analysis/china-trade-steps-seen-as-good-start-but-leave-core-u-s-demands-untouched-idUSKBN1OG0GA.

91. Bu et al., "China Digital Consumer Trends," 2.

92. "'Stage One' U.S.-Japan Trade Agreements." Congressional Research Service, 2019. https://fas.org/sgp/crs/row/R46140.pdf.

93. Stearns, Jonathan. "EU Gives Trump Trade Gift to U.S. Lobster Industry, GOP Senator." *Bloomberg,* August 21, 2020. https://www.bloomberg.com/news/articles/2020-08-21/eu-gives-trump-trade-gift-to-u-s-lobster-industry-gop-senator?sref=hF44HboC.

94. Lu, Zhiyao (Lucy), and Jeffrey J. Schott. "How Is China Retaliating for U.S. National Security Tariffs on Steel and Aluminum?" Peterson Institute for International Economics, April 9, 2018. https://www.piie.com/research/piie-charts/how-china-retaliating-us-national-security-tariffs-steel-and-aluminum.

95. U.S. Census Bureau, Foreign Trade Division. "Trade in Goods with China," April 2, 2021. https://www.census.gov/foreign-trade/balance/c5700.html; Bown, Chad P., and Melina Kolb. "Trump's Trade War Timeline: An Up-to-Date Guide." Peterson Institute for International Economics, February 8, 2021. https://www.piie.com/sites/default/files/documents/trump-trade-war-timeline.pdf.

96. Dorning, Mike. "U.S. Farm Bankruptcies Surge 24% on Strain from Trump Trade War." *Bloomberg,* October 30, 2019. https://www.bloomberg.com/news/articles/2019-10-30/u-s-farm-bankruptcies-surge-24-on-strain-from-trump-trade-war?sref=hF44HboC.

97. U.S. Bureau of Labor Statistics, "Employment, Hours, and Earnings: All Employees, Thousands, Manufacturing"; U.S. Bureau of Labor Statistics. "Employment, Hours, and Earnings from the Current Employment Statistics Survey (National): All Employees, Thousands, Iron and Steel Mills and Ferroalloy Production, Seasonally Adjusted." Accessed April 3, 2021. https://data.bls.gov/timeseries/CES3133110001. Author's calculations based on U.S. Bureau of Labor Statistics data.

98. Coren, Michael J. "Two Companies Petitioned for Trump's Solar Tariffs—

Now They're Both out of Business." *Quartz,* June 18, 2019. http://qz.com/1644846 /two-companies-that-petitioned-for-trumps-solar-tariffs-are-out-of-business/; Groom, Nichola. "U.S. Solar Group Says Trump Tariff Killing Jobs; White House Says 'Fake News.'" *Reuters,* December 3, 2019. https://www.reuters.com/article/uk-usa-solar -tariffs/u-s-solar-industry-to-lose-62000-jobs-due-to-trump-tariffs-study-idUSKBN 1Y71V8.

99. SEIA. "Study: Solar Tariffs Cause Devastating Harm to U.S. Market, Economy and Jobs," December 3, 2019. https://www.seia.org/news/solar-tariff-impacts.

100. "Solar Energy: Frequently Asked Questions." Congressional Research Service, October 2020. https://fas.org/sgp/crs/misc/R46196.pdf.

101. U.S. Bureau of Labor Statistics. "Employment, Hours, and Earnings: All Employees, Thousands, Iron and Steel Mills and Ferroalloy Production." Quoted in Cox, Lydia, and Kadee Russ. "Will Steel Tariffs Put U.S. Jobs at Risk?" Econofact, February 26, 2018. https://econofact.org/will-steel-tariffs-put-u-s-jobs-at-risk.

102. Flaaen, Aaron, and Justin Pierce. "Disentangling the Effects of the 2018– 2019 Tariffs on a Globally Connected U.S. Manufacturing Sector." Finance and Economics Discussion Series. Federal Reserve Board, 2019. https://www.federalreserve .gov/econres/feds/files/2019086pap.pdf. Quoted in Cox, Lydia, and Kadee Russ. "Steel Tariffs and U.S. Jobs Revisited." Econofact, February 6, 2018. https://econo fact.org/steel-tariffs-and-u-s-jobs-revisited.

103. Cox and Russ, "Will Steel Tariffs Put U.S. Jobs at Risk?"

104. McEleney, John. "Ford CEO Says Metals Tariffs Took $1 Billion of Profit." *Bloomberg,* September 26, 2018. https://www.industryweek.com/leadership/article /22026410/ford-ceo-says-metals-tariffs-took-1-billion-of-profit; Boehm, Eric. "After Losing $1 Billion to Tariffs, General Motors Announces 14,000 Layoffs." *Reason,* November 26, 2018. https://reason.com/2018/11/26/after-losing-1-billion-to-tariffs -genera/.

105. Long, Heather. "Trump's Steel Tariffs Cost U.S. Consumers $900,000 for Every Job Created, Experts Say." *Washington Post.* May 7, 2019. https://www.wash ingtonpost.com/business/2019/05/07/trumps-steel-tariffs-cost-us-consumers -every-job-created-experts-say/.

106. Congressional Budget Office. "The Economic Outlook." In *The Budget and Economic Outlook: 2020 to 2030.* Washington, DC: Congressional Budget Office, 2020, 31, 33. https://www.cbo.gov/system/files/2020-01/56020-CBO-Outlook.pdf.

107. Handley, Kyle, Fariha Kamal, and Ryan Monarch. "Rising Import Tariffs, Falling Export Growth: When Modern Supply Chains Meet Old-Style Protectionism." National Bureau of Economic Research, January 2020, 3. https://doi.org/10.3386 /w26611.

108. European Union. "Negotiations and Agreements." Accessed April 23, 2021. https://ec.europa.eu/trade/policy/countries-and-regions/negotiations-and-agree ments/; Dalton, Matthew. "Salty Issue in U.S.-European Trade Talks: Feta Cheese." *Wall Street Journal,* October 9, 2015. https://www.wsj.com/articles/regional-food -names-are-stumbling-block-in-u-s-european-trade-talks-1445298063.

109. Russell, Jon. "Vietnam's New Cyber Security Law Draws Concern for Restricting Free Speech." *TechCrunch,* June 12, 2018. https://techcrunch.com/2018/06/12/vietnams-new-cyber-security-law-draws-concern-for-restricting-free-speech/.

110. Chandran, Nyshka. "American Farmers Brace for More Pain as Pacific Trade Deal Kicks In without the US." *CNBC,* January 2, 2019. https://www.cnbc.com/2018/12/31/cptpp-american-farmers-set-for-pain-as-pacific-trade-deal-kicks-in.html.

111. Wenbo, Liu. 2021. "China, Japan Reach Breakthrough Tariff Reduction under RCEP, Which Products May Cost Less?" Accessed March 26, 2021. https://news.cgtn.com/news/2020-12-01/China-Japan-reach-tariff-reduction-which-products-may-cost-less--VRkd1JKl5S/index.html.

112. World Health Organization. "International Food Standards," October 2020. https://www.who.int/foodsafety/areas_work/food-standard/en/; IAPP. "ISO Publishes First International Standards for Privacy Information Management," August 7, 2019. https://iapp.org/news/a/iso-publishes-first-international-standards-for-privacy-information-management/; WIPO. "Geographical Indications," October 2020. https://www.wipo.int/geo_indications/en/; Better Buildings Solutions Center. "What Is ISO 50001?," October 2020. https://betterbuildingssolutioncenter.energy.gov/iso-50001/what-iso-50001.

113. Plumer, Brad, and Nadja Popovich. "How U.S. Fuel Economy Standards Compare with the Rest of the World's." *New York Times,* April 3, 2018. https://www.nytimes.com/interactive/2018/04/03/climate/us-fuel-economy.html; Farrell, Maria. "Quietly, Symbolically, U.S. Control of the Internet Was Just Ended." *Guardian,* March 14, 2016. https://www.theguardian.com/technology/2016/mar/14/icann-internet-control-domain-names-iana; Maharrey, Michael. "SWIFT and the Weaponization of the U.S. Dollar." *FEE Stories,* October 6, 2018. https://fee.org/articles/swift-and-the-weaponization-of-the-us-dollar/.

114. ISO. "Members," October 2020. https://www.iso.org/members.html.

115. American Institute of Physics. "FYI: Science Policy News," October 2020. https://www.aip.org/fyi/2020/fy21-budget-request-national-institute-standards-and-technology%2523:~:text=The%252520Trump%252520administration%252520proposes%252520to,build%252520out%252520quantum%252520networking%252520capabilities.

116. U.S-China Business Council. "China in International Standards Setting," February 2020. https://www.uschina.org/sites/default/files/china_in_international_standards_setting.pdf; Ryugen, Hideaki, and Hiroyuki Akiyama. "China Leads the Way on Global Standards for 5G and Beyond." *Financial Times,* August 4, 2020. https://www.ft.com/content/858d81bd-c42c-404d-b30d-0be32a097f1c?desktop=true&segmentId=7c8f09b9-9b61-4fbb-9430-9208a9e233c8#myft:notification:daily-email:content.

117. Montgomery, Erika. "How Does GDPR Affect Marketing in the United States?" Three Girls Media, May 2, 2018. https://www.threegirlsmedia.com/2018/05/02/how-does-gdpr-affect-marketing-in-the-united-states/; Ehret, Todd. "Data Privacy and GDPR at One Year, a U.S. Perspective. Part One—Report Card." *Reuters,* May

22, 2019. https://www.reuters.com/article/bc-finreg-gdpr-one-year-report-card-part
/data-privacy-and-gdpr-at-one-year-a-u-s-perspective-part-one-report-card-idUSKCN
1SS2K5.

6. The United States' Best Bet

1. Rembert, Mark, Michael Betz, Bo Feng, and Mark Partridge. "Taking Measure of Ohio's Opioid Crisis." Ohio State University, Swank Program in Rural-Urban Policy, October 2017. https://aede.osu.edu/sites/aede/files/publication_files/Swank %20-%20Taking%20Measure%20of%20Ohios%20Opioid%20Crisis.pdf; Summit County (OH) Public Health. "Population Health Vital Statistics Brief, Volume 1: Death and Life Expectancy." Vital Statistics Brief. April 2018. https://www.scph.org/sites/default /files/editor/Death_Data_Brief_0817.pdf.

2. Statista. "Exports of Goods and Services from the United States from 1990 to 2019, as a Percentage of GDP," Accessed July 26, 2021. https://www.statista.com /statistics/258779/us-exports-as-a-percentage-of-gdp/; Suominen, Kati. *Revolutionizing World Trade: How Disruptive Technologies Open Opportunities for All*. Emerging Frontiers in the Global Economy. Stanford, CA: Stanford University Press, 2019. https:// doi.org/10.1515/9781503610729; California Inland Empire District Export Council. "U.S. Exporting Facts." 2015. http://www.ciedec.org/resources/exporting-facts/.

3. Istrate, Emilia, Jonathan Rothwell, and Bruce Katz. "Export Nation: How U.S. Metros Lead National Export Growth and Boost Competitiveness." Brookings, 2010. https://www.brookings.edu/wp-content/uploads/2016/06/0726_exports_istrate _rothwell_katz.pdf; Clerides, Sofronis K., Saul Lach, and James R. Tybout. "Is Learning by Exporting Important? Micro-Dynamic Evidence from Colombia, Mexico, and Morocco." *Quarterly Journal of Economics* 113, no. 3 (August 1, 1998): 903–47. https:// doi.org/10.1162/003355398555784; Aw, Bee Yan, Sukkyun Chung, and Mark J. Roberts. "Productivity and Turnover in the Export Market: Micro-Level Evidence from the Republic of Korea and Taiwan (China)." *World Bank Economic Review* 14, no. 1 (2000): 65–90. https://www.jstor.org/stable/3990035; Delgado, Miguel A., Jose C. Fariñas, and Sonia Ruano. "Firm Productivity and Export Markets: A Non-Parametric Approach." *Journal of International Economics* 57, no. 2 (August 1, 2002): 397–422. https://doi.org/10.1016/S0022-1996(01)00154-4. Studies show that the positive correlation between exporting corporations and employee pay holds across many economies, including several for which exports are a larger portion of overall GDP, including Spain, Germany, Mexico, South Korea, and Taiwan.

4. Slaughter, Matthew J. "The 'Exporting Jobs' Canard." *Wall Street Journal*, June 14, 2017, sec. Opinion. https://www.wsj.com/articles/the-exporting-jobs-canard -1497482039; Bernard, Andrew B., J. Bradford Jensen, and Peter K. Schott. "Importers, Exporters and Multinationals: A Portrait of Firms in the U.S. That Trade Goods." Tuck School of Business at Dartmouth, May 8, 2007, 51. http://mba.tuck.dartmouth .edu/pages/faculty/andrew.bernard/imex.pdf.

5. CIA. "The World Factbook." October 5, 2020. https://www.cia.gov/the -world-factbook/.

6. World Bank. "GDP per Capita, PPP (Current International $)—Germany, Mexico, Bulgaria, United States, France, Latvia, Romania." Accessed April 2, 2021. https://data.worldbank.org/indicator/NY.GDP.PCAP.PP.CD?end=2019&locations =DE-MX-BG-US-FR-LV-RO&start=1994. In the early to mid-1990s, the wage differentials between Germany, France, and the UK and Bulgaria, Romania, Latvia, and others were fairly similar to that between the United States and Mexico.

7. OECD. "Trade in Value Added: China." December 2018. https://www.oecd .org/industry/ind/TIVA-2018-China.pdf.

8. Daboub, Juan José, and Daniel F. Runde. "Turning the Covid-19 Crisis into an Opportunity for the Central American Textile Sector." Center for Strategic & International Studies, June 17, 2020. https://www.csis.org/analysis/turning-covid-19 -crisis-opportunity-central-american-textile-sector; data on U.S. exports to Central America from U.S. Census Bureau, author's calculation.

9. Moran, Theodore H., and Lindsay Oldenski. "How U.S. Investments in Mexico Have Increased Investment and Jobs at Home." Peterson Institute for International Economics, July 11, 2015. https://www.piie.com/blogs/realtime-economic -issues-watch/how-us-investments-mexico-have-increased-investment-and-jobs.

10. World Bank. "Tariff Rate, Applied, Weighted Mean, All Products (%)." October 2020. https://data.worldbank.org/indicator/tm.tax.mrch.wm.ar.zs. In 2018, imported goods faced an average tariff rate of 2.6 percent globally and an average rate of 3.4 percent in China. By comparison, goods imported into the United States only faced an average tariff rate of 1.6 percent. See World Bank, "Tariff Rate, Applied."

11. Added together, the countries that the United States has free-trade agreements with account for 9.43 percent of world GDP and 6 percent of the global population. Author's calculations based on the twenty nations that the United States maintains formal agreements with and World Bank data. See International Trade Administration. "Free Trade Agreements." Accessed April 2, 2021. http://www.trade .gov/free-trade-agreements; World Bank. "GDP (Current US$)." Accessed April 2, 2021. https://data.worldbank.org/indicator/NY.GDP.MKTP.CD; World Bank. "Population, Total." Accessed April 2, 2021. https://data.worldbank.org/indicator/SP .POP.TOTL.

12. U.S. Trade Representative. "NAFTA: A Decade of Success." July 2004. https:// ustr.gov/about-us/policy-offices/press-office/fact-sheets/archives/2004/july /nafta-decade-success; Flatness, Anne, and Chris Rasmussen. "U.S.-Produced Value in U.S. Imports from NAFTA." Office of Trade and Economic Analysis, International Trade Administration, Department of Commerce, September 22, 2017. https://www .commerce.gov/sites/default/files/us-produced-value-in-us-imports-from-nafta.pdf. In the first ten years of NAFTA, U.S. exports to Canada and Mexico grew from $134 billion ($46 billion to Mexico and $87.8 billion to Canada) to $251 billion ($105 and $146 billion, respectively). In 2003, Mexico and Canada accounted for 36 percent of total U.S. exports.

13. White House. "Building Resilient Supply Chains, Revitalizing American Manufacturing, and Fostering Broad-Based Growth." 100-Day Reviews under Executive

Order 14017. June 2021. https://www.whitehouse.gov/wp-content/uploads/2021/06/100-day-supply-chain-review-report.pdf.

14. Tetakawi. "Comprehensive List of Mexico's Free Trade Agreements (FTAs)," November 7, 2019. https://insights.tetakawi.com/mexicos-free-trade-agreements; Global Affairs Canada. "Expand Your Business Horizons with Canada's Free Trade Agreements." Accessed April 2, 2021. https://www.tradecommissioner.gc.ca/canad export/0003849.aspx?lang=eng.

15. OECD. "Import Content of Exports." Accessed April 2, 2021. https://doi .org/10.1787/5834f58a-en.

16. For instance, a study by Michael Waugh showed that higher car prices (in the study, due to Chinese retaliatory tariffs) led to an estimated $2.5 billion in lost auto sales just between July 2018 and June 2019. Waugh, Michael E. "The Consumption Response to Trade Shocks: Evidence from the U.S.-China Trade War." National Bureau of Economic Research, 2019. https://www.nber.org/papers/w26353.

17. U.S. Bureau of Labor Statistics. "Employment Projections—2019–2029." September 1, 2020. https://www.bls.gov/news.release/pdf/ecopro.pdf.

18. Waugh, "Consumption Response"; Lund, Susan, Anu Madgavkar, James Manyika, Sven Smit, Kweilin Ellingrud, Mary Meaney, and Olivia Robinson. "The Future of Work after Covid-19." McKinsey Global Institute, February 18, 2021. https:// www.mckinsey.com/featured-insights/future-of-work/the-future-of-work-after -covid-19.

19. McKinnon, Tricia. "How Kroger Uses Artificial Intelligence (AI) to Innovate." Indigo9 Digital Inc., June 10, 2019. https://www.indigo9digital.com/blog//kroger -use-artificial-intelligence-to-innovate-in-its-store-of-the-future.

20. CONAHEC: Consortium for North American Higher Education Collaboration. Accessed April 2, 2021. https://conahec.org/; U.S. Department of State. "100,000 Strong Educational Exchange Initiatives." Accessed April 2, 2021. https:// 2009-2017.state.gov/100k//index.htm; Robertson, Angela, and Duncan Wood. "Building on Early Success: Next Steps in U.S.-Mexico Education Cooperation." Wilson Center Mexico Institute, August 2017. https://www.wilsoncenter.org/sites /default/files/media/documents/publication/building_on_early_success_next _steps_in_u.s.-mexico_educational_cooperation.pdf. The Consortium for North American Higher Education Collaboration (CONAHEC) began in 1994 with NAFTA. It grew from 13 higher-education leaders in the three countries to 150 by 2007, primarily hosting exchange programs among the three countries. However, the organization remains small, with limited government support.

21. Statistics Canada. "Focus on Geography Series, 2016 Census," 2017. https:// www12.statcan.gc.ca/census-recensement/2016/as-sa/fogs-spg/Facts-can-eng.cfm ?Lang=Eng&GK=CAN&GC=01&TOPIC=7.

22. Thomas, Katie. "U.S. Hospitals Wrestle with Shortages of Drug Supplies Made in Puerto Rico." *New York Time,* October 23, 2017, sec. Health. https://www.nytimes .com/2017/10/23/health/puerto-rico-hurricane-maria-drug-shortage.html; Palmer, Eric. "Shortages of Drugs and Saline Reported as Puerto Rico Hurricane Damage

Lingers." Fierce Pharma, October 12, 2017. https://www.fiercepharma.com/pharma/shortages-drugs-and-saline-reported-as-puerto-rico-hurricane-damage-lingers.

23. Saad, Lydia. "Americans' Views on Trade in the Trump Era." Gallup, October 25, 2019. https://news.gallup.com/opinion/gallup/267770/americans-views-trade-trump-era.aspx.

Index

Figures are indicated by "*f*" following the page number.